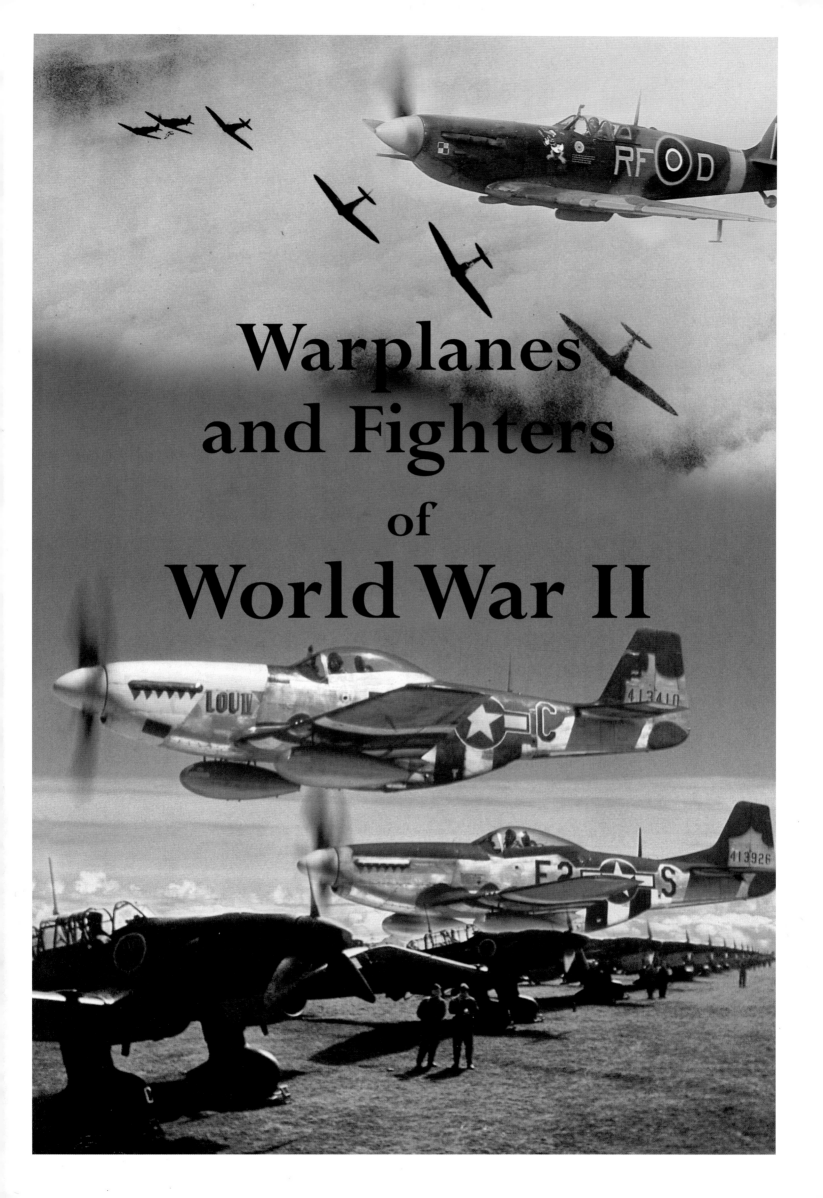

Warplanes
and Fighters
of
World War II

The three titles listed below were first published in 1982 by Octopus Publishing Group Ltd

This 2002 compilation edition published by Chancellor Press
an imprint of Bounty Books, a division of Octopus Publishing Group Ltd,
2–4 Heron Quays, London E14 4JP

A CIP catalogue record for this book is available from the British Library

ISBN 0 7537 05370
Printed in China

Authors:

American Fighters of World War II: David A. Anderton

British Fighters of World War II: Bill Gunston

German Warplanes of World War II: Francis K. Mason

General editors: Paul E. Eden and Soph Moeng
Designer: Nathalie Macdonald

Foreword

Germany entered World War II with what was arguably the most advanced air force in the world. Fine aircraft, good training and clever tactics, together with the combat experience gained over Spain during that country's civil war, combined to make the Luftwaffe unstoppable as Hitler waged his Blitzkrieg across Western Europe. The best Britain's RAF could do was to hold off the German offensive with a motley collection of obsolete aircraft and the first examples of its new generation of warplanes. As these new machines, including the Hurricane and Spitfire matured, the balance of airpower began to change in favour of the Allies. When the Americans arrived in the European theatre to add their might to that of the British, no amount of German technological advantage could save the Luftwaffe.

In the Pacific a similar situation prevailed, with Allied forces eventually overcoming the initial Japanese onslaught. It was in the Pacific that the US Navy engaged in some of the greatest naval engagements ever fought, many of them being decided by carrier aircraft alone.

"The danger inherent in any report confined to one aspect of the war is that it may mislead the reader into forgetting that the conflict was won by a combination of ground, naval and air forces…" So said the United States Navy's Vice Admiral Forrest Sherman in 1947, when he was Deputy Chief of Naval Operations, and it is worth keeping that in mind as we begin this survey of American fighters of World War II. When war came, the fighter strength of the United States lagged behind those of its future allies and enemies. Its service aircraft were either obsolete or at the end of their potential development. New types neared production, but a long and difficult period of maturing lay ahead before they could tangle with the enemy on anything but a very unequal footing. Armament was hardly better than it had been in World War I, and altitude performance, range, speed and manoeuvrability were generally poor.

By the end of the war, American designers had produced several fighter aircraft since recognised as classics. American production lines, untouched by the daily reality of war, enjoyed the twin luxuries of time and distance. Because of them, US factories were able to build an unequalled capacity that turned out combat aircraft by the thousands.

Without exception, though, the US fighters that helped wind up the long conflict had been ordered into development before war began for America. In some cases, the aircraft were in design before September 1939, when all hell broke loose on the Polish border with Germany.

So here it is, a galaxy of American fighters. Some were classics, and some were clunkers. But – as part of a brave company – they helped to hold, and then to roll back, a fearsome, ruthless and cruel enemy.

Judge them on their merits, in the context of their times.

The very fact that in the Battle of Britain the pilots of RAF Fighter Command unquestionably defeated the superior numbers of the previously invincible Luftwaffe shows that British fighters must have been pretty good. Yet in fact, they were in many respects technically inferior to their opposite numbers, and available in far smaller quantities and all are described in British Fighters of World War II.

However, in the skilled hands of the RAF the Hurricanes and Spitfires inflicted the first military defeat Hitler's Third Reich had ever suffered, and made it possible for the Western democracies to build up their strength until, on 6 June 1944, they were able to start the reconquest of Western Europe. By this time the Spitfire had changed so much it ought to have been given a new name. The Hawker Hurricane had at last been replaced by Typhoons and Tempests, which were used mainly in the ground-attack role.

From autumn 1940, the Bristol Beaufighter had served on all fronts and proved its ability to launch everything from bullets to torpedoes. Its partner, the wooden de Havilland Mosquito, matured as the best night interdiction aircraft of the war. Thanks to Frank Whittle, Britain was the pioneer of the turbojet, and the world's first regular jet fighter squadron was not a Luftwaffe unit, but No. 616 Sqn, Royal Air Force. Yet the Meteor was ordered in such small numbers that it made little impact on the war. The new German jets could do little to stem the tide of Allied advance but represented a new technology that had for years been in Britain's possession and should have been applied with far more determination and vigour. This volume tells the story of the trials and tribulations of Britain's struggle for air supremacy: a struggle as much with its own bureaucracy as with the enemy. Nonetheless it was a victorious struggle and one which contains many remarkable and fascinating aspects.

When the German Blitzkrieg struck Poland in 1939, the world watched in awe as Hitler's war machine wrought instant havoc against the traditional equipment of the defending Poles. This was not to be a single occurrence; soon Norway and Denmark fell, then the Low Countries and France. This was something new and different from the long drawn-out trench warfare of World War I. The new ingredient was air power. And Germany's Luftwaffe was the finest air force in the world. Its combat-proven warplanes were piloted by war-hardened, well trained pilots; the aircraft were deployed in optimum formations and available in quantity, as detailed in German Warplanes of World War II.

The German aircraft industry surpassed the rest of the world in ingenuity and in production technique. Its products were classic: Messerschmitt and Focke-Wulf fighters, Stuka dive-bombers, and bombers from Junkers, Dornier and Heinkel. There were also excellent maritime reconnaissance aircraft, seaplanes, giant transports, observation aircraft and trainers. And towards the latter stages of the war, the Luftwaffe was deploying potentially war-winning jet- and rocket-powered combat aircraft. But these came too little and too late to avoid defeat.

When the curtain finally fell on Germany in May 1945 the once-vaunted Luftwaffe was a spent force. Most of its best pilots were dead, its bases in ruins, the aircraft factories destroyed or captured and its aircraft grounded by lack of fuel. Yet in six years of war its aircrew and aircraft had matched anything the Allies had thrown at them. And much of the new technology developed for the Luftwaffe laid the foundations for post-war developments.

Undoubtedly the world breathed a sigh of relief when Hitler was defeated. But there is no denying that Hitler's Luftwaffe and other arms of the German war machine flew some excellent aircraft. This volume amply portrays their magnificence and dreadful potency.

Contents

American Fighters

of

World War II

The First Round

The Americans had come up with some neat ideas in the 1930s. But the blooding of Europe in 1939 shows that these ideas had not been put together in the right packages.

Before World War II, the United States was a country that seemed to want only to live in splendid and impossible isolation from the rest of the world. It was secure behind friendly borders to the north and south, and protected by vast expanses of ocean to the east and west. With no plans of territorial expansion, or of attacking another country, America's security policy was based solely on defence.

The US Navy was the primary agent of that policy, assigned to defend the coasts in co-operation with strategically placed batteries of the US Army's Coast Artillery. The US Army itself was small, and still largely equipped with the rifles, machine-guns, artillery and personal gear used in World War I.

Subordinate service

Air power was a very subordinate arm of both major services. In the US Army, very limited availability of funding had forced some cruel choices, including a concentration on the bomber as the selected tool of the projection of air power. It made sense in light of the assumed security policy. Any attacker would have to invade, and would have to amass forces for that invasion. Bombers would seek out, attack and destroy the accumulation of ordnance, supplies and troops needed for such an invasion. No enemy aircraft capable of intercepting bombers so far from its own home bases was known to exist, and so it was assumed that the bombers would make their way to the target free of harassment. That assumption cost dearly over Europe, just a few years later.

US Navy requirements

The US Navy needed aircraft for scouting, and provision had been made long before 1939 for catapult operations of aircraft from cruisers and battleships. The five fleet carriers in commission were equipped with the very latest biplane fighters and bombers, and their mission was fleet defence.

In September 1939, the US Army Air Corps was equipped with a total of about 1,500 aircraft, of which 800 were claimed as first-line strength. The US Navy had a few more

Left: A pre-war line-up of snarling P-26 pursuits, resplendent in blue bodies and Chrome Yellow wings and tails. By the time of the Japanese attack on Pearl Harbor, the P-26 had been almost entirely replaced by other types and equipped just one unit, the 31st Sqn of the 37th Pursuit Group.

Below: Grumman established an enviable reputation for supplying the US Navy with fighters throughout the 1930s. The F3F was in the process of being transferred to training units when the US entered the war, with nearly 180 examples still on the Navy and Marine inventory. This is an F3F-2.

Curtiss P-36

Curtiss P-36A of the 79th Pursuit Squadron, 20th Pursuit Group, Moffet Field, California, November 1939.

A line-up of Curtiss P-36Cs of the 27th Pursuit Squadron, US Army Air Corps.

Curtiss P-36A (dotted wing guns show P-36C)

than 900 claimed as first line, but several hundred of that number were obsolescent biplanes. Across the wide Atlantic, the Royal Air Force numbered about 2,000 first-line aircraft, plus reserves, and the Luftwaffe counted approximately 4,000 aircraft ready for combat, plus reserve strengths estimated as high as an additional 1,000. Personnel strength of the USAAC was less than 27,000 officers and men; that was about one-quarter of the RAF's strength, and one-twentieth of the Luftwaffe's personnel.

US Army fighter types

About 700 of the US Army's 800 first-line aircraft were three types: the standard fighter was the Curtiss P-36A, a graceful aircraft designed in 1934 and very near the end of its operational life; the standard bomber was the lumbering Douglas B-18A, a modified DC-3 with a misshapen nose and a design that also dated back to 1934;

and the standard attacker was the Northrop A-17A, a light two-seater that – after much later improvement and modification – eventually became the Douglas SBD, the US Navy's best bomber of the war.

The US Navy's first-line fighter in late 1939 was the stubby Grumman F3F, last of the biplane fighters in US service. Flown by US Marine Corps and US Navy pilots, the Grummans were based on four of the fleet carriers. Development of the US Navy's first monoplane fighter, the Brewster F2A, was under way, but that ill-fated craft was a long way from service, and had a dismal battle record when it finally did fight.

The rude awakening began in September 1939, with the frightening Blitzkrieg that slashed through Poland. It left behind a swathe of destroyed cavalry units, obsolescent aircraft and defeated foot soldiers. The speed of the German advance, the combined use of air and ground

The Boeing F4B-3 biplane was one of the first fighters in the world to have a semi-monocoque stressed-skin fuselage. Three are seen after being passed from Navy fighter squadron VF-1B to shore service with the US Marines.

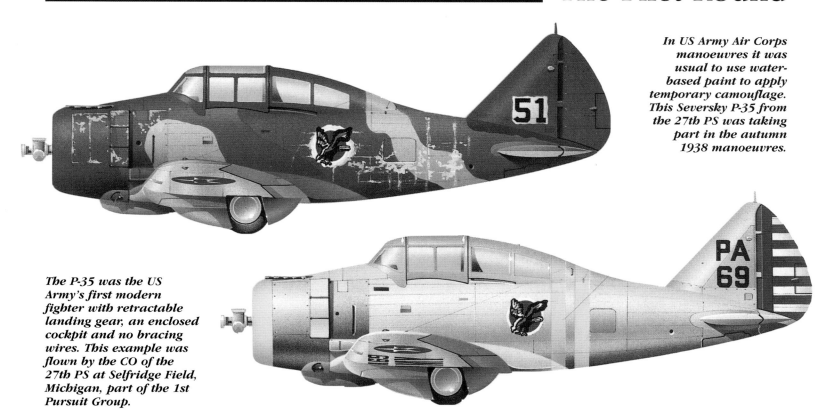

In US Army Air Corps manoeuvres it was usual to use water-based paint to apply temporary camouflage. This Seversky P-35 from the 27th PS was taking part in the autumn 1938 manoeuvres.

The P-35 was the US Army's first modern fighter with retractable landing gear, an enclosed cockpit and no bracing wires. This example was flown by the CO of the 27th PS at Selfridge Field, Michigan, part of the 1st Pursuit Group.

forces, and the outstanding performance of the fledgling Luftwaffe - all amplified considerably by a very efficient propaganda machine - caused serious concern among the planners and builders of American defence industries.

New types in the pipeline

Fortunately for the final outcome of the war, there had been a few determined backers of advanced fighters before the Germans made the need crystal clear. By the time the war began in Europe, the USAAC had placed its first orders for the Lockheed P-38, the Bell P-39 and the Curtiss P-40. All had made their first flights before September 1939. The US Navy was receiving its first monoplane fighter, the Brewster F2A-1, and had ordered the rugged Grumman F4F-3

Wildcat into production. Both prototypes had flown during 1937. The experimental Vought XF4U-1, first of the 400-mph (645-km/h) class of fighters, had been ordered by mid-1938.

Between the launching of Germany's lightning war and the Japanese attack at Pearl Harbor, three additional aircraft entered the design process to become the most significant American fighters of the war. Republic's XP-47

The Bell P-39 Airacobra promised much in 1939, but proved to be very much an also-ran. The P-39 saw only limited service with US forces but instead found its niche as a ground-attack machine with the Soviet air forces. No longer front-line types, these P-39Ds are seen from an unusual angle with a training unit in 1942.

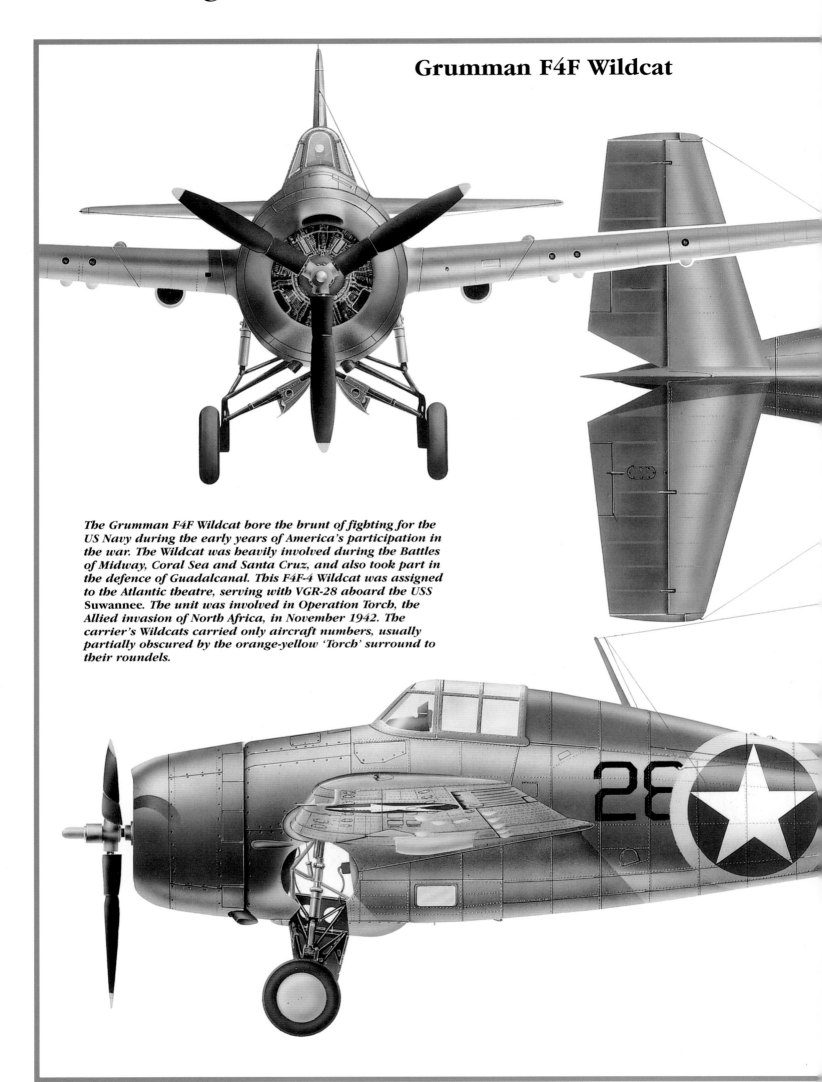

Grumman F4F Wildcat

The Grumman F4F Wildcat bore the brunt of fighting for the US Navy during the early years of America's participation in the war. The Wildcat was heavily involved during the Battles of Midway, Coral Sea and Santa Cruz, and also took part in the defence of Guadalcanal. This F4F-4 Wildcat was assigned to the Atlantic theatre, serving with VGR-28 aboard the USS Suwannee. The unit was involved in Operation Torch, the Allied invasion of North Africa, in November 1942. The carrier's Wildcats carried only aircraft numbers, usually partially obscured by the orange-yellow 'Torch' surround to their roundels.

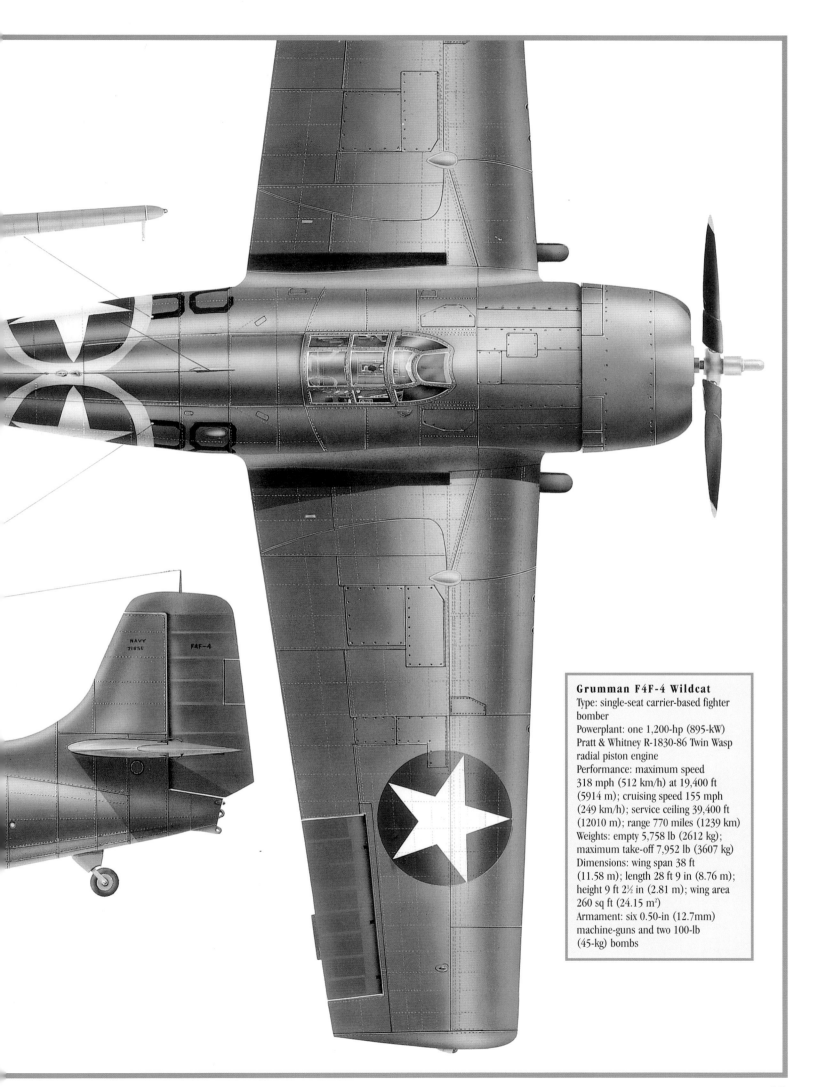

Grumman F4F-4 Wildcat
Type: single-seat carrier-based fighter
bomber
Powerplant: one 1,200-hp (895-kW)
Pratt & Whitney R-1830-86 Twin Wasp
radial piston engine
Performance: maximum speed
318 mph (512 km/h) at 19,400 ft
(5914 m); cruising speed 155 mph
(249 km/h); service ceiling 39,400 ft
(12010 m); range 770 miles (1239 km)
Weights: empty 5,758 lb (2612 kg);
maximum take-off 7,952 lb (3607 kg)
Dimensions: wing span 38 ft
(11.58 m); length 28 ft 9 in (8.76 m);
height 9 ft 2½ in (2.81 m); wing area
260 sq ft (24.15 m²)
Armament: six 0.50-in (12.7mm)
machine-guns and two 100-lb
(45-kg) bombs

Curtiss P-36 Hawk

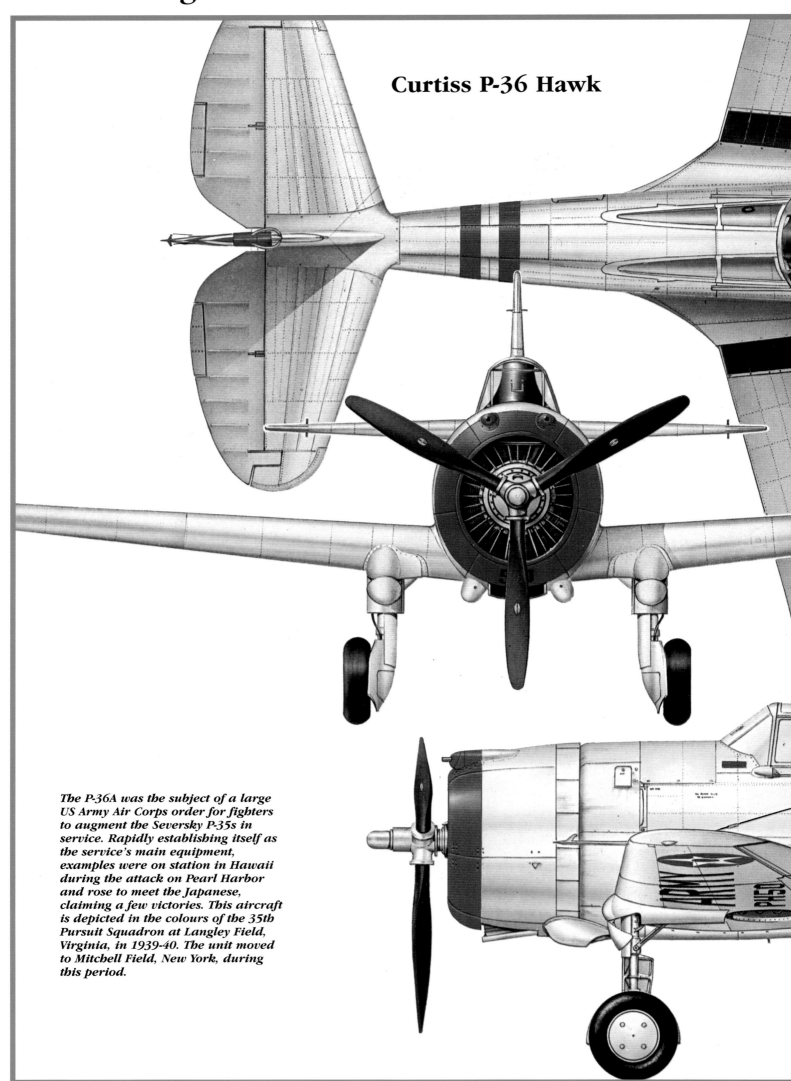

The P-36A was the subject of a large US Army Air Corps order for fighters to augment the Seversky P-35s in service. Rapidly establishing itself as the service's main equipment, examples were on station in Hawaii during the attack on Pearl Harbor and rose to meet the Japanese, claiming a few victories. This aircraft is depicted in the colours of the 35th Pursuit Squadron at Langley Field, Virginia, in 1939-40. The unit moved to Mitchell Field, New York, during this period.

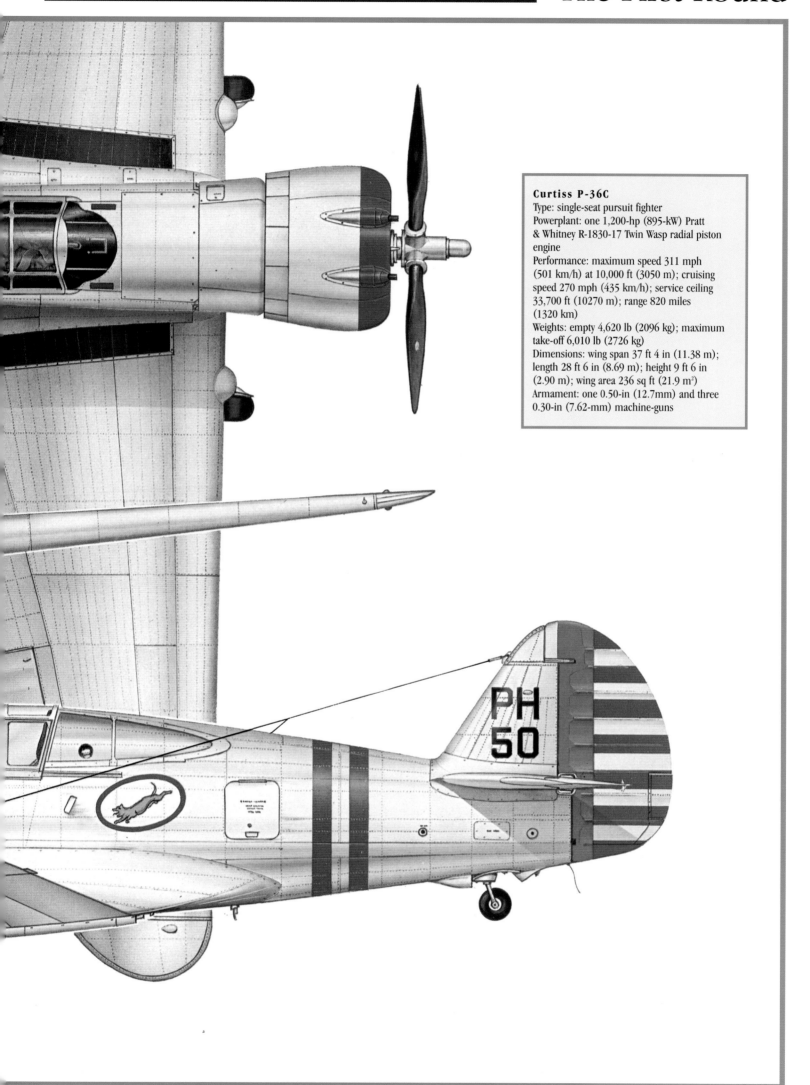

Curtiss P-36C
Type: single-seat pursuit fighter
Powerplant: one 1,200-hp (895-kW) Pratt
& Whitney R-1830-17 Twin Wasp radial piston
engine
Performance: maximum speed 311 mph
(501 km/h) at 10,000 ft (3050 m); cruising
speed 270 mph (435 km/h); service ceiling
33,700 ft (10270 m); range 820 miles
(1320 km)
Weights: empty 4,620 lb (2096 kg); maximum
take-off 6,010 lb (2726 kg)
Dimensions: wing span 37 ft 4 in (11.38 m);
length 28 ft 6 in (8.69 m); height 9 ft 6 in
(2.90 m); wing area 236 sq ft (21.9 m²)
Armament: one 0.50-in (12.7mm) and three
0.30-in (7.62-mm) machine-guns

American Fighters of World War II

Due to its sheer weight and size, some fighter designers thought the Republic XP-47B, first flown on 6 May 1941, a very mistaken answer to the fighter design problem. Nevertheless, the P-47 evolved into an effective fighter and an impressive fighter-bomber.

In the 100-odd days of the Battle of Britain North American Aviation conceived this new fighter, the NA-73X. From it stemmed a type that is widely regarded as the best all-round fighter of the war, the P-51 Mustang.

began to take shape early in 1940. It was followed a few months later by the North American NA-73, forerunner of the P-51 Mustang. On the US Navy side, Grumman's F6F Hellcat, slated to become the primary fighter in the Pacific theatre, was first defined by a simple request from the US Navy: put a larger engine in the Wildcat so that its performance might be improved.

And so, when war finally came to the United States, the renamed US Army Air Force had on hand a fighter strength composed largely of Curtiss P-40s, with a few Curtiss P-36s and Republic P-35s in overseas locations, and a very few

Bell P-39s defending the west coast against a feared enemy air attack. The US Navy and US Marines had the majority of their fighter squadrons equipped with Grumman Wildcats. A single squadron of Brewster F2A-3 aircraft was operating from the USS *Lexington*, flown by enlisted chief petty officer pilots of Fighting Squadron (VF) 2. The US Marine Corps also flew a mix of Wildcats and Brewsters.

With this force of unproven fighters, American pilots lifted off to meet the tough and determined onslaught of highly-skilled, well trained Japanese pilots flying a very superior fighter: the Mitsubishi Zero.

The Lightning was one of the first Lockheed designs in which the famous Skunk Works designer Clarence L. 'Kelly' Johnson had a hand. Here the first of these strange twin-boomed fighters, the XP-38 prototype, is parked at March Field on 31 December 1938, having been trucked to the airfield from the Lockheed plant at Burbank, California.

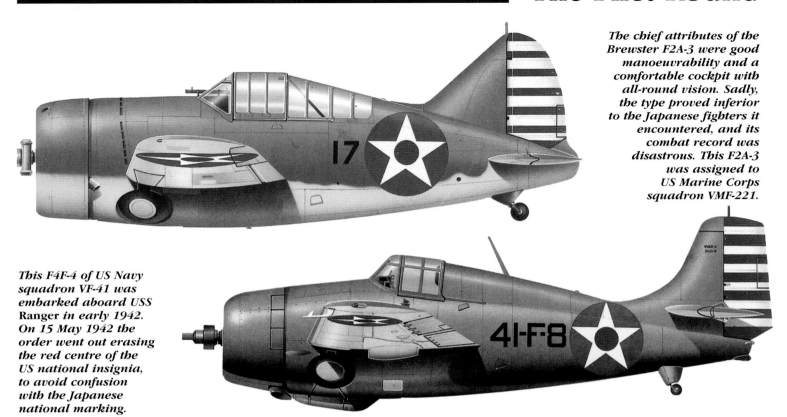

The chief attributes of the Brewster F2A-3 were good manoeuvrability and a comfortable cockpit with all-round vision. Sadly, the type proved inferior to the Japanese fighters it encountered, and its combat record was disastrous. This F2A-3 was assigned to US Marine Corps squadron VMF-221.

This F4F-4 of US Navy squadron VF-41 was embarked aboard USS Ranger in early 1942. On 15 May 1942 the order went out erasing the red centre of the US national insignia, to avoid confusion with the Japanese national marking.

Fighter sketches

Seversky (Republic) P-35

Designed originally as the Seversky SEV-1XP for a USAAC competition of August 1935, this fighter was re-engined and redesignated as the P-35. The USAAC ordered 77 examples on 16 June 1936, the type becoming the service's first operational single-seat all-metal purusit aircraft with retractable landing gear and enclosed cockpit. The P-35 served with the 17th, 27th and 94th Pursuit Squadrons (1st Pursuit Group) between 1938 and 1940, sharing flight time with Curtiss P-36s assigned to the same squadrons in a service test competition. The USAAC diverted 48 from a Swedish order for the defence of the Philippines in October 1940. By 7 December 1941, the P-35 equipped only the 34th Pursuit Squadron based near Manila. The little fighters saw combat in the area during December, and two survived to join the 'Bamboo Fleet' on Bataan. Both were subsequently lost to enemy action.

Curtiss P-36

Derived from the fixed-gear Hawk 75 of 1934, this trim pursuit lost an initial competition to the P-35, but won the later and more important one of May 1937. The USAAC ordered 210 on 6 June 1937, in the largest US fighter order since World War I. Deliveries began in April 1938, with early assignments to the 1st, 8th, 16th, 18th and 20th Pursuit Groups. The P-36A was a sound type, with good handling and manoeuvrability but by December 1941, it was already considered obsolescent. The type was relegated to the training role in the USA, but some were still on active duty in the Panama Canal Zone and Hawaii. Several of the latter survived the initial Japanese attack at Pearl Harbor, intercepted a group of torpedo aircraft and flamed two.

The US Navy's best fighter at the outbreak of war was the Grumman F4F Wildcat. A contemporary of the Japanese Zero, the F4F had an inferior performance in several respects, yet proved capable of holding its own thanks to its superior armament, rugged construction and well-trained pilots.

American Fighters of World War II

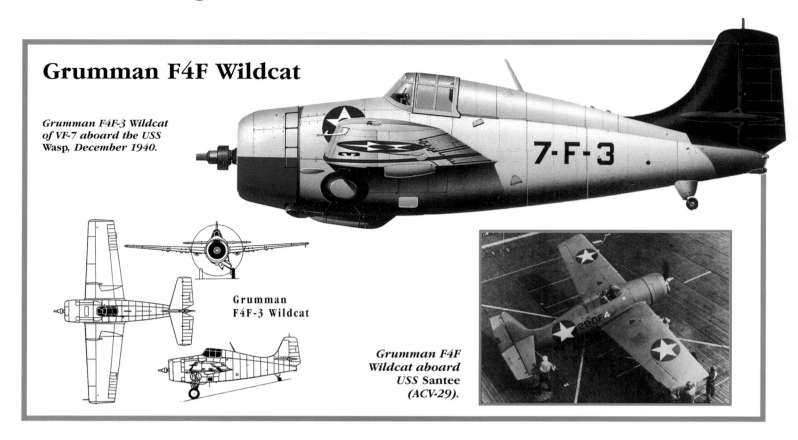

Grumman F4F Wildcat

Grumman F4F-3 Wildcat of VF-7 aboard the USS Wasp, December 1940.

7-F-3

Grumman F4F-3 Wildcat

Grumman F4F Wildcat aboard USS Santee (ACV-29).

Brewster F2A

The US Navy's first monoplane fighter began development on 15 November 1935 and flew first in December 1937. Deliveries to the fleet began in July 1939, but early tests aboard the USS *Lexington* showed landing gear weaknesses. As a stripped, test aircraft its performance matched those of its 1938 contemporaries; but equipped with armour, extra guns and radio to make it combat-ready, it was only mediocre. By 7 December 1941, US Navy F2As were operational only with VF-2, and that unit was disbanded soon after. The US Marines flew them against overwhelming Japanese air strength during the Battle of Midway, on 4 June 1942, and lost 13 out of 20 Brewsters in air combat. Total production was 509 examples.

Curtiss P-40 Warhawk

Starting from the basis of a re-engined P-36, the P-40 became the standard USAAC pursuit, replacing both the P-35 and the P-36. A rugged airframe and low cost kept it in production as a stop-gap fighter, buying time to tool for more advanced types. It was immortalised by the American Volunteer Group in China and Burma, and was the most important USAAF fighter in the inventory at the start of the war. A total of 16,802 of all variants was built.

The Vought Corsair was a massive aircraft, with the largest diameter propeller then fitted to any fighter. The prototype XF4U-1 first flew on 20 May 1940. Five months later it became the first American fighter to exceed 400 mph (644 km/h), one of the results of this being termination of Pratt & Whitney's programme for liquid-cooled engines in favour of its radials, like that powering the XF4U-1.

Grumman F4F Wildcat

Originally designed as a biplane in a competition – which it lost to the Brewster F2A, the Wildcat went on to become the US Navy's first-line fighter at the start of the war. It had been redesigned and re-engined, and was ordered by the US Navy in September 1938, and delivered to the fleet beginning in late 1940. When the Japanese attacked, the Wildcat was the mainstay of US Navy and US Marine fighting squadrons, equipping 10 out of the established 13. Although easily outmanoeuvred by the lightly loaded Japanese fighters, Wildcats combined heavy armament and rugged build with pilot skills and tactics to rack up a kill ratio of nearly 7:1. Wildcats were especially valuable for their ability to operate from small escort carriers. Production totalled 7,344 examples.

Above: While the Wildcat was holding the fort during the early years of America's war, Grumman was already working hard on a successor. Apart from the fairings for the main landing gears this might be a production F6F Hellcat. In fact it was the prototype, with designation XF6F-3, flown with the Double Wasp engine on 30 July 1942.

On 10 April 1942, when this photograph was taken over the Pacific, many Allied pilots could expect to come off worse if they met Japanese fighters. Two exceptions were Lt Cdr J.S. Thach (nearest) and Lt Edward H. 'Butch' O'Hare, of VF-3. Flying these F4F-3s, they already had three and four victories respectively. O'Hare was the first US Navy ace of the war.

The Army Attackers

The USAAF fighters of 1941 had serious shortcomings. But in the pipeline were some classic aircraft that soon gave the service real teeth in the escort and ground-attack missions.

Five American aircraft shouldered the bulk of the fighter combat action for the US Army Air Force (USAAF) during World War II: the Bell P-39 Airacobra, Curtiss P-40 Warhawk, Lockheed P-38 Lightning, North American P-51 Mustang and Republic P-47 Thunderbolt. Additionally, a substantial and often overlooked share of the fighting was done with Supermarine Spitfires, equipping a number of American units through a reverse Lend-Lease arrangement.

Each of these fighters had been under development, and at least one prototype of each had flown and been tested, before war affected the United States in December 1941. Furthermore, production lines – spurred on by enormous support from foreign orders, particularly from the British and French – were beginning to turn out quantities of fighters, as well as other types.

American fighters were, at that stage of their develop-ment, almost universally unsuitable for contemporary combat: their armament was light; the use of armour was minimal; self-sealing tanks were still being developed; and radio equipment was very basic. The fighter force of the United States was then best suited for daytime, good-weather fighting against inferior numbers.

Freelance operations

In retrospect, one wonders just what tactical thinking was behind the specifications often issued by the USAAC for its fighters. They seem to have been written for some unimagined contest, where the enemy flew straight and level in bright sunshine at no higher than 10,000 ft (3050 m) and no faster than 200 mph (320 km/h). Moreover, enemy aircraft apparently were assumed to be incapable of defending themselves. The reality of air combat never intruded into the paragraphs of the pre-war

Left: This post-6 June 1944 image illustrates the primary US fighters flying from British bases in the later war years. The P-51 came to dominate, as the P-47 faded away. The P-38 was never a great success over Northern Europe.

Illustrated here wearing the short-lived (July-September 1943) red-bordered insignia, the F-5B was the final form of the unarmed photo-reconnaissance Lightning. A P-38J fighter, in Olive Drab over Neutral Gray finish, keeps company.

Curtiss P-40 Warhawk

Curtiss P-40C Warhawk of the 39th Fighter Squadron, 31st Pursuit Group, Selfridge Field, Michigan, 1941.

Curtiss P-40N Warhawk
Type: single-seat fighter-bomber
Powerplant: one 1,200-hp (895-kW) Allison V-1710-81 piston engine
Performance: maximum speed 343 mph (552 km/h) at 15,000 ft (4570 m); service ceiling 31,000 ft (9480 m); range with auxiliary fuel at 10,000 ft (3050 m) 1,080 miles (1738 km)
Weights: empty 6,200 lb (2812 kg); maximum take-off 8,850 lb (4014 kg)
Dimensions: wing span 37 ft 4 in (11.38 m); length 33 ft 4 in (10.16 m); height 12 ft 4 in (3.76 m); wing area 236 sq ft (21.92 m²)
Armament: six 0.50-in (12.7-mm) machine-guns, plus up to 1,500 lb (680 kg) of bombs

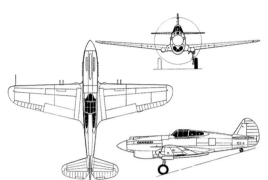

Curtiss P-40K Warhawk

Curtiss P-40N-20, Burma 1944.

specifications that defined the shape and performance of an entire generation of American combat aircraft.

As a result, Americans got the worst of it in the early air fighting. There was, happily for national morale at the time, one exception: the American Volunteer Group (AVG). That organisation, brilliantly led by Claire Chennault, a fighter tactician retired from the USAAC, racked up an astonishing victory string against first-ranked Japanese pilots in China and Burma. The unit used Chennault's basic concepts for effective defensive fighter operations: first, detect and

Built as P-40Bs to be supplied through Lend-Lease to the RAF, where they became Tomahawk Mk IIBs, 100 of the Curtiss fighters were diverted for use by the American Volunteer Group in China - Chennault's famed 'Flying Tigers'.

report the target; second, intercept it; third, shoot it down. The AVG's early model P-40s, universally regarded as mediocre fighters by everybody else, became terrible weapons in the hands of skilled and daring pilots who flew their aircraft unusually well.

Tactics and the proper use of fighters made the AVG effective, though outnumbered, and that lesson had to be learned over and over again by young pilots coming into combat for the first time. Those who learned, survived.

As one result of improperly written requirements, and the evolution of tactics, specific fighters designed to do one task often found their best employment in another. Republic's P-47 Thunderbolt was one example. Designed as a high-altitude fighter, it first became a bomber escort,

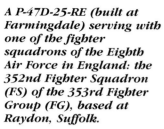

A P-47D-25-RE (built at Farmingdale) serving with one of the fighter squadrons of the Eighth Air Force in England: the 352nd Fighter Squadron (FS) of the 353rd Fighter Group (FG), based at Raydon, Suffolk.

A colourful P-47D-30-RA with dorsal fin, serving with the occupation forces in Germany in the summer of 1945. The unit was the 512th FS of the 406th Fighter Group.

One of the last of the 'razorback' Thunderbolts, this Evansville-built P-47D was assigned to the Pacific theatre. It served with the 19th FS, 318th Fighter Group, based on Saipan island in the summer of 1944. Though generally adequate, the P-47D's original cockpit produced a 20° blind spot at the rear.

Below: These are six of the first Republic P-47B Thunderbolts to be delivered to a fighting unit, the 56th Fighter Group, USAAF. Commanded by the outstanding fighter leader, Lt Col 'Hub' Zemke, this unit transferred to England in 1943 and eventually notched up 674½ 'kills', the highest air combat score of all US forces in World War II.

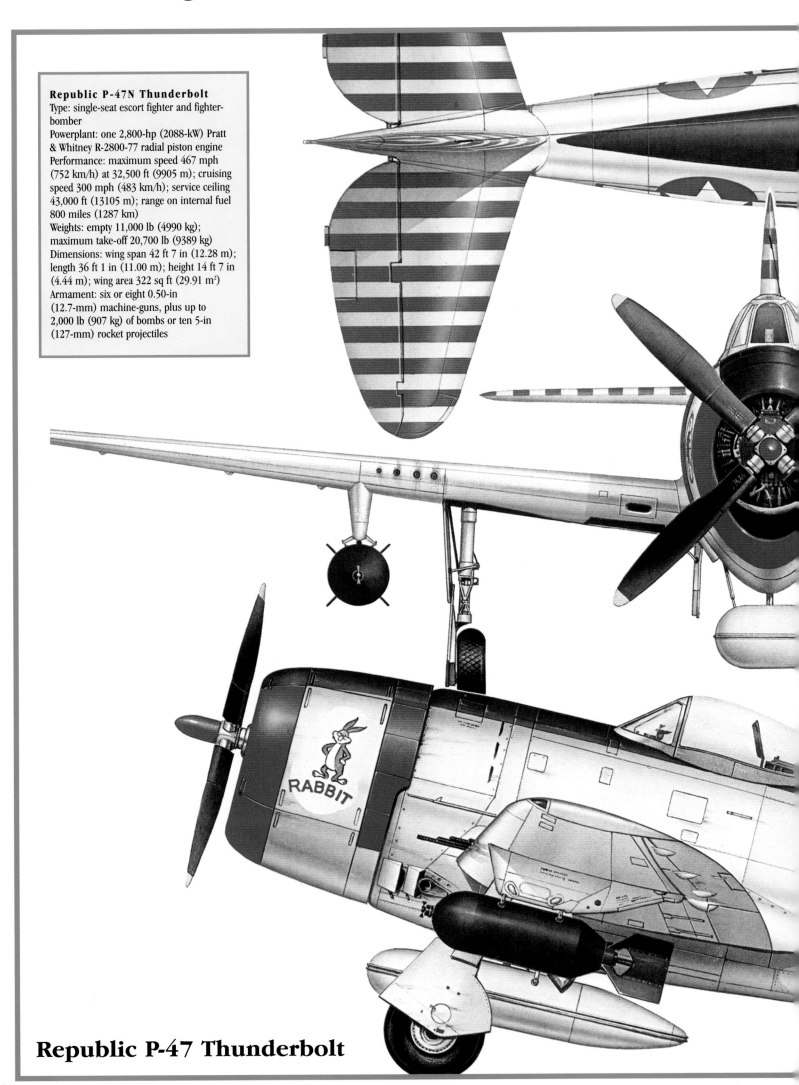

Republic P-47N Thunderbolt
Type: single-seat escort fighter and fighter-bomber
Powerplant: one 2,800-hp (2088-kW) Pratt & Whitney R-2800-77 radial piston engine
Performance: maximum speed 467 mph (752 km/h) at 32,500 ft (9905 m); cruising speed 300 mph (483 km/h); service ceiling 43,000 ft (13105 m); range on internal fuel 800 miles (1287 km)
Weights: empty 11,000 lb (4990 kg); maximum take-off 20,700 lb (9389 kg)
Dimensions: wing span 42 ft 7 in (12.28 m); length 36 ft 1 in (11.00 m); height 14 ft 7 in (4.44 m); wing area 322 sq ft (29.91 m²)
Armament: six or eight 0.50-in (12.7-mm) machine-guns, plus up to 2,000 lb (907 kg) of bombs or ten 5-in (127-mm) rocket projectiles

RABBIT

Republic P-47 Thunderbolt

One of the finest fighter-bombers of the war, the P-47D had adequate range and firepower to excel in the bomber escort role, but really found its niche as a ground attack platform. Extremely fast and very tough, the Thunderbolt was a stable gunnery platform and was deadly with rockets or bombs at low level. This aircraft was assigned to the 527th Fighter Squadron, 86th Fighter Group, and was based at Pisa during 1944. In addition to fighter and attack work in support of the slow advance through the tough Italian theatre, the P-47s also flew bomber-escort missions, sometimes as far as Berlin.

Republic P-47D-10 Thunderbolt

1 Rudder upper hinge
2 Aerial attachment
3 Fin flanged ribs
4 Rudder post/aft spar
5 Fin front spar
6 Rudder trim tab worm and screw actuating mechanism (chain driven)
7 Rudder centre hinge
8 Rudder trim tab
9 Rudder structure
10 Tail navigation light
11 Elevator fixed tab
12 Elevator trim tab

13 Starboard elevator structure
14 Elevator outboard hinge
15 Elevator torque tube
16 Elevator trim tab worm and screw actuating mechanism
17 Chain drive
18 Starboard tailplane
19 Tail jacking point
20 Rudder control cables
21 Elevator control rod and linkage
22 Fin spar/fuselage attachment point
23 Port elevator
24 Aerial
25 Port tailplane structure (two spars and flanged ribs)
26 Tailwheel retraction worm gear
27 Tailwheel anti-shimmy gear
28 Tailwheel oleo
29 Tailwheel doors
30 Retractable and steerable tailwheel
31 Tailwheel fork
32 Tailwheel mount and pivot
33 Rudder cables
34 Rudder and elevator trim control cables
35 Lifting tube
36 Elevator rod linkage
37 Semi-monocoque all-metal fuselage construction
38 Fuselage dorsal 'razorback' profile
39 Aerial lead-in
40 Fuselage stringers
41 Supercharger air filter
42 Supercharger
43 Turbine casing
44 Turbo-supercharger compartment air vent
45 Turbo-supercharger exhaust hood fairing (stainless steel)
46 Outlet louvres
47 Intercooler exhaust doors (port and starboard)
48 Exhaust pipes
49 Cooling air ducts
50 Intercooler unit (cooling and supercharged air)
51 Radio transmitter and receiver packs (Detrola)
52 Canopy track
53 Elevator rod linkage
54 Aerial mast
55 Formation light
56 Rear-vision frame cut-out and glazing
57 Oxygen bottles
58 Supercharged and cooling air pipe (supercharger to carburettor) port
59 Elevator linkage

60 Supercharged and cooling air pipe (supercharger to carburettor) starboard
61 Central duct (to intercooler unit)
62 Wingroot air louvres
63 Wingroot fillet
64 Auxiliary fuel tank (100 US gal; 379 litres)
65 Auxiliary fuel filler point
66 Rudder cable turnbuckle
67 Cockpit floor support
68 Seat adjustment lever
69 Pilot's seat
70 Canopy emergency release (port and starboard)
71 Trim tab controls
72 Back and head armour
73 Headrest
74 Rearward-sliding canopy
75 Rear-view mirror fairing
76 Vee windshields with central pillar
77 Internal bulletproof glass screen
78 Gunsight
79 Engine control quadrant (cockpit port wall)
80 Control column
81 Rudder pedals
82 Oxygen regulator
83 Underfloor elevator control quadrant
84 Rudder cable linkage
85 Wing rear spar/fuselage attachment (tapered bolts/bushings)
86 Wing supporting lower bulkhead section
87 Main fuel tank (205 US gal; 776 litres)
88 Fuselage forward structure
89 Stainless steel/Alclad firewall bulkhead
90 Cowl flap valve
91 Main fuel filler point
92 Anti-freeze fluid tank
93 Hydraulic reservoir
94 Aileron control rod
95 Aileron trim tab control cables
96 Aileron hinge access panels
97 Aileron and tab control linkage
98 Aileron trim tab (port wing only)
99 Frise-type aileron
100 Wing rear (No. 2) spar
101 Port navigation light
102 Pitot head
103 Wing front (No. 1) spar
104 Wing stressed skin

105 Four-gun ammunition troughs (individual bays)
106 Staggered gun barrels
107 Removable panel
108 Inter-spar gun bay access panel
109 Forward gunsight bead
110 Oil feed pipes
111 Oil tank (28.6 US gal; 108 litres)
112 Hydraulic pressure line
113 Engine upper bearers
114 Engine control correlating cam
115 Eclipse pump (anti-icing)
116 Fuel level transmitter
117 Generator
118 Battery junction box
119 Storage battery
120 Exhaust collector ring
121 Cowl flap actuating cylinder
122 Exhaust outlets to collector ring
123 Cowl flaps
124 Supercharged and cooling air ducts to carburettor (port and starboard)
125 Exhaust upper outlets
126 Cowling frame
127 Pratt & Whitney R-2800-59 18-cylinder two-row radial engine

128 Cowling nose panel
129 Magnetos
130 Propeller governor
131 Propeller hub
132 Reduction gear casing
133 Spinner
134 Propeller cuffs
135 Four-bladed Curtiss constant-speed electric propeller
136 Oil cooler intakes (port and starboard)
137 Supercharger intercooler (central) air intake
138 Ducting
139 Oil cooler feed pipes
140 Starboard oil cooler

141 Engine lower bearers
142 Oil cooler exhaust variable shutter
143 Fixed deflector
144 Excess exhaust gas gate
145 Belly stores/weapons shackles
146 Metal auxiliary drop tank (75 US gal; 284 litres)
147 Inboard mainwheel well door
148 Mainwheel well door actuating cylinder
149 Camera gun port
150 Cabin air conditioning intake (starboard wing only)
151 Wingroot fairing
152 Wing front spar/fuselage attachment (tapered bolts/bushings)

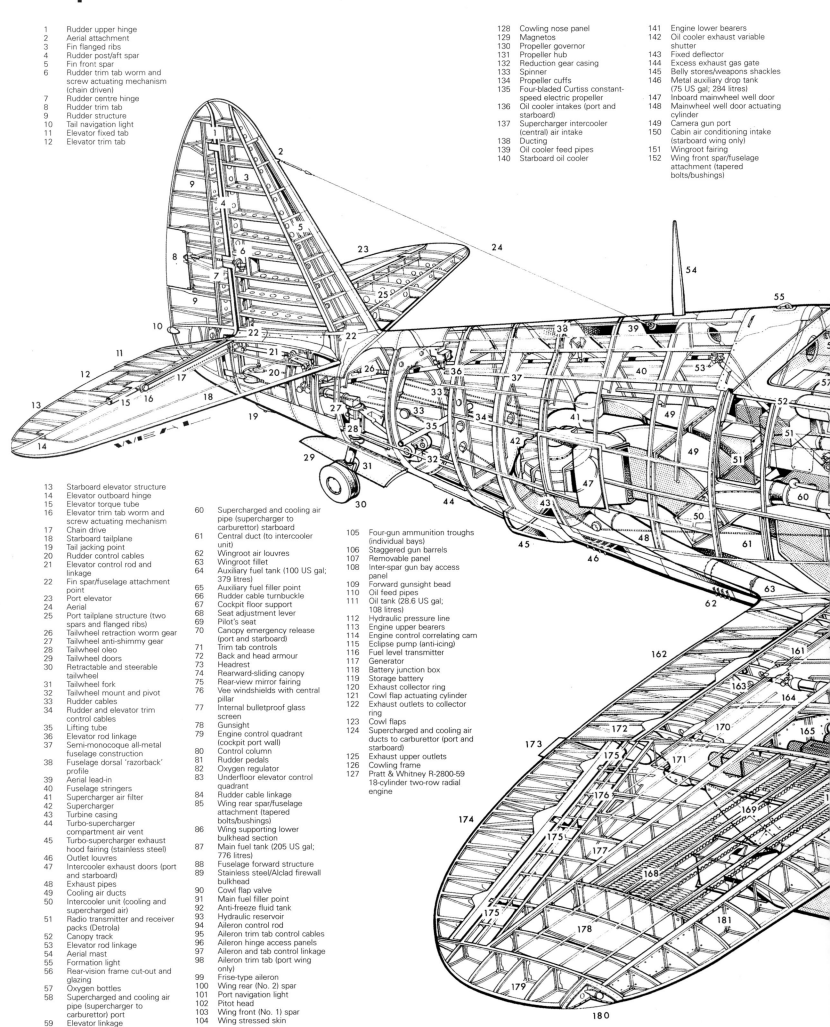

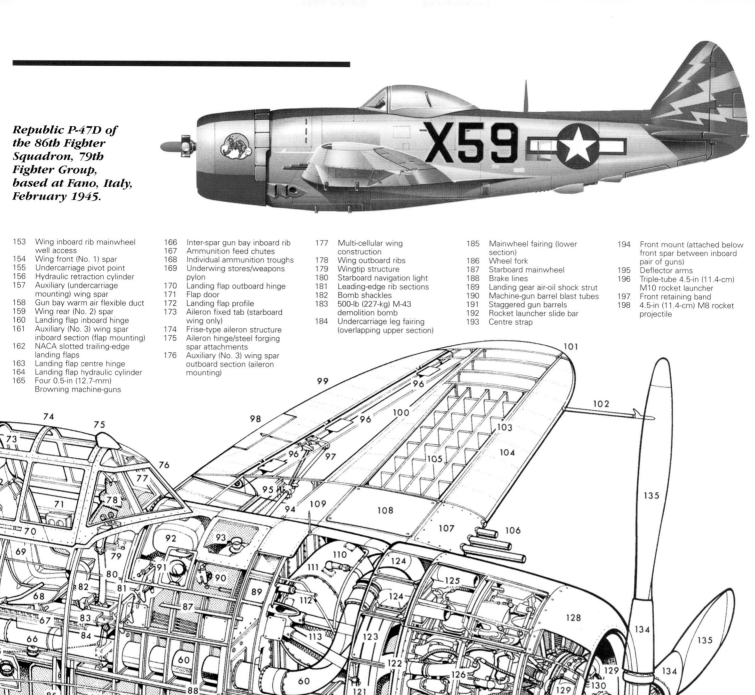

Republic P-47D of the 86th Fighter Squadron, 79th Fighter Group, based at Fano, Italy, February 1945.

153 Wing inboard rib mainwheel well access
154 Wing front (No. 1) spar
155 Undercarriage pivot point
156 Hydraulic retraction cylinder
157 Auxiliary (undercarriage mounting) wing spar
158 Gun bay warm air flexible duct
159 Wing rear (No. 2) spar
160 Landing flap inboard hinge
161 Auxiliary (No. 3) wing spar inboard section (flap mounting)
162 NACA slotted trailing-edge landing flaps
163 Landing flap centre hinge
164 Landing flap hydraulic cylinder
165 Four 0.5-in (12.7-mm) Browning machine-guns

166 Inter-spar gun bay inboard rib
167 Ammunition feed chutes
168 Individual ammunition troughs
169 Underwing stores/weapons pylon
170 Landing flap outboard hinge
171 Flap door
172 Landing flap profile
173 Aileron fixed tab (starboard wing only)
174 Frise-type aileron structure
175 Aileron hinge/steel forging spar attachments
176 Auxiliary (No. 3) wing spar outboard section (aileron mounting)

177 Multi-cellular wing construction
178 Wing outboard ribs
179 Wingtip structure
180 Starboard navigation light
181 Leading-edge rib sections
182 Bomb shackles
183 500-lb (227-kg) M-43 demolition bomb
184 Undercarriage leg fairing (overlapping upper section)

185 Mainwheel fairing (lower section)
186 Wheel fork
187 Starboard mainwheel
188 Brake lines
189 Landing gear air-oil shock strut
190 Machine-gun barrel blast tubes
191 Staggered gun barrels
192 Rocket launcher slide bar
193 Centre strap

194 Front mount (attached below front spar between inboard pair of guns)
195 Deflector arms
196 Triple-tube 4.5-in (11.4-cm) M10 rocket launcher
197 Front retaining band
198 4.5-in (11.4-cm) M8 rocket projectile

Bell P-39 Airacobra

Bell P-39M Airacobra
Type: single-seat monoplane fighter/fighter-bomber
Powerplant: one 1,200-hp (895-kW) Allison V-1710-83 piston engine
Performance: maximum speed 386 mph (621 km/h) at 9,500 ft (2895 m); cruising speed 200 mph (322 km/h); service ceiling 36,000 ft (10970 m); range 650 miles (1046 km)
Weights: empty 5,610 lb (2545 kg); maximum take-off 8,400 lb (3810 kg)
Dimensions: wing span 34 ft (10.36 m); length 30 ft 2 in (9.19 m); height 11 ft 10 in (3.61 m); wing area 213 sq ft (19.79 m²)
Armament: one 37-mm T9 cannon, two 0.50-in (12.7-mm) machine-guns and four 0.30-in (7.62-mm) machine-guns, plus provision for one 500-lb (227-kg) bomb

Bell P-39L of the 93rd Fighter Squadron, 81st Fighter Group, based in Tunisia in 1943.

The Airacobra was a radical design that was found to perform best at low altitudes.

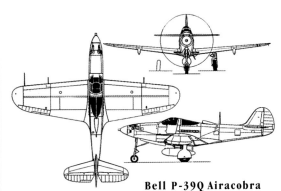

Bell P-39Q Airacobra

These well-worn Bell P-39Ds were photographed in 1942 while assigned to a training unit at Dale Mabry Field near Tallahassee, Florida. The numbering of the 31st Pursuit Group is showing faintly under the large numerals. Designed around the massive T9 37-mm cannon, the P-39 packed a good punch but had unimpressive performance.

Below: The P-38H was one of the last of the Lightning family to come off the Burbank line with the old engine installation comprising only flush oil-cooler inlets under the engine and seperate intercooler radiators. Deep chin radiators followed on the P-38J.

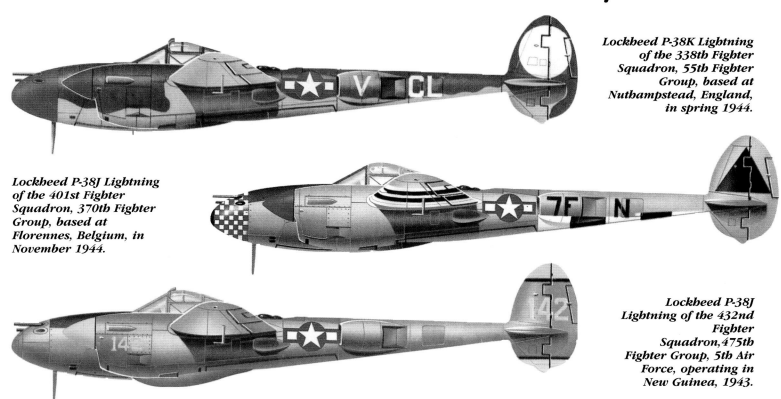

Lockheed P-38K Lightning of the 338th Fighter Squadron, 55th Fighter Group, based at Nuthampstead, England, in spring 1944.

Lockheed P-38J Lightning of the 401st Fighter Squadron, 370th Fighter Group, based at Florennes, Belgium, in November 1944.

Lockheed P-38J Lightning of the 432nd Fighter Squadron, 475th Fighter Group, 5th Air Force, operating in New Guinea, 1943.

and then a superb ground-support aircraft, able to haul enormous loads of ordnance and deliver bombs on target.

The Lockheed P-38 Lightning was another. Designed as an interceptor, it lacked some of the manoeuvrability needed for one-on-one combat against its principal adversary in the Pacific. But it was used as a superlative long-range fighter-bomber in that theatre, although in Europe it struggled as a bomber escort.

Escort fighter missions

As the war situation changed, so did the general role of fighters. One early mission was escorting and protecting bombers. The pre-war USAAC had blundered badly in not appreciating the need for special escort fighters for the heavyweights. Pressed into service, although incapable of performing the mission effectively, the fighters and their pilots received undeserved criticism every time a bomber was lost. But the fighters at that time were range-limited, and could not go with the bombers to the targets deep in

Germany. Drop tanks, hurriedly developed and employed, were some help, but the truly effective use of escorts had to await the long-range Mustang.

Increasingly, fighters were turned toward ground support as a major mission. They became, in effect, a winged heavy artillery, an added supporting strength that enabled ground forces to move more rapidly and securely. With an air umbrella above, and other aircraft down 'in the mud' with the infantry, air power made major contributions to all the ground battles.

As the war moved to its inevitable conclusion, both German and Japanese air strength waned rapidly. With little opposition in the skies of Europe, American fighters ranged across the continent, bombing and strafing ground targets on interdiction missions, or hammering a German armoured column in support; with guidance in the subtleties of long-range cruise control by the famous pilot Charles Lindbergh, they also smashed Japanese air power on the ground at one Pacific island base after another.

Lockheed P-38 Lightning

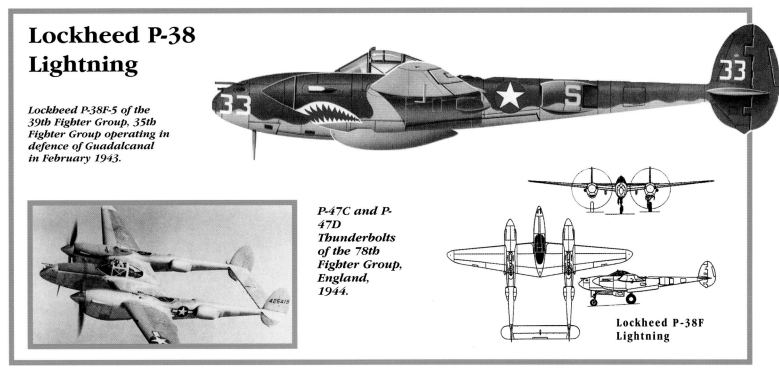

Lockheed P-38F-5 of the 39th Fighter Group, 35th Fighter Group operating in defence of Guadalcanal in February 1943.

P-47C and P-47D Thunderbolts of the 78th Fighter Group, England, 1944.

Lockheed P-38F Lightning

Lockheed P-38J Lightning
Type: single-seat long-range escort fighter
Powerplant: two 1,425-hp (1063-kW) Allison V-1710-89/91 piston engines
Performance: maximum speed 414 mph (666 km/h) at 25,000 ft (7620 m); cruising speed 290 mph (467 km/h); service ceiling 44,000 ft (13410 m); range with internal fuel 475 miles (764 km)
Weights: empty 12,780 lb (5797 kg); maximum take-off 21,600 lb (9798 kg)
Dimensions: wing span 52 ft (15.85 m); length 37 ft 10 in (11.53 m); height 9 ft 10 in (3.00 m); wing area 327.5 sq ft (30.42 m²)
Armament: one 20-mm cannon and four 0.50-in (12.7mm) machine-guns, plus up to 3,200 lb (1451 kg) of bombs

Lockheed P-38 Lightning

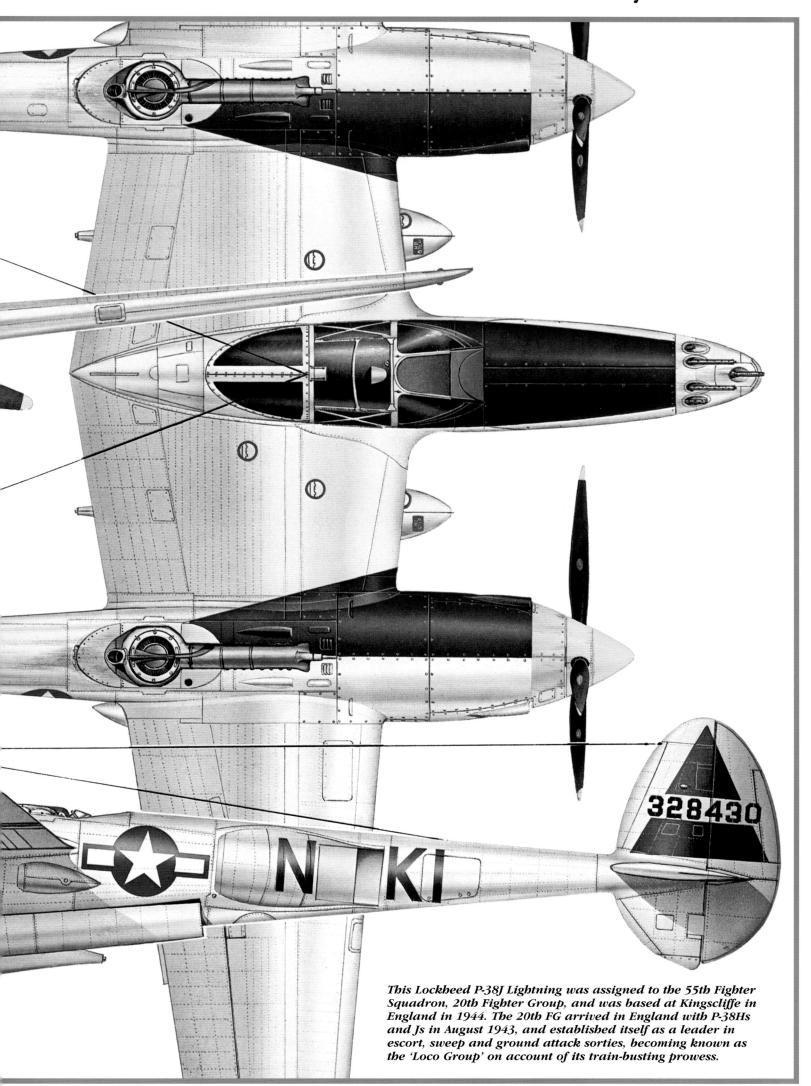

This Lockheed P-38J Lightning was assigned to the 55th Fighter Squadron, 20th Fighter Group, and was based at Kingscliffe in England in 1944. The 20th FG arrived in England with P-38Hs and Js in August 1943, and established itself as a leader in escort, sweep and ground attack sorties, becoming known as the 'Loco Group' on account of its train-busting prowess.

328430

N KI

Lockheed P-38J Lightning

1 Starboard navigation light
2 Wingtip trailing edge strake
3 Landing light (underwing) location
4 Starboard aileron
5 Aileron control rod/quadrant
6 Wing outer spar

20 Engine bearer/bulkhead upper attachment
21 Firewall
22 Triangulated tubular engine bearer supports
23 Polished mirror surface panel (undercarriage visual check)
24 Cantilever engine bearer
25 Intake fairing
26 Accessories cooling intake

36 Four 0.5-in (12.7-mm) machine-guns
37 Cannon flexible hose hydraulic charger
38 Chatellerault-feed cannon magazine (150 rounds)
39 Machine-gun firing solenoid
40 Cannon ammunition feed chute
41 Nose armament cowling clips
42 Case ejection chute (port lower machine-gun)
43 Ammunition box and feed chute (port lower machine-gun)
44 Case ejection chute (port upper machine-gun)

45 Ammunition box and feed chute (port upper machine-gun)
46 Radio antenna
47 Ejection chute exit (shrouded when item 52 attached)
48 Nosewheel door
49 Nosewheel shimmy damper assembly and reservoir
50 Torque links
51 Towing eye
52 Type M10 triple-tube 4.5-in (11.4-cm) rocket-launcher
53 Rearward-retracting nosewheel
54 Alloy spokes cover plate
55 Fork
56 Rocket-launcher forward attachment (to 63)
57 Nosewheel lower drag struts
58 Nosewheel oleo leg
59 Nosewheel pin access
60 Side struts and fulcrum
61 Actuating cylinder
62 Upper drag strut
63 Rocket-launcher forward attachment bracket
64 Rudder pedal assembly
65 Engine controls quadrant

66 Instrument panel
67 Spectacle grip cantilevered control wheel
68 Non-reflective shroud
69 Lynn-3 reflector sight mounting
70 Optically-flat bullet-proof windscreen (P-38J-10 and later)
71 External rear-view mirror
72 Armoured headrest
73 Rearward-hinged canopy
74 Pilot's armoured seat back
75 Canopy bracing
76 Downward-winding side windows
77 Wing root fillets
78 Nosewheel well
79 Port reserve fuel tank, capacity 50 Imp gal (227 litres)
80 Fuel filler cap
81 Main (double I-beam) spar
82 Fuel filler cap
83 Flap inner carriage
84 Port main fuel tank, capacity 75 Imp gal (341 litres)
85 Flap control access

7 Aileron tab drum
8 Aileron tab control pulleys
9 Aileron tab control rod
10 Aileron trim tab
11 Fixed tab
12 Tab cable access
13 Flap extension/retraction cables
14 Control pulleys
15 Flap outer carriage
16 Fowler-type flap (extended)
17 Control access panel
18 Wing spar transition
19 Outer section leading-edge fuel tanks (P-38J-5 and subsequent) capacity 46 Imp gal (208 litres) each

27 Oil radiator (outer sections) and intercooler (centre section) triple intake
28 Spinner
29 Curtiss-Electric three-bladed (left) handed propeller
30 Four machine-gun barrels
31 Cannon barrel
32 Camera-gun aperture
33 Nose panel
34 Bulkhead
35 Machine-gun blast tubes

34

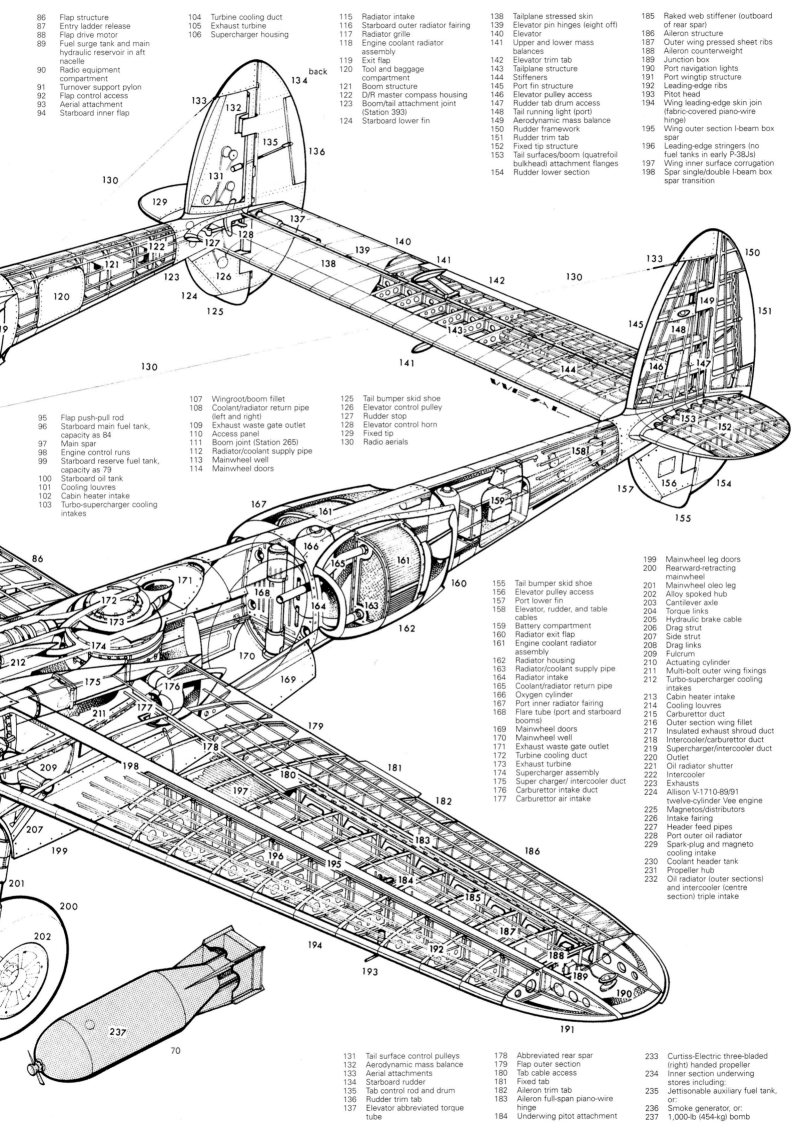

86 Flap structure
87 Entry ladder release
88 Flap drive motor
89 Fuel surge tank and main hydraulic reservoir in aft nacelle
90 Radio equipment compartment
91 Turnover support pylon
92 Flap control access
93 Aerial attachment
94 Starboard inner flap

104 Turbine cooling duct
105 Exhaust turbine
106 Supercharger housing

back
134

115 Radiator intake
116 Starboard outer radiator fairing
117 Radiator grille
118 Engine coolant radiator assembly
119 Exit flap
120 Tool and baggage compartment
121 Boom structure
122 D/R master compass housing
123 Boom/tail attachment joint (Station 393)
124 Starboard lower fin

138 Tailplane stressed skin
139 Elevator pin hinges (eight off)
140 Elevator
141 Upper and lower mass balances
142 Elevator trim tab
143 Tailplane structure
144 Stiffeners
145 Port fin structure
146 Elevator pulley access
147 Rudder tab drum access
148 Tail running light (port)
149 Aerodynamic mass balance
150 Rudder framework
151 Rudder trim tab
152 Fixed tip structure
153 Tail surfaces/boom (quatrefoil bulkhead) attachment flanges
154 Rudder lower section

185 Raked web stiffener (outboard of rear spar)
186 Aileron structure
187 Outer wing pressed sheet ribs
188 Aileron counterweight
189 Junction box
190 Port navigation lights
191 Port wingtip structure
192 Leading-edge ribs
193 Pitot head
194 Wing leading-edge skin join (fabric-covered piano-wire hinge)
195 Wing outer section I-beam box spar
196 Leading-edge stringers (no fuel tanks in early P-38Js)
197 Wing inner surface corrugation
198 Spar single/double I-beam box spar transition

95 Flap push-pull rod
96 Starboard main fuel tank, capacity as 84
97 Main spar
98 Engine control runs
99 Starboard reserve fuel tank, capacity as 79
100 Starboard oil tank
101 Cooling louvres
102 Cabin heater intake
103 Turbo-supercharger cooling intakes

107 Wingroot/boom fillet
108 Coolant/radiator return pipe (left and right)
109 Exhaust waste gate outlet
110 Access panel
111 Boom joint (Station 265)
112 Radiator/coolant supply pipe
113 Mainwheel well
114 Mainwheel doors

125 Tail bumper skid shoe
126 Elevator control pulley
127 Rudder stop
128 Elevator control horn
129 Fixed tip
130 Radio aerials

155 Tail bumper skid shoe
156 Elevator pulley access
157 Port lower fin
158 Elevator, rudder, and table cables
159 Battery compartment
160 Radiator exit flap
161 Engine coolant radiator assembly
162 Radiator housing
163 Radiator/coolant supply pipe
164 Radiator intake
165 Coolant/radiator return pipe
166 Oxygen cylinder
167 Port inner radiator fairing
168 Flare tube (port and starboard booms)
169 Mainwheel doors
170 Mainwheel well
171 Exhaust waste gate outlet
172 Turbine cooling duct
173 Exhaust turbine
174 Supercharger assembly
175 Super charger/ intercooler duct
176 Carburettor intake duct
177 Carburettor air intake

199 Mainwheel leg doors
200 Rearward-retracting mainwheel
201 Mainwheel oleo leg
202 Alloy spoked hub
203 Cantilever axle
204 Torque links
205 Hydraulic brake cable
206 Drag strut
207 Side strut
208 Drag links
209 Fulcrum
210 Actuating cylinder
211 Multi-bolt outer wing fixings
212 Turbo-supercharger cooling intakes
213 Cabin heater intake
214 Cooling louvres
215 Carburettor duct
216 Outer section wing fillet
217 Insulated exhaust shroud duct
218 Intercooler/carburettor duct
219 Supercharger/intercooler duct
220 Outlet
221 Oil radiator shutter
222 Intercooler
223 Exhausts
224 Allison V-1710-89/91 twelve-cylinder Vee engine
225 Magnetos/distributors
226 Intake fairing
227 Header feed pipes
228 Port outer oil radiator
229 Spark-plug and magneto cooling intake
230 Coolant header tank
231 Propeller hub
232 Oil radiator (outer sections) and intercooler (centre section) triple intake

131 Tail surface control pulleys
132 Aerodynamic mass balance
133 Aerial attachments
134 Starboard rudder
135 Tab control rod and drum
136 Rudder trim tab
137 Elevator abbreviated torque tube

178 Abbreviated rear spar
179 Flap outer section
180 Tab cable access
181 Fixed tab
182 Aileron trim tab
183 Aileron full-span piano-wire hinge
184 Underwing pitot attachment

233 Curtiss-Electric three-bladed (right) handed propeller
234 Inner section underwing stores including:
235 Jettisonable auxiliary fuel tank, or:
236 Smoke generator, or:
237 1,000-lb (454-kg) bomb

American Fighters of World War II

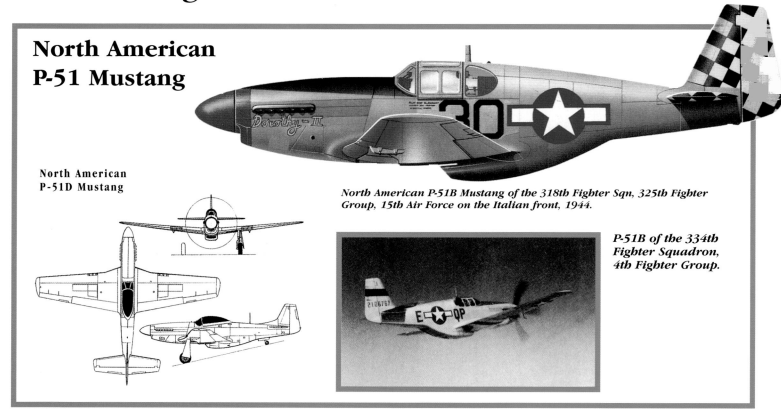

North American
P-51 Mustang

North American
P-51D Mustang

North American P-51B Mustang of the 318th Fighter Sqn, 325th Fighter Group, 15th Air Force on the Italian front, 1944.

P-51B of the 334th Fighter Squadron, 4th Fighter Group.

Fighter sketches

Bell P-39 Airacobra

Another radical design, the P-39 featured an engine in the fuselage behind the pilot. Designed as an interceptor, it was destined to be developed without turbo-supercharging and, as a result, it never achieved good high-altitude performance. It was reported to be a dream to fly with near-perfect control harmony. 'Think the turn,' said one pilot, 'and around she goes.' It had a low service ceiling, a low rate of climb, and a relative lack of manoeuvrability. But it had a rugged airframe. Properly flown, it became an important ground-support aircraft, with the firepower to inflict great damage, and the capacity to absorb punishment. It failed miserably in its first European deployment, and was quickly replaced there, but in the Pacific. It served well as a bomber escort, interceptor

of Japanese air raids, and as an attacker against ground targets. The US Army accepted 9,558 examples, most of which were sent to the Russians. USAAF peak inventory was 2,150. By 1944, the P-39's unit cost was about $50,000.

Curtiss P-40 Warhawk

Begun as a basically simple re-engining of the tenth P-36, the P-40 gained a combat record that won it final and grudging respect from its detractors. It was the standard pursuit aircraft when the USA entered the war, and had already been in combat with the Flying Tigers in China. It entered combat with the USAAF on 7 December 1941, and stayed in service until VJ-Day. Operationally, it was used best from an advantage in altitude, speed and position. If a p-40 attack began with a 2,000-ft (610-m) altitude advantage, the aircraft could make four passes through an enemy formation before having to leave the fight to climb back to

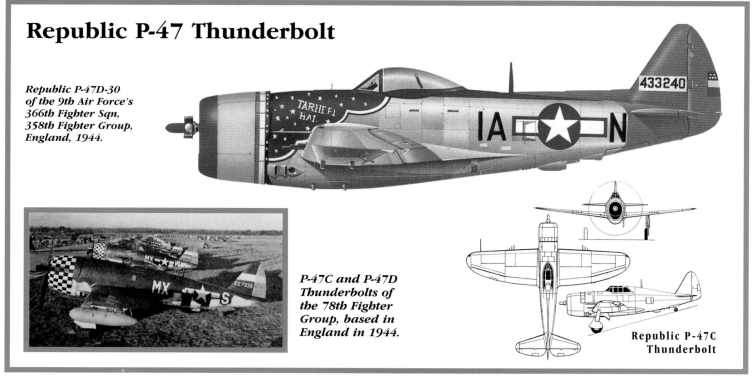

Republic P-47 Thunderbolt

Republic P-47D-30 of the 9th Air Force's 366th Fighter Sqn, 358th Fighter Group, England, 1944.

P-47C and P-47D Thunderbolts of the 78th Fighter Group, based in England in 1944.

Republic P-47C
Thunderbolt

This P-51A was flown by the 1st Air Commando's CO, Colonel Philip Cochran, in Burma in 1944. It was armed with four 12.7-mm (0.50-in) guns and had a direction-finding loop antenna on the rear fuselage.

This aircraft represents the original USAAF production variant of the North American P-51 with four 20-mm cannon; this example served with the 154th Fighter Sqn in Tunisia and Sicily in 1943.

Below: The Curtiss P-40 was built in enormous numbers until as late as 1944. Although its performance was poor by the standards of its more advanced contemporaries, the type nevertheless continued to give sterling service with US forces as well as with a large number of Allied units. This P-40E of the 11th Fighter Squadron, 343rd FG, served in the Aleutians, North Pacific in 1942. The nose art was adopted as a tribute to Claire Chennault, leader of the 'Flying Tigers'.

Above: This is one of the best photographs ever taken of P-51s on an operational flight in World War II. Three of the aircraft are Inglewood-built P-51D-5s, 44-13926 having the dorsal fin which was added to many P-51Ds built without it. Furthest away is a P-51B-15 with the original framed canopy. The Mustangs flew with the 8th Air Force's 375th Fighter Squadron, 361st Fighter Group. The unit was assigned a bomber escort mission.

American Fighters of World War II

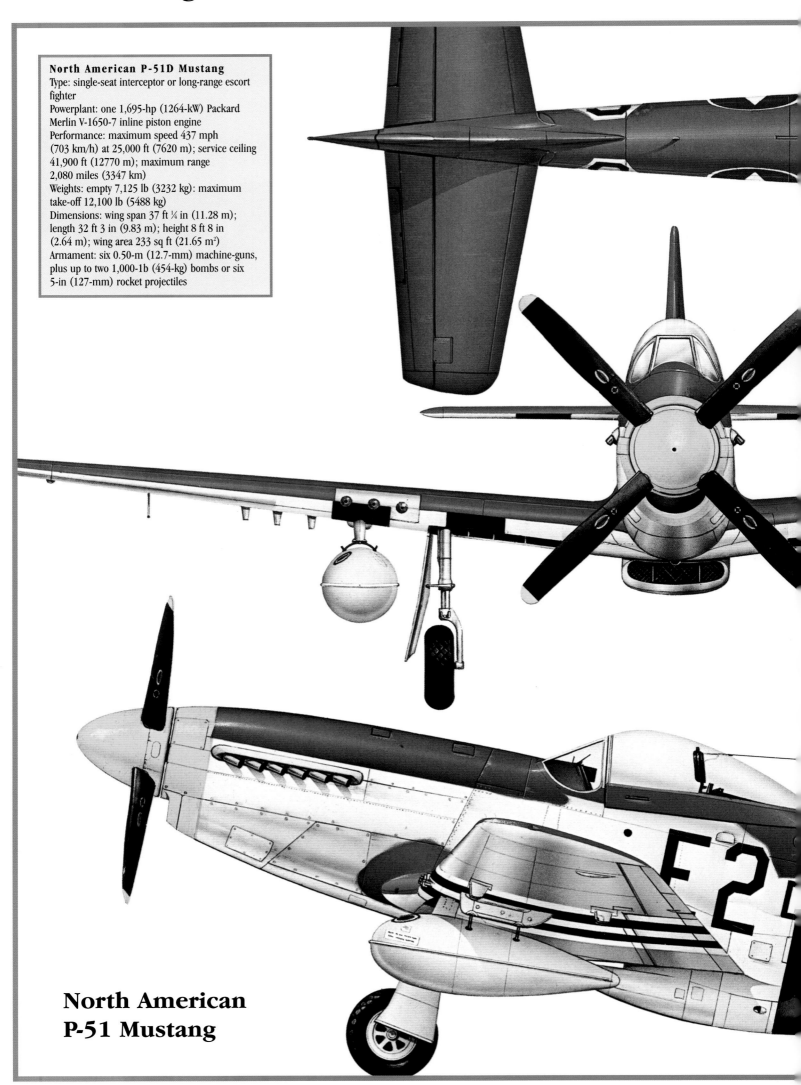

North American P-51D Mustang
Type: single-seat interceptor or long-range escort fighter
Powerplant: one 1,695-hp (1264-kW) Packard Merlin V-1650-7 inline piston engine
Performance: maximum speed 437 mph (703 km/h) at 25,000 ft (7620 m); service ceiling 41,900 ft (12770 m); maximum range 2,080 miles (3347 km)
Weights: empty 7,125 lb (3232 kg): maximum take-off 12,100 lb (5488 kg)
Dimensions: wing span 37 ft ¼ in (11.28 m); length 32 ft 3 in (9.83 m); height 8 ft 8 in (2.64 m); wing area 233 sq ft (21.65 m²)
Armament: six 0.50-m (12.7-mm) machine-guns, plus up to two 1,000-1b (454-kg) bombs or six 5-in (127-mm) rocket projectiles

**North American
P-51 Mustang**

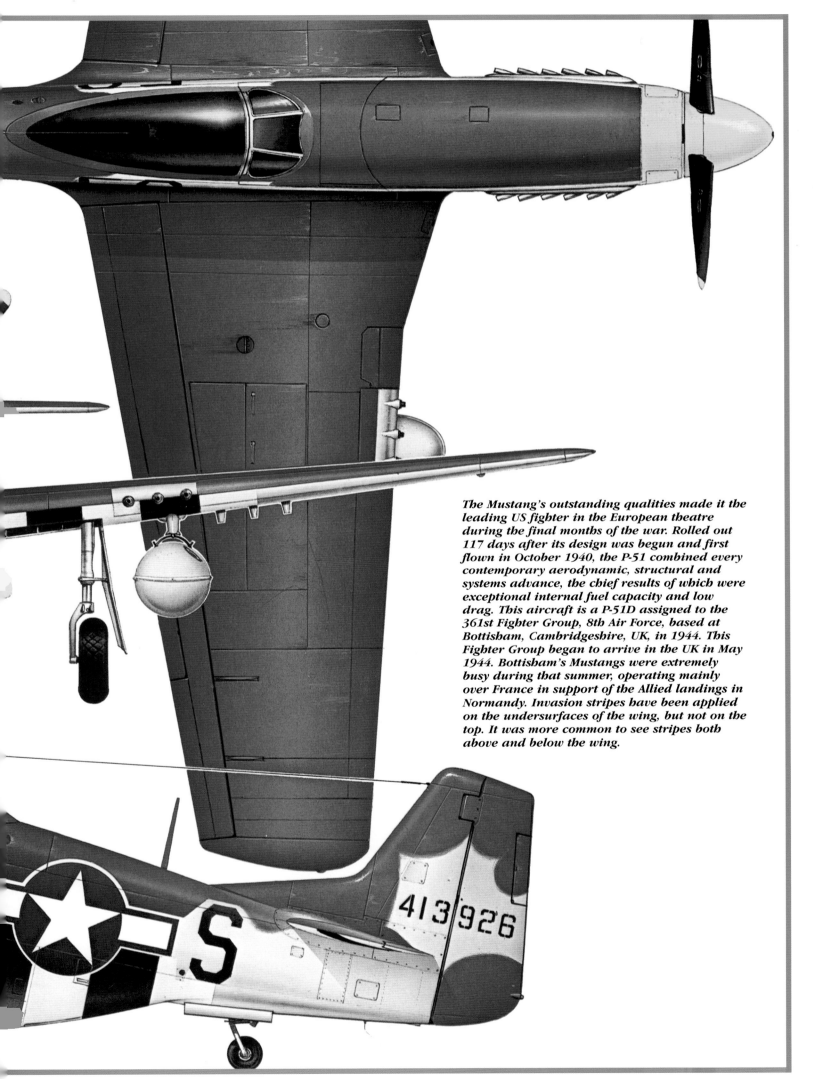

The Mustang's outstanding qualities made it the leading US fighter in the European theatre during the final months of the war. Rolled out 117 days after its design was begun and first flown in October 1940, the P-51 combined every contemporary aerodynamic, structural and systems advance, the chief results of which were exceptional internal fuel capacity and low drag. This aircraft is a P-51D assigned to the 361st Fighter Group, 8th Air Force, based at Bottisham, Cambridgeshire, UK, in 1944. This Fighter Group began to arrive in the UK in May 1944. Bottisham's Mustangs were extremely busy during that summer, operating mainly over France in support of the Allied landings in Normandy. Invasion stripes have been applied on the undersurfaces of the wing, but not on the top. It was more common to see stripes both above and below the wing.

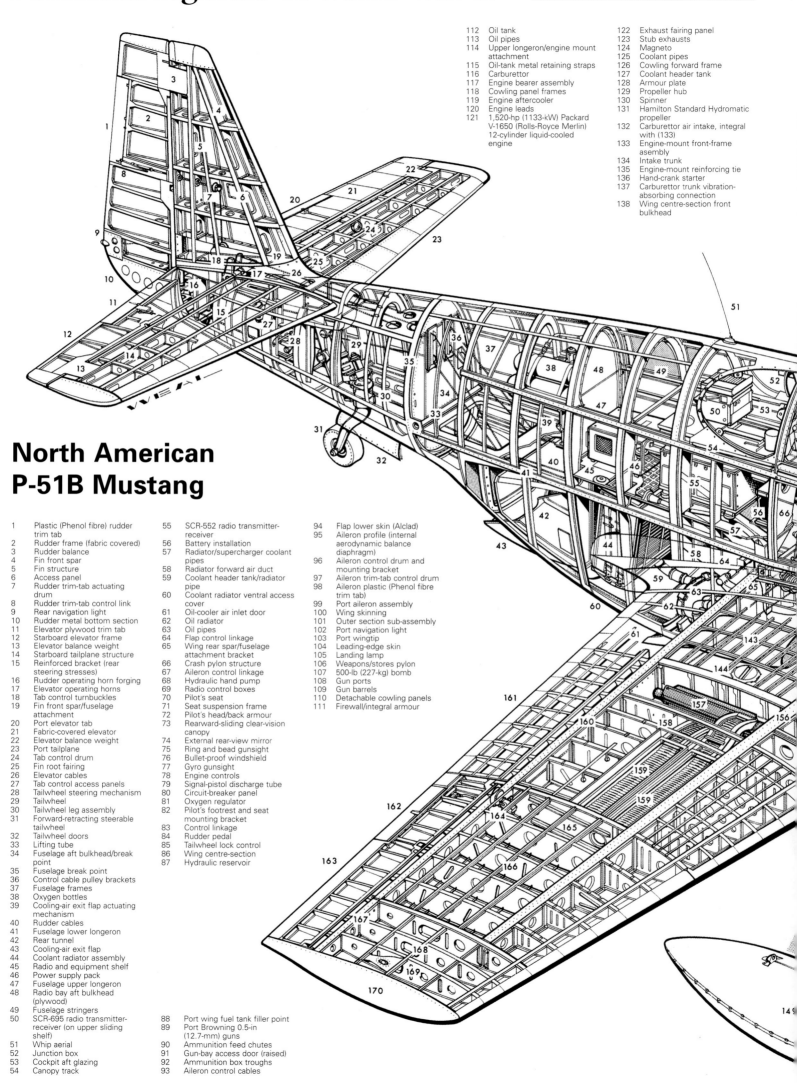

North American
P-51B Mustang

1. Plastic (Phenol fibre) rudder trim tab
2. Rudder frame (fabric covered)
3. Rudder balance
4. Fin front spar
5. Fin structure
6. Access panel
7. Rudder trim-tab actuating drum
8. Rudder trim-tab control link
9. Rear navigation light
10. Rudder metal bottom section
11. Elevator plywood trim tab
12. Starboard elevator frame
13. Elevator balance weight
14. Starboard tailplane structure
15. Reinforced bracket (rear steering stresses)
16. Rudder operating horn forging
17. Elevator operating horns
18. Tab control turnbuckles
19. Fin front spar/fuselage attachment
20. Port elevator tab
21. Fabric-covered elevator
22. Elevator balance weight
23. Port tailplane
24. Tab control drum
25. Fin root fairing
26. Elevator cables
27. Tab control access panels
28. Tailwheel steering mechanism
29. Tailwheel
30. Tailwheel leg assembly
31. Forward-retracting steerable tailwheel
32. Tailwheel doors
33. Lifting tube
34. Fuselage aft bulkhead/break point
35. Fuselage break point
36. Control cable pulley brackets
37. Fuselage frames
38. Oxygen bottles
39. Cooling-air exit flap actuating mechanism
40. Rudder cables
41. Fuselage lower longeron
42. Rear tunnel
43. Cooling-air exit flap
44. Coolant radiator assembly
45. Radio and equipment shelf
46. Power supply pack
47. Fuselage upper longeron
48. Radio bay aft bulkhead (plywood)
49. Fuselage stringers
50. SCR-695 radio transmitter-receiver (on upper sliding shelf)
51. Whip aerial
52. Junction box
53. Cockpit aft glazing
54. Canopy track

55. SCR-552 radio transmitter-receiver
56. Battery installation
57. Radiator/supercharger coolant pipes
58. Radiator forward air duct
59. Coolant header tank/radiator pipe
60. Coolant radiator ventral access cover
61. Oil-cooler air inlet door
62. Oil radiator
63. Oil pipes
64. Flap control linkage
65. Wing rear spar/fuselage attachment bracket
66. Crash pylon structure
67. Aileron control linkage
68. Hydraulic hand pump
69. Radio control boxes
70. Pilot's seat
71. Seat suspension frame
72. Pilot's head/back armour
73. Rearward-sliding clear-vision canopy
74. External rear-view mirror
75. Ring and bead gunsight
76. Bullet-proof windshield
77. Gyro gunsight
78. Engine controls
79. Signal-pistol discharge tube
80. Circuit-breaker panel
81. Oxygen regulator
82. Pilot's footrest and seat mounting bracket
83. Control linkage
84. Rudder pedal
85. Tailwheel lock control
86. Wing centre-section
87. Hydraulic reservoir

88. Port wing fuel tank filler point
89. Port Browning 0.5-in (12.7-mm) guns
90. Ammunition feed chutes
91. Gun-bay access door (raised)
92. Ammunition box troughs
93. Aileron control cables

94. Flap lower skin (Alclad)
95. Aileron profile (internal aerodynamic balance diaphragm)
96. Aileron control drum and mounting bracket
97. Aileron trim-tab control drum
98. Aileron plastic (Phenol fibre trim tab)
99. Port aileron assembly
100. Wing skinning
101. Outer section sub-assembly
102. Port navigation light
103. Port wingtip
104. Leading-edge skin
105. Landing lamp
106. Weapons/stores pylon
107. 500-lb (227-kg) bomb
108. Gun ports
109. Gun barrels
110. Detachable cowling panels
111. Firewall/integral armour

112. Oil tank
113. Oil pipes
114. Upper longeron/engine mount attachment
115. Oil-tank metal retaining straps
116. Carburettor
117. Engine bearer assembly
118. Cowling panel frames
119. Engine aftercooler
120. Engine leads
121. 1,520-hp (1133-kW) Packard V-1650 (Rolls-Royce Merlin) 12-cylinder liquid-cooled engine

122. Exhaust fairing panel
123. Stub exhausts
124. Magneto
125. Coolant pipes
126. Cowling forward frame
127. Coolant header tank
128. Armour plate
129. Propeller hub
130. Spinner
131. Hamilton Standard Hydromatic propeller
132. Carburettor air intake, integral with (133)
133. Engine-mount front-frame assembly
134. Intake trunk
135. Engine-mount reinforcing tie
136. Hand-crank starter
137. Carburettor trunk vibration-absorbing connection
138. Wing centre-section front bulkhead

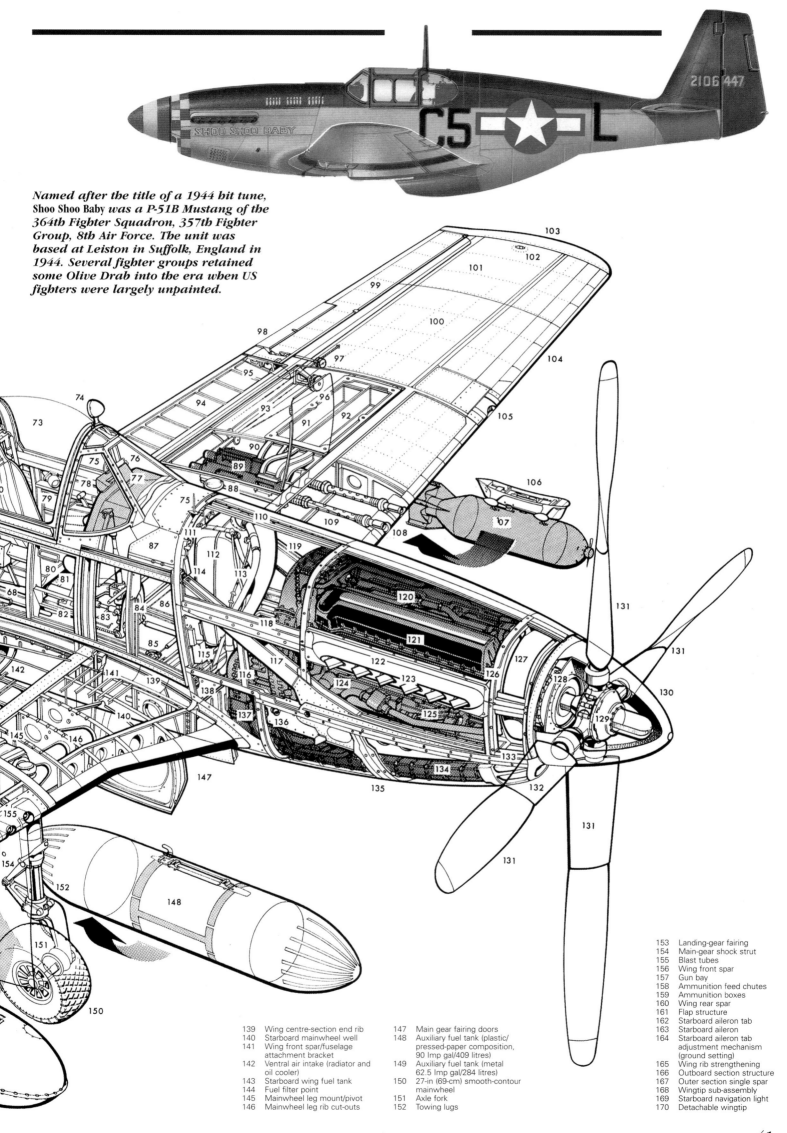

Named after the title of a 1944 hit tune,
Shoo Shoo Baby was a P-51B Mustang of the
364th Fighter Squadron, 357th Fighter
Group, 8th Air Force. The unit was
based at Leiston in Suffolk, England in
1944. Several fighter groups retained
some Olive Drab into the era when US
fighters were largely unpainted.

139	Wing centre-section end rib	147	Main gear fairing doors
140	Starboard mainwheel well	148	Auxiliary fuel tank (plastic/
141	Wing front spar/fuselage		pressed-paper composition,
	attachment bracket		90 Imp gal/409 litres)
142	Ventral air intake (radiator and	149	Auxiliary fuel tank (metal
	oil cooler)		62.5 Imp gal/284 litres)
143	Starboard wing fuel tank	150	27-in (69-cm) smooth-contour
144	Fuel filter point		mainwheel
145	Mainwheel leg mount/pivot	151	Axle fork
146	Mainwheel leg rib cut-outs	152	Towing lugs

153	Landing-gear fairing
154	Main-gear shock strut
155	Blast tubes
156	Wing front spar
157	Gun bay
158	Ammunition feed chutes
159	Ammunition boxes
160	Wing rear spar
161	Flap structure
162	Starboard aileron tab
163	Starboard aileron
164	Starboard aileron tab
	adjustment mechanism
	(ground setting)
165	Wing rib strengthening
166	Outboard section structure
167	Outer section single spar
168	Wingtip sub-assembly
169	Starboard navigation light
170	Detachable wingtip

The P-38 Lightning was exceptionally versatile; its roles included fighter, bomber, night-fighter, reconnaissance, casualty evacuation and torpedo-bombing, to name but a few. This is a P-38H-5-LO in mid-1943 Olive Drab/Neutral Gray finish.

the perch again. Defensive tactics were to quickly perform a split-S manoeuvre and dive down to gain speed and pull away. An alternative was to turn into the enemy or, if at low altitude, to skid violently. When production ended in December 1944, the US Army had accepted 12,302 P-40s. Unit cost was c.$60,552.

Lockheed P-38 Lightning

The P-38 was a daring departure from the state of the design art in 1936, when the programme began. The prototype first flew 27 January 1939, but was written off

Above: This particularly attractive colour scheme identified the P-51D Mustangs of the 4th Fighter Squadron, 52nd Fighter Group. This outfit served with the 15th Air Force, and finished the war operating from Torretto and Piagiolino, Italy.

Taken in early 1944, this fine study of a P-51D shows the underwing racks for drop tanks or bombs. The Millie P flew with the 343rd Fighter Squadron, 55th Fighter Group with yellow/green nose and spinner, Olive Drab rear fuselage and yellow rudder.

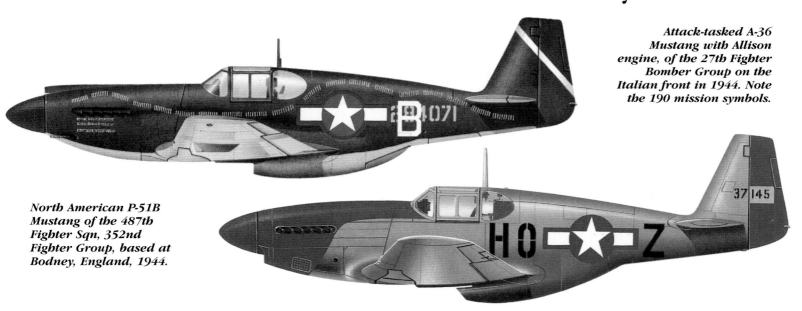

Attack-tasked A-36 Mustang with Allison engine, of the 27th Fighter Bomber Group on the Italian front in 1944. Note the 190 mission symbols.

North American P-51B Mustang of the 487th Fighter Sqn, 352nd Fighter Group, based at Bodney, England, 1944.

hardly two weeks later following a grandstanding transcontinental speed run. First production quantities were for the British, but without turbo-superchargers and with inevitable weight increases, performance was poor. Deliveries to the USAAF began in June 1941, and by the following April, about 350 were in service but under flight restrictions. Manoeuvrability was sluggish, especially in rolls, so that a P-38 was slow to switch from one manoeuvre to another, and slow to break off combat. Best combat tactics were to bounce the enemy from above at high speed, make one pass through the formation, and climb out. Their final kill ratio in the Pacific was 12:1. By 1944, P-38s cost $134,284 each in production, and the USAAF accepted 9,395 of the type.

Republic P-47 Thunderbolt

After a couple of false starts which cost almost a year's delay, Republic's proposal for a new fighter was accepted in mid-1940. Orders for production aircraft followed, and the first prototype flew on 6 May 1941. In April 1943 the Thunderbolt entered combat. 'She really can dive!' said one startled pilot. 'She'd damn well better,' said his commander, 'she sure as hell can't climb!' The P-47 escorted bombers for a while in Europe, until the North American P-51 Mustang came along. And then the

Thunderbolt found its true role as a powerful fighter-bomber. In deep interdiction strikes against rail and road targets, it destroyed thousands of locomotives, railway rolling stock, trucks, tanks and other vehicles. The P-47 was also a potent fighter, racking up an overall kill ratio of nearly 5:1. By the end of the war, a P-47 cost around $83,000.

North American P-51 Mustang

If it had not been for the UK's desperate need for fighters, the Mustang might never have been designed. And once it had been built, the USAAF did almost everything it could to avoid looking at it, Designed in 1940 in response to a British request, the prototype NA-73 first flew 26 October 1940. It featured use of a daringly different NACA 'low-drag, laminar-flow' aerofoil section. It became an exceptional fighter after its sleek airframe was married to the British Rolls-Royce Merlin engine. In this new guise, finally bought by the USAAF, it became the fighter par excellence, escorting bombers to Berlin and beyond, hammering at ground targets in glide-bombing attacks, and tangling with the best the Luftwaffe could put up, including jets and even the rocket-propelled Messerschmitt Me 163. The US Army purchased 14,068 Mustangs. In 1945, a P-51 Mustang cost $50,985.

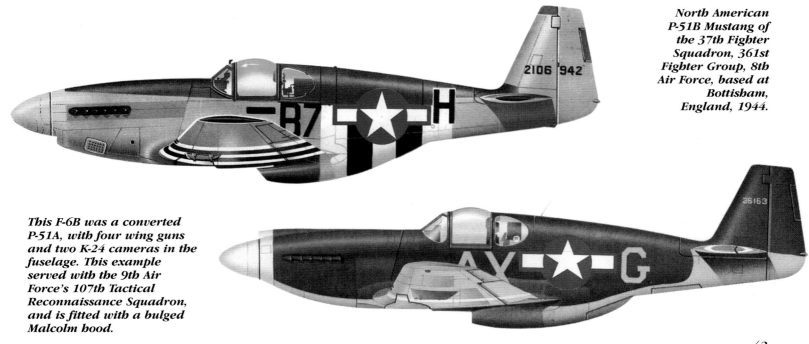

North American P-51B Mustang of the 37th Fighter Squadron, 361st Fighter Group, 8th Air Force, based at Bottisham, England, 1944.

This F-6B was a converted P-51A, with four wing guns and two K-24 cameras in the fuselage. This example served with the 9th Air Force's 107th Tactical Reconnaissance Squadron, and is fitted with a bulged Malcolm hood.

Pacific Pugilists

The US Navy fielded some poor fighter types at the beginning of the war, only initially holding its own with the Grumman F4F Wildcat. Then came two of the all-time greats, the Hellcat and Corsair that swept all before them.

If there were any lingering prejudices against the effectiveness of air power in the minds of high-level US Navy officers, they were erased at one stroke by the stunning Japanese attack on Pearl Harbor on the morning of 7 December 1941. The US Navy's principal Pacific base was devastated, and the bulk of its capital ships – proud battleships with the entire tradition of the US Navy behind them – was destroyed.

The US Navy was forced to fight its war with carriers, the only capital ships left. But it was a pitifully small force that faced a preponderance of Japanese naval strength. In the Pacific, the US Navy had two carriers, neither near Pearl Harbor. The USS *Enterprise* was returning from a ferry run to Wake Island, having just delivered the doomed Marine

Fighting Squadron (VMF) 211, with a dozen Grumman F4F-3 Wildcats as complement. She carried her own fighter force of 18 Wildcats. The USS *Lexington* was headed for Midway Island, to deliver a Marine scout bomber squadron. She was defended by 18 Brewster F2A-3s.

A new weapon

The carriers *Ranger*, *Wasp* and *Yorktown* were on station in the Atlantic, with a total complement of 90 Grumman F4Fs. The USS *Hornet* was also in Atlantic waters on her shakedown cruise; she had been commissioned two months before. Her fighters were 18 Wildcats. The USS *Saratoga* was lying at anchor in San Diego harbour, having just come out of overhaul.

Left: More than any other fighter, Grumman's F6F Hellcat turned the tide against the Japanese in the Pacific. The F6F's combat record is unmatched. Of the total of 6,477 confirmed victories by US Navy carrier-based pilots, the F6F (which only entered the fray on 31 August 1943) gained 4,947.

Though its development began much later than that of the Corsair, the Hellcat was in action by 1943 in greater numbers. Here F6F-3s start their engines aboard the USS Yorktown. Each of these aircraft carries a 150-US gal (568-litre) drop tank on its centreline position.

Brewster F2A Buffalo

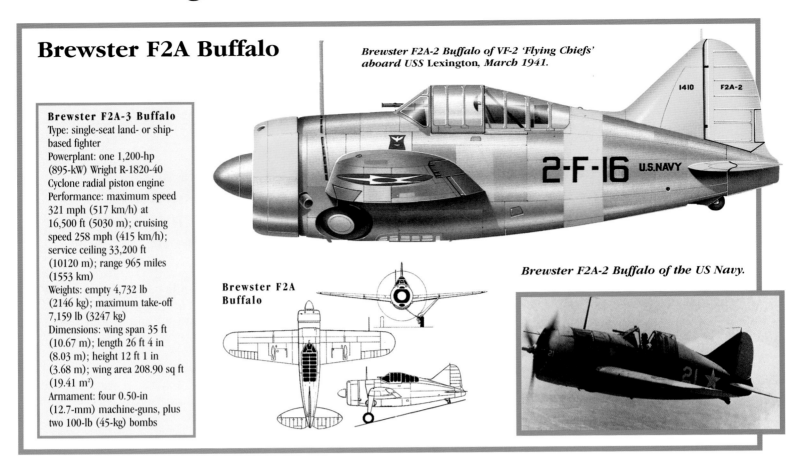

Brewster F2A-2 Buffalo of VF-2 'Flying Chiefs' aboard USS Lexington, March 1941.

Brewster F2A-3 Buffalo
Type: single-seat land- or ship-based fighter
Powerplant: one 1,200-hp (895-kW) Wright R-1820-40 Cyclone radial piston engine
Performance: maximum speed 321 mph (517 km/h) at 16,500 ft (5030 m); cruising speed 258 mph (415 km/h); service ceiling 33,200 ft (10120 m); range 965 miles (1553 km)
Weights: empty 4,732 lb (2146 kg); maximum take-off 7,159 lb (3247 kg)
Dimensions: wing span 35 ft (10.67 m); length 26 ft 4 in (8.03 m); height 12 ft 1 in (3.68 m); wing area 208.90 sq ft (19.41 m²)
Armament: four 0.50-in (12.7-mm) machine-guns, plus two 100-lb (45-kg) bombs

Brewster F2A Buffalo

Brewster F2A-2 Buffalo of the US Navy.

Two carriers with 36 fighters, plus 12 Wildcats on Wake Island, faced the Japanese attack in the Pacific. It was one of the two wars, both different, that the United States Navy waged. In the Atlantic, the campaign was to be one of blockade and protection of shipping, plus support of three future amphibious assaults (North Africa, southern France and Normandy). In the Pacific, the objectives were to stop the Japanese drive, and then to roll it back to the home islands.

Distance and time were to work in favour of the United States, so that the arsenal of democracy could get production lines moving at a high volume. Early Japanese conquests, which seemed absolutely overwhelming when first studied, placed their forces out at the ends of a number of thin supply lines that were vulnerable to sea and air attack. Cut them, even one at a time, and Japan would begin to feel defeat.

Photographed on 3 August 1942, this peel-off by F2A-2 fighters took place at a training unit in the United States. By that time no F2As were left in front-line US service, the last being with the USAAF in Australia. The F2A was never officially named Buffalo in US service.

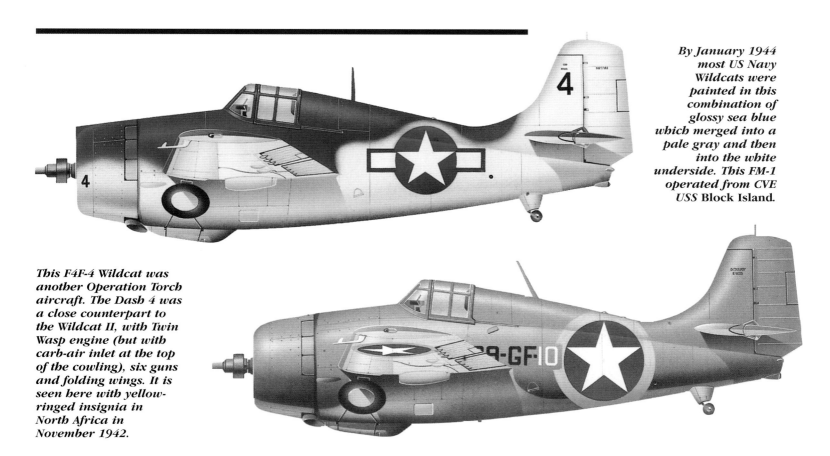

By January 1944 most US Navy Wildcats were painted in this combination of glossy sea blue which merged into a pale gray and then into the white underside. This FM-1 operated from CVE USS Block Island.

This F4F-4 Wildcat was another Operation Torch aircraft. The Dash 4 was a close counterpart to the Wildcat II, with Twin Wasp engine (but with carb-air inlet at the top of the cowling), six guns and folding wings. It is seen here with yellow-ringed insignia in North Africa in November 1942.

The US Navy had an ace up its sleeve: radar. Close co-operation and technology transfer with the British had been naval policy for several years before the war, and the basic concepts of shipboard use of radar had been explored and developed by December 1941. During 1940, the US Navy had been conducting experiments with ship-based search radar, and *Yorktown* had reported successfully detecting and tracking aircraft as far as 100 miles (161 km) distant. In July 1941 the US Navy approved the construction of radar plots (the equivalent of the later combat intelligence centres) for carriers, and started on

the first aboard the *Hornet*. Within two weeks, the Chief of Naval Operations ordered that fighter direction centres be established on all carriers.

Ironically, it was the Navy among US services that first put Chennault's basic concepts of air defence into operation. The ships had radar, the basic means of detection, and radar plots, which were a method of reporting information.

This photograph of a squadron of F4F-3A Hellcats was taken on 12 May 1942. Despite its narrow track the F4F was adequately stable on a pitching deck. Note the Douglas SBD Dauntlesses in the background.

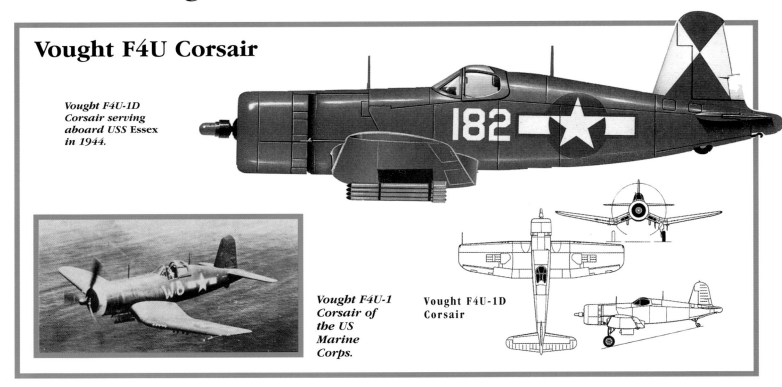

Vought F4U Corsair

Vought F4U-1D Corsair serving aboard USS Essex in 1944.

Vought F4U-1 Corsair of the US Marine Corps.

Vought F4U-1D Corsair

That information was used by the fighter director to vector combat elements to intercept the incoming threat. Once in sight of their targets, it was left to the fighters to apply their team tactics and to destroy the enemy aircraft.

Less than two months after the attack at Pearl Harbor, the US Navy steamed its first carrier offensive westward to the Gilbert and Marshall Islands. Two task forces, with their flagships *Enterprise* and *Yorktown*, raided those islands, and then went on to hit Wake and Marcus Islands. More carrier strikes hit Japanese shipping that was supporting landings at Lae and Salamaua, on New Guinea. And then the first of many sea-air battles erupted in the Coral Sea. Neither side's ships ever saw each other, the fight was a series of air attacks. The Japanese were frustrated in their attempt to land troops at Port Moresby, New Guinea, the US Navy lost the *Lexington*.

The key battle developed off Midway island in June 1942. There, the Japanese lost control of the air, their fighters and bombers hammered out of the sky by Grumman Wildcats. It was the turning point of the naval war in the Pacific. The *Yorktown* was abandoned after attack, but the Japanese lost four carriers and, more importantly, the best of their pilots. From then on, Japanese pilot quality was markedly inferior to its level earlier in the war

Guadalcanal

In August, the long campaign to seize and hold Guadalcanal began, and during subsequent naval battles, four US carriers – the entire Pacific fleet strength – were put out of service. *Enterprise* was bombed on 24 August and *Saratoga* was damaged a week later by a torpedo; both left the theatre for repairs. *Wasp* was sunk by a submarine on 15 September, and *Hornet* was lost to air attack on 26 October. In the meantime, *Enterprise* had been repaired and had returned to become the only carrier in the Pacific one year after war came to the United States.

As in legends, the US Marines came to the rescue. With their new Vought F4U Corsairs they operated out of land

As of 11 Septmber 1943 (the date of this photograph) Espiritu Santo on the New Hebrides was the home of VMF-214 'Black Sheep', the most famous of all US Marine fighter squadrons. Leading his men out to battle in their F4U-1s is 'Pappy' Boyington, the greatest of all US Marine Corps fighter aces of World War II.

Above: By far the most important operators of the Corsair in World War II were the fighter squadrons of the US Marine Corps, based on island airstrips in the Pacific. This bombing mission was photographed leaving parking areas on Majuro Atoll, in the Marshalls, on 29 August 1944. The squadron was assigned to the 4th Marine Air Wing.

Below: Taken on 18 June 1944, this dramatic photograph shows a flaming Kawanishi J1N1, probably a kamikaze, attacking the escort carrier USS Kitkun Bay off Leyte in October 1944.

Vought F4U Corsair

Vought F4U-4 Corsair
Type: single-seat carrier-based fighter/fighter-bomber
Powerplant: one 2,450-hp (1827-kW), with water
injection, Pratt & Whitney R-2800-18W Double Wasp
radial piston engine
Performance: maximum speed 446 mph (718 km/h)
at 26,200 ft (7985 m); service ceiling 41,500 ft
(12650 m); normal range 1,005 miles (1617 km);
maximum range 1,560 miles (2511 km)
Weights: empty 9,205 lb (4175 kg); maximum take-off
14,670 lb (6654 kg)
Dimensions: wing span 40 ft 11 in (12.47 m); length
33 ft 8 in (10. 26 m); height 14 ft 9 in (4.50 m); wing
area 314 sq ft (29.17 m²)
Armament: six 0.50-in (12.7-mm) machine-guns, plus
two 1,000-lb (454-kg) bombs or eight 5-in (127-mm)
rocket projectiles

*The F4U Corsair rapidly established itself as the
premier air combat fighter in the Pacific theatre;
indeed, subsequent tests in the USA proved that on
many counts it was the best air combat fighter
extant. This F4U-1A Corsair was flown by
Lieutenant Ira C. 'Ike' Kepford, the US Navy's
leading ace in the Pacific, with VF-17. Known as
the 'Jolly Roger' the unit was assigned to USS
Bougainville between November 1943 and
February 1944 and became the first to see action
with the F4U Corsair. Flown by pilots of the US
Marine Corps, Corsairs first won air supremacy in
the battle zones and then went on to prove
themselves as the Marines' best friends in their
secondary role as fighter-bombers as US forces
advanced deep into enemy territory in the Pacific
theatre. Kepford was one of 15 aces to go to war
in the Corsair. He had a total of 16 victories
recorded by the 'rising suns' on the fuselage side,
forward of the cockpit.*

Vought F4U-1A Corsair

1 Spinner
2 Three-bladed Hamilton Standard constant-speed propeller
3 Reduction gear housing
4 Nose ring
5 Pratt & Whitney R-2800-8W Double Wasp 18-cylinder two-row engine
6 Exhaust pipes
7 Hydraulically-operated cowling
8 Fixed cowling panels
9 Wing leading-edge unprotected integral fuel tank, capacity 62 US gal (235 litres)
10 Truss-type main spar
11 Leading-edge rib structure
12 Starboard navigation light
13 Wingtip
14 Wing structure
15 Wing ribs
16 Wing outer-section (fabric skinning aft of main spar)
17 Starboard aileron
18 Ammunition boxes (maximum total capacity 2,350 rounds)

51 Trim tab control wheels
52 Wing folding lever
53 Centre/aft fuselage bulkhead
54 Radio shelf
55 Radio installation
56 Canopy track
57 Bulkhead
58 Aerial lead-in
59 Aerial mast
60 Aerials
61 Heavy sheet skin plating
62 Dorsal identification light
63 Longeron
64 Control runs
65 Aft fuselage structure
66 Compass installation
67 Lifting tube
68 Access/inspection panels
69 Fin/fuselage forward attachment
70 Starboard tailplane
71 Elevator balance
72 Fin structure
73 Inspection panels
74 Rudder balance
75 Aerial stub

76 Rudder upper hinge
77 Rudder structure
78 Diagonal bracing
79 Rudder trim tab
80 Trim tab actuating rod
81 Access panel
82 Rudder post
83 Tailplane end rib
84 Elevator control runs
85 Fixed fairing root
86 Elevator trim tabs (port and starboard)
87 Tail cone
88 Rear navigation light
89 Port elevator
90 Elevator balance
91 Port tailplane structure
92 Arrester hook (stowed)
93 Tail section frames
94 Fairing
95 Tailwheel (retracted)
96 Arrester hook (lowered)
97 Tailwheel/hook doors
98 Tailwheel/hook attachment/pivot

99 Mooring/tie-down lug
100 Rearward-retracting tailwheel
101 Tailwheel oleo
102 Support strut
103 Arrester hook actuating strut
104 Aft/tail section bulkhead
105 Arrester hook shock absorber
106 Tailwheel/arrester hook cylinder
107 Tailwheel retraction strut
108 Bulkhead attachment points
109 Fuselage skinning
110 Bulkhead frame
111 Elevator/rudder control runs
112 Entry hand/foothold
113 Hydraulically-operated flap inboard section
114 Wing fold line
115 'Flap gap' closure plate
116 Hydraulically-operated flap outboard section
117 Aileron balance tab (port only)
118 Aileron trim tab

119 Port aileron
120 Deck landing grip
121 Port wingtip
122 Port navigation light
123 Pitot head
124 Leading-edge ribs
125 Wing outer section structure
126 Ammunition boxes
127 Three 0.5-in (12.7-mm) Colt-Browning MG53-2 wing machine-guns with 400 rpg (inboard pair) and 375 rpg (outboard)
128 Wing fold outboard cylinder

19 Aileron trim tab
20 Aerial mast
21 Forward bulkhead
22 Oil tank, capacity 28 US gal (106 litres)
23 Oil tank forward armour plate
24 Fire suppressor cylinder
25 Supercharger housing
26 Exhaust trunking
27 Blower assembly
28 Engine support frame
29 Engine control runs
30 Wing main spar carry-through structure
31 Engine support attachment
32 Upper cowling deflection plate (0.1-in/0.25-cm aluminium)
33 Fuel filler cap
34 Fuselage main fuel tank, capacity 237 US gal (897 litres)
35 Upper longeron
36 Fuselage forward frames
37 Rudder pedals
38 Heelboards
39 Control column
40 Instrument panel
41 Reflector sight
42 Armoured-glass windshield
43 Rear-view mirror
44 Rearward-sliding cockpit canopy
45 Handgrip
46 Headrest
47 Pilot's head and back armour
48 Canopy frame
49 Pilot's seat
50 Engine control quadrant

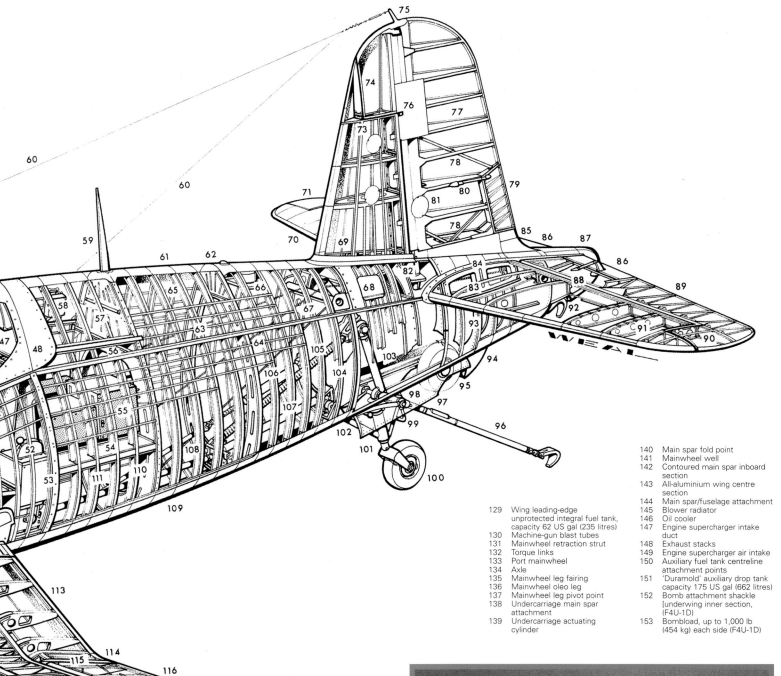

129 Wing leading-edge
    unprotected integral fuel tank,
    capacity 62 US gal (235 litres)
130 Machine-gun blast tubes
131 Mainwheel retraction strut
132 Torque links
133 Port mainwheel
134 Axle
135 Mainwheel leg fairing
136 Mainwheel oleo leg
137 Mainwheel leg pivot point
138 Undercarriage main spar
    attachment
139 Undercarriage actuating
    cylinder

140 Main spar fold point
141 Mainwheel well
142 Contoured main spar inboard
    section
143 All-aluminium wing centre
    section
144 Main spar/fuselage attachment
145 Blower radiator
146 Oil cooler
147 Engine supercharger intake
    duct
148 Exhaust stacks
149 Engine supercharger air intake
150 Auxiliary fuel tank centreline
    attachment points
151 'Duramold' auxiliary drop tank
    capacity 175 US gal (662 litres)
152 Bomb attachment shackle
    [underwing inner section,
    (F4U-1D)
153 Bombload, up to 1,000 lb
    (454 kg) each side (F4U-1D)

*The standard US Navy combat
formation comprised two two-
ship elements. Here a quartet
of Vought F4U-1 Corsairs
wearing the markings of the
celebrated US Marine Corps
'Black Sheep' squadron
(VMF-124) banks left over the
island of Bougainville in the
Solomons group. In such
operational conditions, the
Corsair soon proved a potent
and versatile fighter-bomber.*

Grumman F6F Hellcat

Grumman F6F-5 Hellcat of US Navy VF-12 aboard USS Randolph (CV-15), early 1945.

Grumman F6F Hellcat launching from USS Randolph.

Grumman F6F-3 Hellcat

More than any other single type it was the Grumman F6F Hellcat that defeated Japan in the skies. Immediately after recovering aboard the USS Hornet (CV-11) after a raid on the Marianas in the spring of 1944, this F6F-3 has its wings folded. The action was wholly manual; the wings pivoted as they were folded aft to lie, upper surfaces outwards, along the fuselage sides.

Below: This is one a series of air-to-air shots of an F6F-3 Hellcat secured during manufacturer's testing over the Grumman 'Iron Works' on Long Island, New York.

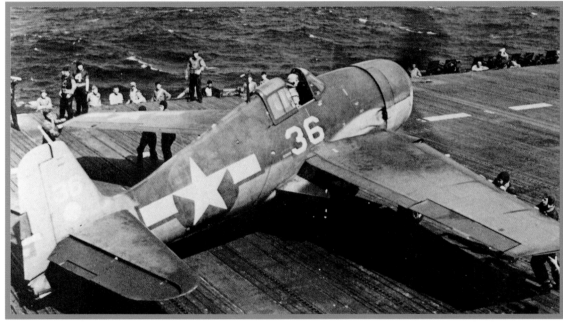

bases in the Solomons chain, honing the tactics and manoeuvres that made the F4U into a deadly killing machine. Their continuous fighting, shared with US Army Air Force units, first held the Japanese at bay and then drove them out of island after island.

New strike force

In August 1943 the US Navy played another ace: the Grumman F6F-3 Hellcat. Rugged, heavily armed, manned by a fresh crop of well-trained pilots and based on a rapidly increasing number of new and fast carriers of the 'Essex' - and 'Independence'-classes, the Hellcats became the spearhead of a new naval strength. The mobile, powerful, fast carrier strike force of air and surface groups was born.

In this new teaming of naval arms, the fighter grew in importance, reflected in the change in aircraft complement approved in October 1943. It raised fighter numbers aboard 'Essex'-class carriers to 36, equal to bomber strength and twice that of the torpedo bombers.

Two years after war began, the US Navy was able to

assemble fast carrier task forces around new carriers. In January 1944, when raids were begun to support the occupation of the Marshall Islands, Task Force 58 sailed in four groups including six heavy and six light carriers. Six months later, TF 58 steamed against the Marianas with seven heavy and eight light carriers. In that campaign, US Navy air power scored its greatest victory: the 'great Marianas turkey shoot'.

The greatest battle

It was the largest naval air battle in history. The antagonists were about equal in air strength at the start: approximately 1,000 Japanese aircraft and pilots faced about 1,100 American machines. But when it was over, the US held the Philippine Sea and the sky above it, and had hammered the Japanese so fiercely that there was no possibility of their recovery. Only 35 aircraft remained operational in the Japanese fleet; the rest were lost to American action, either shot out of the sky, at the bottom with their sunken carriers, or damaged beyond repair. Three Japanese

The family resemblance is obvious between the F6F-3 Hellcats on the right (the port side of the deck of this escort carrier) and the TBF Avenger torpedo-bombers in the foreground. The flat-top was the USS Monterey, seen in January 1944.

carriers were sunk, and another pair had been hit too badly to regain capability for action. The greatest Japanese loss was among the aircrews. More than three-quarters of the Japanese naval airmen in that battle never went back home. It was the end of Japan's naval air arm; there were no reserves, and no filled pipeline of trained pilots.

More fighters

Within two months after that great air battle, the fighter complement of each fleet carrier was raised again to 54, this time outnumbering both the bomber strength of 24 aircraft and the torpedo-bomber strength of 18.

The war rolled on. Landings in southern France were supported by US carrier air teams. The Philippines were invaded and occupied, as the Japanese continued their retreat. Task Force 38 used 17 carriers in its pre-invasion assault on Leyte; an additional 18 escort carriers supplied air support for the landing itself. And again the fighter complement increased, this time to 73 for the 'Essex'-class

ships, against 15 each of the bombers and torpedo-bombers. The US Marines came aboard in December 1944 with fighter squadrons, and in January fighter-bomber units were established.

Japan held on tenaciously, while the carriers steamed inexorably westward. In July 1945 Task Force 38 began air strikes against Japan from Hokkaido in the north to Kyushu in the south. Hellcats bombed and strafed, rocketed ground targets, shot down the occasional interceptor and escorted the bombers. It was a one-sided affair, with light US Navy losses and tremendous damage done to the Japanese. The war was lost, and had the Japanese admitted the fact that the bombs at Hiroshima and Nagasaki might not have been necessary.

The final devastation of Japan and its once-sprawling network of bases and sea lanes had been hastened by powerful air forces available on the mobile bases of the fleet. And for the last year and more of the war, the predominant component of that air force was the fighter.

Another deck filled with products from the Grumman 'Ironworks', TBF Avengers on the left and F6F Hellcats on the right. The Hellcats are carrying drop tanks and are probably preparing for an escort mission, as the wing racks are clean of either bombs or rockets.

With its radar pod out of view on the starboard wing, this F4U-2 Corsair served with Marine night-fighter squadron VMF(N)-532. It was based at Roi island, Kwajalein Atoll, in 1943-44, and was flown by the CO, Major Everett H. Vaughan.

Naval fighter sketches

Grumman F4F Wildcat

Although it was the first-line strength in the Pacific and Atlantic when war came, the Wildcat was being phased out of that role by the Hellcat and the Corsair by mid-1943. Built in great quantities by both Grumman and General Motors (as the FM series), the tubby F4F fighters served on more than 100 escort carriers. They protected convoys in the wild waters of the North Atlantic and also supported amphibious landings in the Pacific with rockets, bombs and gunnery. Final kill ratio was 7:1. The US Navy accepted 7,415 of all models, F4F and FM. General Motors built 1,151 FM-1s and 4,777 FM-2s respectively.

Grumman F6F Hellcat

Big brother of the Wildcat, the Hellcat was defined on 15 January 1941. Construction was ordered on 30 June 1941 and the first XF6F-1 flew 26 June 1942. Deliveries of the production F6F-3 version began 3 October 1942 and by August 1943 the Hellcat was ready for combat. Within a few months, it was the only fighter embarked on the rapidly growing number of new fast carriers. The cutting edge of the US Navy's sea-air assault forces, it was rugged, reasonably fast, and a stable gunnery platform with a battery of six 0.5-in (12.7-mm) machine-guns. It served as a

This portrait of a quintet of F4U-1As was caught on camera in April 1944. The skull and crossbones identifies the unit as the famed VF-17 'Jolly Rogers'.

Grumman F6F Hellcat

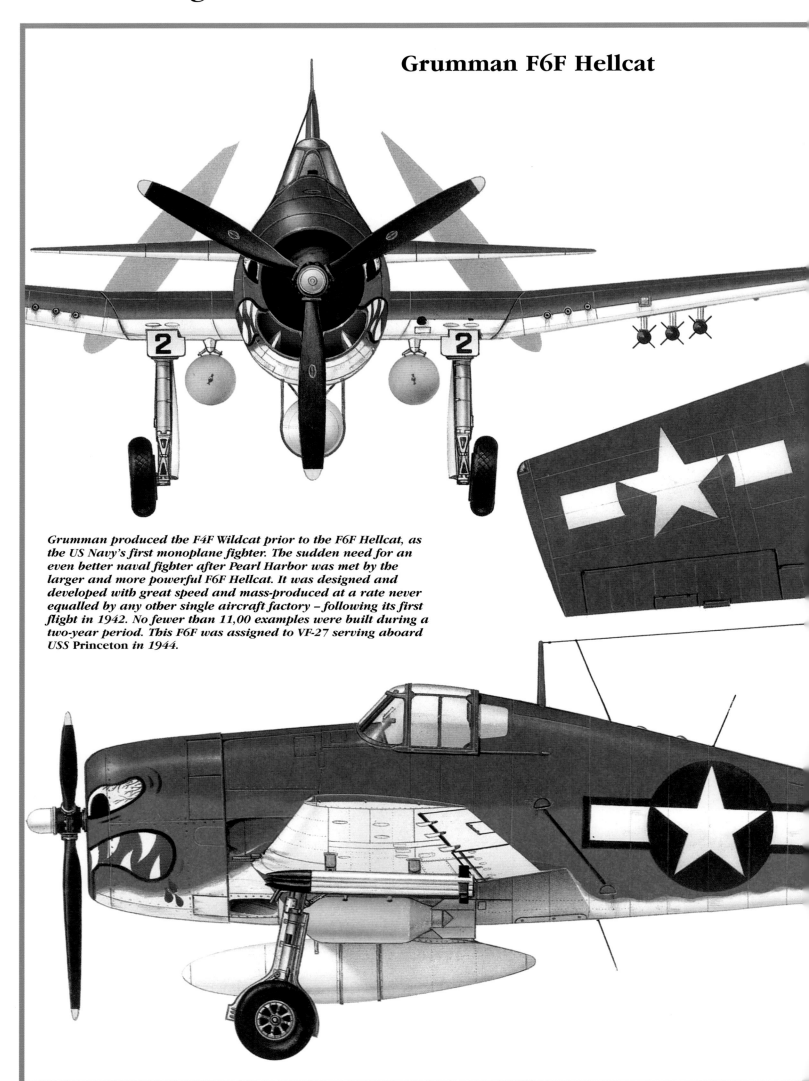

Grumman produced the F4F Wildcat prior to the F6F Hellcat, as the US Navy's first monoplane fighter. The sudden need for an even better naval fighter after Pearl Harbor was met by the larger and more powerful F6F Hellcat. It was designed and developed with great speed and mass-produced at a rate never equalled by any other single aircraft factory – following its first flight in 1942. No fewer than 11,00 examples were built during a two-year period. This F6F was assigned to VF-27 serving aboard USS Princeton *in 1944.*

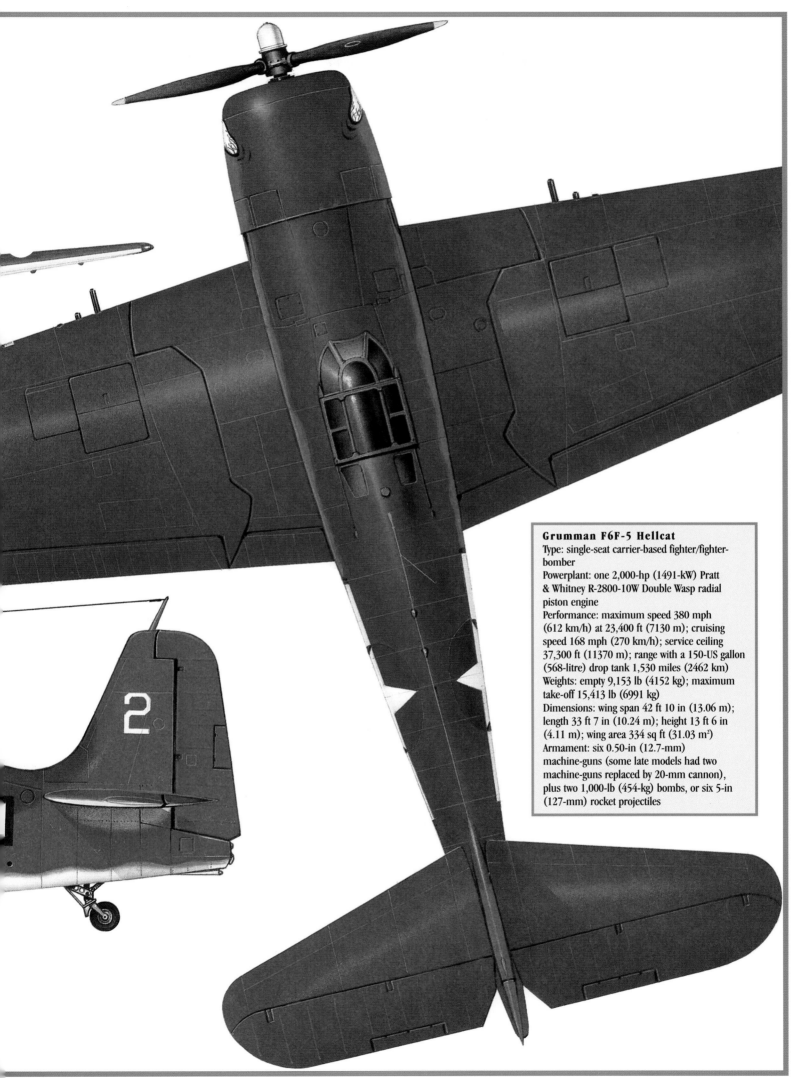

Grumman F6F-5 Hellcat

Type: single-seat carrier-based fighter/fighter-bomber

Powerplant: one 2,000-hp (1491-kW) Pratt & Whitney R-2800-10W Double Wasp radial piston engine

Performance: maximum speed 380 mph (612 km/h) at 23,400 ft (7130 m); cruising speed 168 mph (270 km/h); service ceiling 37,300 ft (11370 m); range with a 150-US gallon (568-litre) drop tank 1,530 miles (2462 km)

Weights: empty 9,153 lb (4152 kg); maximum take-off 15,413 lb (6991 kg)

Dimensions: wing span 42 ft 10 in (13.06 m); length 33 ft 7 in (10.24 m); height 13 ft 6 in (4.11 m); wing area 334 sq ft (31.03 m²)

Armament: six 0.50-in (12.7-mm) machine-guns (some late models had two machine-guns replaced by 20-mm cannon), plus two 1,000-lb (454-kg) bombs, or six 5-in (127-mm) rocket projectiles

Grumman F6F-5 Hellcat

1 Radio mast
2 Rudder balance
3 Rudder upper hinge
4 Aluminium alloy fin ribs
5 Rudder post
6 Rudder structure
7 Rudder trim tab
8 Rudder middle hinge
9 Diagonal stiffeners
10 Aluminium alloy elevator trim tab
11 Fabric-covered (and taped) elevator surfaces
12 Elevator balance
13 Flush-riveted leading-edge strip
14 Arrester hook (extended)
15 Tailplane ribs
16 Tail navigation (running) light
17 Rudder lower hinge
18 Arrester hook (stowed)
19 Fin main spar lower cut-out
20 Tailplane end rib
21 Fin forward spar
22 Fuselage/finroot fairing
23 Port elevator
24 Aluminium alloy-skinned tailplane
25 Section light
26 Fuselage aft frame
27 Control access
28 Bulkhead
29 Tailwheel hydraulic shock-absorber

30 Tailwheel centring mechanism
31 Tailwheel steel mounting arm
32 Rearward-retracting tailwheel (hard rubber tyre)
33 Fairing
34 Steel plate door fairing
35 Trestling sling support tube
36 Hydraulic actuating cylinder
37 Flanged ring fuselage frames
38 Control cable runs
39 Fuselage longerons
40 Relay box
41 Dorsal rod antenna
42 Dorsal recognition light
43 Radio aerial
44 Radio mast
45 Aerial lead-in
46 Dorsal frame stiffeners
47 Junction box
48 Radio equipment (upper rack)
49 Radio shelf
50 Control cable runs
51 Transverse brace
52 Remote radio compass
53 Ventral recognition lights (three)
54 Ventral rod antenna
55 Destructor device
56 Accumulator
57 Radio equipment (lower rack)
58 Entry hand/footholds
59 Engine water injection tank
60 Canopy track
61 Water filler neck
62 Rear-view window
63 Rearward-sliding cockpit canopy (open)
64 Headrest
65 Pilot's head/shoulder armour
66 Canopy sill (reinforced)
67 Fire extinguisher
68 Oxygen bottle (port fuselage wall)
69 Water tank mounting
70 Underfloor self-sealing fuel tank (60 US gal; 227 litres)
71 Armoured bulkhead
72 Starboard console
73 Pilot's seat
74 Hydraulic handpump
75 Fuel filler cap and neck
76 Rudder pedals
77 Central console
78 Control column

79 Chart board (horizontal stowage)
80 Instrument panel
81 Panel coaming
82 Reflector gunsight
83 Rear-view mirror
84 Armoured glass windshield
85 Deflection plate (pilot forward protection)
86 Main bulkhead (armour-plated)

upper section with hoisting sling attachments port and starboard)
87 Aluminium alloy aileron trim tab
88 Fabric-covered (and taped) aileron surfaces
89 Flush-riveted outer wing skin
90 Aluminium alloy sheet wingtip (riveted to wing outer rib)
91 Port navigation (running) light
92 Formed leading-edge

(approach/landing light and camera gun inboard)
93 Fixed cowling panel
94 Armour plate (oil tank forward protection)
95 Oil tank (19 US gal/72 litres)
96 Welded engine mount fittings
97 Fuselage forward bulkhead
98 Aileron control linkage
99 Engine accessories bay
100 Engine mounting frame (hydraulic fluid reservoir attached to port frames)
101 Controllable cooling gills
102 Cowling ring (removable servicing/ access panels)
103 Pratt & Whitney R-2800-10W

twin-row radial air-cooled engine
104 Nose ring profile
105 Reduction gear housing
106 Three-bladed Hamilton Standard Hydromatic controllable-pitch propeller
107 Propeller hub
108 Engine oil cooler (centre) and supercharger intercooler
109 Oil cooler deflection plate

under-protection
110 Oil cooler duct
111 Intercooler intake duct
112 Mainwheel fairing
113 Port mainwheel
114 Auxiliary tank support/attachment arms
115 Cooler outlet and fairing
116 Exhaust cluster
117 Supercharger housing
118 Exhaust outlet scoop
119 Wing front spar web
120 Wing front spar/fuselage

attachment bolts
121 Undercarriage mounting/pivot point on front spar
122 Inter-spar self-sealing fuel tanks (port and starboard: 87.5 US gal (133 litres) each)
123 Wing rear spar/fuselage attachment bolts
124 Structural end rib
125 Slotted wing flap profile
126 Wing flap centre-section
127 Wing fold line
128 Starboard wheel well (doubler-plate reinforced edges)
129 Gun bay
130 Removable diagonal brace

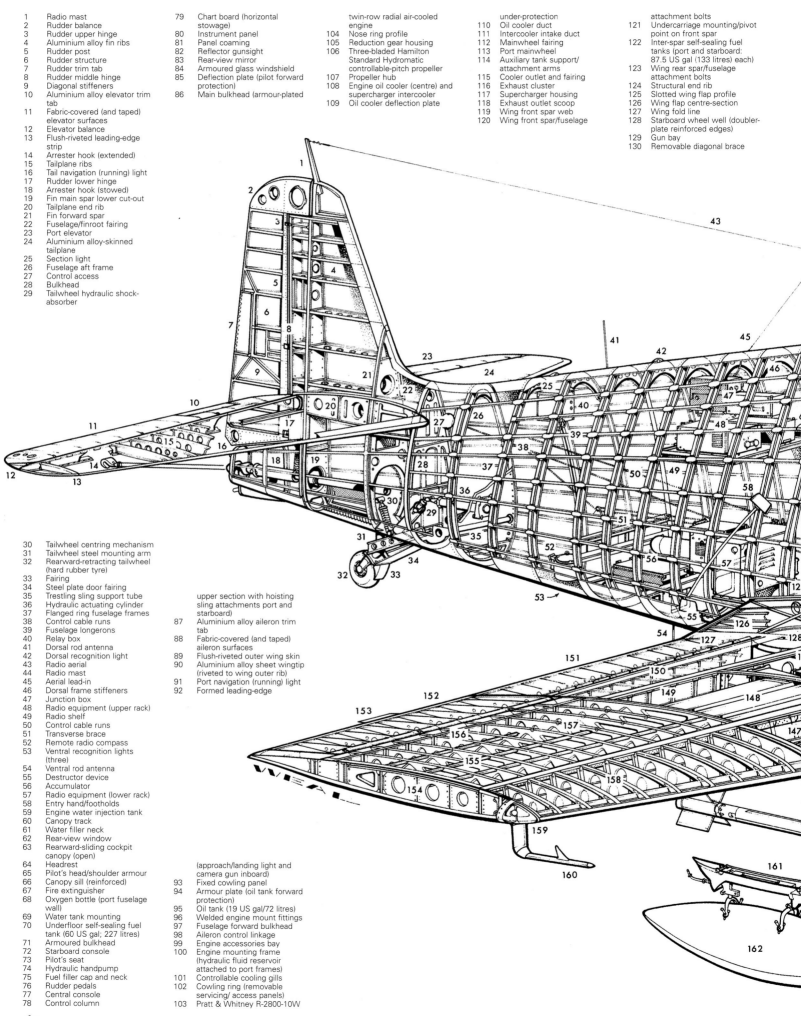

strut
131 Three 0.5-in (12.7-mm) Colt Browning machine-guns
132 Auxiliary tank aft support
133 Blast tubes
134 Folding wing joint (upper surface)
135 Machine-gun barrels

136 Fairing
137 Undercarriage actuating strut
138 Mainwheel leg oleo hydraulic shock strut
139 Auxiliary tank sling/brace
140 Long-range auxiliary fuel tank (jettisonable)
141 Mainwheel aluminium alloy fairing
142 Forged steel torque link
143 Low pressure balloon tyre
144 Cast magnesium wheel
145 Underwing 5-in (12.7-cm) air-to-ground RPs

146 Mark V zero-length rocket launcher installation
147 Canted wing front spar
148 Inter-spar ammunition box bay (lower surface access)
149 Wing rear spar (normal to plane of wing)
150 Rear sub spar
151 Wing flap outer-section
152 Frise-type aileron
153 Aileron balance tab
154 Wing outer rib
155 Wing lateral stiffeners

156 Aileron spar
157 Wing outer-section ribs
158 Leading-edge rib cut-outs
159 Starboard navigation (running) light
160 Pitot head
161 Underwing stores pylon (mounted on fixed centre-section inboard of mainwheel leg)
162 Auxiliary fuel tank

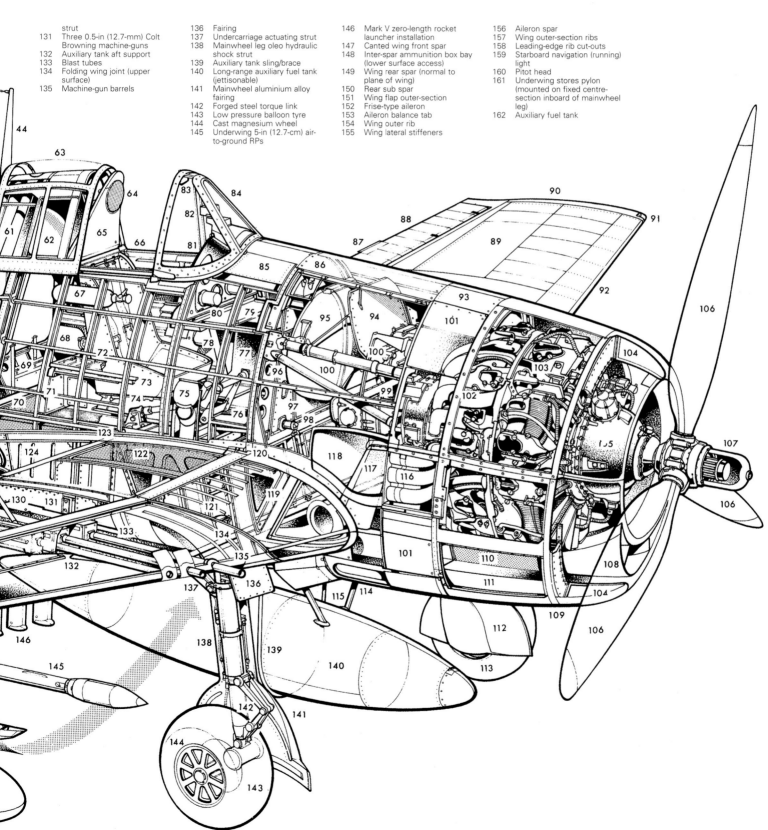

Commander David S. McCampbell was, by some margin the top-scoring US Navy ace of World War II with 34 confirmed victories. He gained them all in a succession of F6Fs named Minsi after late May 1944! On 24 October 1944 he was credited with the destruction of nine Japanese aircraft – a US record. McCampbell was the third highest-scoring American ace of World War II after the USAAF's Dick Bong (40 kills) and Thomas McGuire (38 kills).

Below: This early production F6F-3 was photographed over Calafornia in May 1943. The aircraft belongs to VF-4 and its pristine condition suggests that it was fresh out of the box.

bomber escort, thereby greatly increasing bomber crew life expectancy. Hellcats established an umbrella of air superiority in the Pacific, and also worked close to the beaches, ploughing paths through Japanese defences with guns, rockets and bombs. The F6F was easily maintained, so it was almost always available. Its overall kill ratio was an astonishing 19:1, a figure out of reach of any other contemporary fighter. Production reached 12,275.

Vought F4U Corsair

Delayed by what have always been called 'teething troubles', the Corsair won a 1938 design competition, and first flew on 29 May 1940. It first equipped Marine Fighting Squadron 124, commissioned 7 September 1942, and sailed early in 1943 for Guadalcanal via Espiritu Santu. The Corsair had great potential which was first realised by the US Marines. They operated the bent-winged birds from dirt strips in the Solomons and the other island chains, swooping down on unsuspecting Japanese outposts. Initially barred from carrier operations because of landing gear bounce, the Corsair finally made it aboard, and proved a fitting team-mate for the Hellcat. Built by both Brewster (although in small quantities as the F3A) and Goodyear (as the FG) as well as Vought, it became the longest-lived of the US Navy's fighters, ending its service career in the Korean War. Like the Hellcat, it was modified to become a night-fighter and a photo-reconnaissance aircraft. Corsairs flew more than 64,000 combat sorties with the US Navy and the US Marines, and about two-thirds of these were logged in the Solomons. The Corsair's overall kill ratio was 11:1, and production ceased after 12,571 examples had been built.

This unusual combat photograph shows the final moments of a Japanese 'Zeke'. The Mitsubishi A6M Zero was attacked by a US Navy F6F on 1 November 1944. The smoke trail behind the F6F comes from its six '50-cal' (12.7-mm) machine-guns.

Rapid-fire catapult launches from the fleet carrier USS Randolph as one F6F strives to gain height and two more are readied for launch from the port and starboard catapults alternately. The aircraft are setting out for a strike on the Japanese mainland in July 1945. Underwing rockets are almost hidden by the lowered flaps.

Night-Fighters

At first US forces deemed that there was no need for night fighters. Then both main services saw the advantages – the USAAF procured the mighty Black Widow multi-role aircraft, while the US Navy added small radar sets to its standard fighters.

Well before America entered the war, observers from the US Army and US Navy had seen how the Germans had bombed London by night during the Blitz. Luftwaffe losses were minimal, measured against the results achieved by the bombing, and all the varied means for destroying German aircraft, in combination, hardly posed a serious threat to continuing night operations.

The Americans, impressed with what they had seen, decided that the development of night-fighters was a matter for some priority. The RAF had Bristol Blenheims and Boulton Paul Defiants equipped with airborne interception (AI) radar, tied to ground control of interception (GCI) stations, identification gear to tell friendly aircraft from enemy, radar beacons for navigation and homing in the dark, and VHF radio for communications. Later came Bristol Beaufighters, the hulking aerodynamic beast that had room for radar and a crew to operate it, and Douglas DB-7/A-20 Havocs, converted from light bombers to night fighters by installing radar in the nose. They had seen enough; the Americans went back home and began to agitate for some dedicated night-fighter aircraft.

There were two distinct development trends in those days, one – of course – for each of the major services. The US Army was headed toward the design of a new and large aircraft. The US Navy needed to adapt its contemporary

Left: The classic US World War II night-fighter was the Northrop P-61. About the same size as a medium bomber, the three-seat Black Widow was by far the largest and most powerful fighter of the war. Here, a pair of P-61C-10s lifts off, the air reverberating to the beats of a quartet of 2,800-hp (2088-kW) Double Wasp engines.

Below: USAAF no. 44-27234 was one of the P-38Ls converted by field units in the Pacific as two-seat night-fighters in 1944. Some 76 P-38L-5-LOs were modified as P-38Ms, with AN/APS-6 radar in an undernose radome and an operator in the raised rear cockpit. A load of ten high-velocity aircraft rockets could be carried on distinctive underwing pylons.

This was the second of 59 Douglas A-20 attack bombers rebuilt in 1941 as operational night-fighter trainers with the designation P-70. Equipped with British-supplied AI Mk IV radar (note nose aerial), they packed a quartet of 20-mm cannon in a ventral pack; the fully operational P-70A toted 'six fifties' in the nose.

aircraft to the task; life and logistics were complicated enough aboard carriers without adding to the confusion. But both built on the British experience, learning what they could of tactics and employment of airborne radars.

Army night-fighters

It was the US Army's intent to develop a special-purpose fighter for night interception. That service was convinced that heavy, bulky and complex radar had to be carried in a large aircraft with a multiple-man crew. The pilot would be directed toward the interception by a radar operator and the third man was a defensive gunner. This thinking jelled into a tentative specification which was sent to the Northrop Corporation soon after the initiation of the London Blitz in the late summer of 1940. Northrop turned out a final configuration by 22 November 1940 and submitted it to the USAAC.

A year into the war, the Northrop P-61 (as it was designated) was experiencing troubles, and the USAAF cast about for interim solutions. The first was the Douglas P-70,

an 'instant' conversion from a light bomber, the A-20G. The USAAF did essentially the same things that the British had done to the DB-7; it was, basically, the same aircraft, after all. Radar, based on the British design, was added to the nose and a quartet of 20-mm cannon was boxed under the fuselage. In early 1943, P-70s reached service with the 6th Night-Fighter Squadron: Detachment A was based in the Southwest Pacific; Detachment B served on Guadalcanal.

Mid-Pacific improvisation

The P-70 was intended to be a stop-gap solution until the arrival of the Northrop P-61. But its performance was miserable. It lacked speed, climb and manoeuvrability. So on Guadalcanal, the ingenious mech-anics of Detachment B, aided by one of its pilots, began to modify a standard Lockheed P-38. They borrowed a P-70 radar, installed a second seat for its operator, and tested the result.

While this was happening in the Pacific, some USAAF units with the 12th Air Force in North Africa were operating Bristol Beaufighters, taken over from the British in reverse

Development of radar-equipped night-fighters began in the USA in 1940 using British radar technology. The first US night-fighter was the Douglas P-70, but this saw only limited active service. Until July 1944, the only night-fighters operational with the USAAF were the British-built Beaufighter Mk VIF; this example served with the 12th Air Force.

Night-Fighters

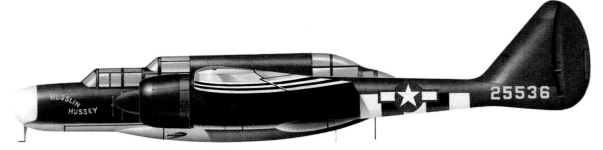

Pending introduction of the P-61 in July 1944 all the front-line night-fighters in the US Army Air Force were British-supplied Beaufighters. The most numerous type was the Beaufighter Mk VIF, which equipped Nos 414, 415, 416 (as seen here in Corsica, late 1943) and 417 Sqns, all with the 12th Air Force.

Hustlin Hussy *was an Olive Drab/ Neutral Gray-painted Northrop P-61A-5 Black Widow assigned to the 422nd Night-Fighter Squadron and based at Scorton, England, in 1944.*

Lend-Lease. Four night-fighter squadrons were so equipped, each with a dozen Beaufighter Mk VIFs carrying British AI Mk VE or Mk VIII, a late-model radar that used centimetric wavelengths. The 'Beau' was never noted for being an exceptionally forgiving machine, and the US units that flew them experienced an exceptionally high casualty rate. It is likely that the pilots had all come to Beaufighters from tricycle-geared light or medium bombers, and they were unfamiliar with landing the tail-dragger 'Beau'.

The USAAF also experimented with a specially modified two-seat Lockheed P-38, with radar slung in external pods at various locations. It was designated P-38M when it was finally built, but it was used only for pilot training during World War II.

P-61s began entering combat in the summer of 1944 in the Mediterranean, European and Southwest Pacific theatres. Properly handled, the Black Widow became an effective night fighter and night intruder; its long range and ability to carry as much as 6,400 lb (2903 kg) of bombs made operations officers cast covetous eyes at whatever P-61s were available to fly.

But because it was a first-generation night-fighter, it was quickly outmoded as radar equipment shrank drastically in size and improved markedly in performance. What the P-61s did in 1944 was duplicated by US Navy night-fighters using far smaller radar equipment tucked into a wing pod.

Army night-fighter sketches

Lockheed P-38M Lightning
The genesis of the P-38M lay in 1943 field modifications to develop a quick stop-gap until delivery of the Northrop P-61. Initial results were inconclusive, although combat tests indicated that the P-38M had great potential. The USAAF ordered a prototype P-38L which led to a production order for 75 two-seat P-38M models. Their performance was superior to that of the P-61 in speed, climb, combat radius and ceding, but the aircraft only reached training units during the war. It was on the verge of combat operations when the war ended.

On the basis of combat victories alone, the P-70 programme could be described as a failure. However, this converted bomber and its crews did much to establish the principles of night fighting within the USAAF. This is one of 65 P-70A-2s (converted A-20Gs). Note the SCR-720 radar arrays in the nose and on the sides of the forward fuselage.

The initial batch of P-61As packed an extremely formidable punch in the form of four 20-mm cannon with 200 rounds apiece in the belly, plus a dorsal turret, which, when fitted, added four 0.50-in (12.7-mm) guns each with 560 rounds. The turret was deleted after the 37th production P-61A. Tabitha is a P-61A-10 and was photographed at Scorton immediately after delivery on 2 June 1944.

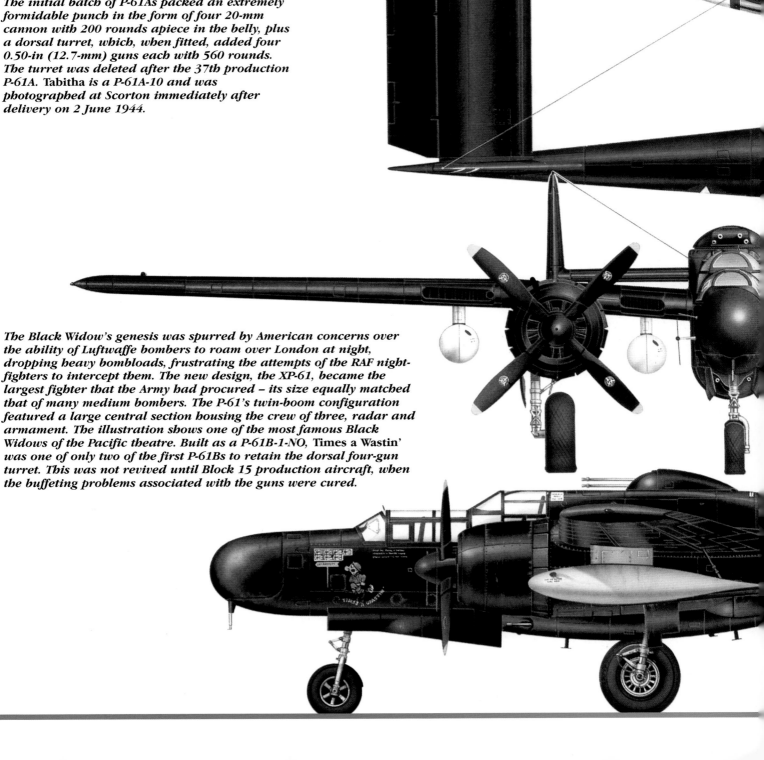

The Black Widow's genesis was spurred by American concerns over the ability of Luftwaffe bombers to roam over London at night, dropping heavy bombloads, frustrating the attempts of the RAF night-fighters to intercept them. The new design, the XP-61, became the largest fighter that the Army had procured – its size equally matched that of many medium bombers. The P-61's twin-boom configuration featured a large central section housing the crew of three, radar and armament. The illustration shows one of the most famous Black Widows of the Pacific theatre. Built as a P-61B-1-NO, Times a Wastin' was one of only two of the first P-61Bs to retain the dorsal four-gun turret. This was not revived until Block 15 production aircraft, when the buffeting problems associated with the guns were cured.

Northrop P-61 Black Widow

Northrop P-61A Black Widow
Type: three-seat night-fighter and intruder
Powerplant: two 2,250-hp (1678-kW) Pratt & Whitney
R-2800-65 Double Wasp radial piston engines
Performance: maximum speed 369 mph (594 km/h) at
20,000 ft (6095 m); service ceiling 33,100 ft (10090 m);
range 1,000 miles (1609 km) on internal fuel or
1,900 miles (3058 km) with maximum external fuel
Weights: empty 20,965 lb (9510 kg); maximum take-off
32,400 lb (14696 kg)
Dimensions: wing span 66 ft (20.12 m); length 48 ft
11 in (14.91 m); height 14 ft 2 in (4.32 m); wing area
664 sq ft (61.69 m²)
Armament: four 20-mm cannon in lower forward
fuselage, supplemented in some aircraft by four 0.50-in
(12.7-mm) machine-guns in dorsal turret

Northrop P-61B Black Widow

1	Starboard navigation light	17	Nacelle ring	34	Bullet-resistant windshield
2	Starboard formation light	18	Starboard outer auxiliary tank	35	Fuselage structural joint
3	Aileron hinge fairing	19	Four-bladed Curtiss Electric		(armour plate deleted for
4	Conventional aileron		propeller		clarity)
5	Aileron tab	20	Propeller cuffs	36	Radar modulator
6	Full-span flaps (Zapp type)	21	Propeller boss	37	Dielectric nosecone
7	Retractable aileron (operable	22	Heater air induction	38	SCR-720 radar scanner
	as spoiler)	23	Front spar	39	Gun camera (gunsight aiming
8	Wing skinning	24	Plexiglas canopy		point)
9	De-icer boot	25	Cannon access bulkhead	40	Mast
10	Intercooler controllable		cut-out	41	Pitot head
	shutters	26	Front gunner's compartment	42	Radar equipment steel support
11	Intercooler and supercharger	27	Sighting station		tube
	induction	28	Bullet-resistant windshield	43	Bulkhead (centre joint)
12	Fuel filler cap	29	Inter-cockpit/ compartment	44	Rudder pedals
13	Starboard outer wing fuel tank		armour (shaded)	45	Drag strut
14	Nacelle fairing	30	Pilot's canopy	46	Torque link
15	Cooling gills	31	Pilot's seat	47	Towing eye
16	Pratt & Whitney R-2800-65	32	Control column	48	Nosewheel
	engine	33	Gunsight (fixed cannon)	49	Cantilever steel strut
				50	Mud guard (often deleted)
				51	Taxi lamp

52	Air-oil shock strut (shimmy damper on forward face)	70	Flush-riveted aluminium alloy skin
53	Nosewheel door	71	Gun mantle (four 0.50-in/
54	Cockpit floor		12.7-mm machine-guns)
55	Radar aerials	72	General Electric remote
56	Gunner's compartment floor		control power turret
	(stepped)	73	Turret drive ring
57	Gunner's seat-swivel	74	Rear spar carry-through
	mechanism	75	Turret support rear armour
58	Cannon ports		plate
59	Heater air induction	76	Radio operator/rear gunner's
60	Cannon ammunition		compartment
	magazines	77	Gunner's seat-swivel
61	Ammunition feed chute		mechanism
62	Four 20-mm cannon in ventral	78	Plexiglas tailcone
	compartment	79	Rear compartment glazing
63	Magazine forward armour	80	Aerial attachment
	plate	81	Sighting station
64	Front spar fuselage cut-out	82	Anti-collision beacon
65	Magazine rear armour plate	83	Tailboom structure (inner
66	Rear spar fuselage cut-out		stringers deleted for clarity)
67	Dorsal turret support/drive	84	Control runs
	motor	85	Tailboom/fin attachment
68	Front spar carry-through	86	Fin spar attachment (inner
69	Turret support forward armour		face)
	plate	87	Rudder lower hinge

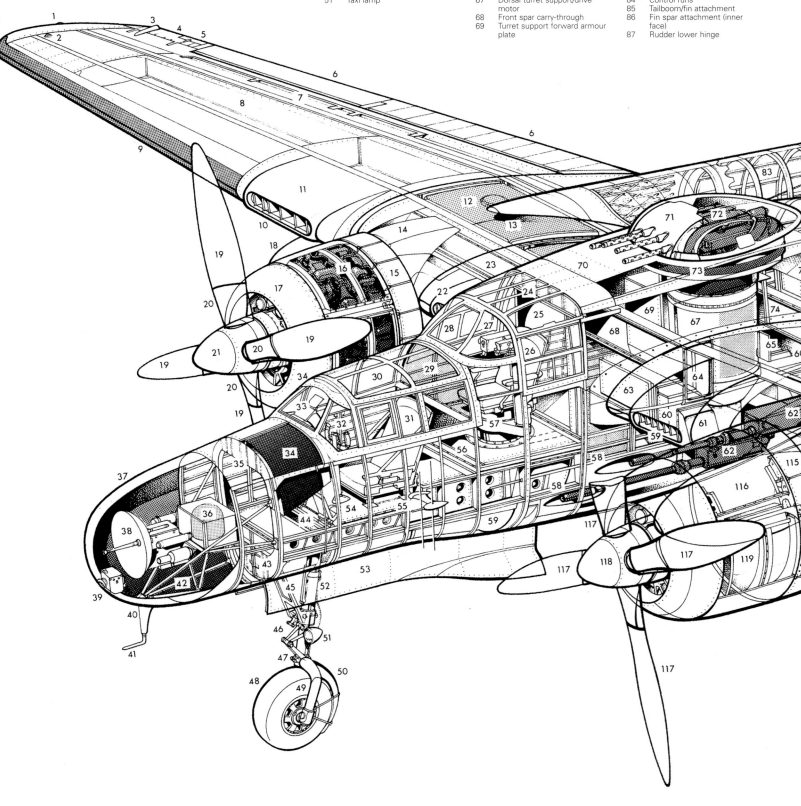

88 De-icer boot
89 Fin structure
90 Rudder upper hinge
91 Rudder
92 Rear navigation light
93 Rudder tab
94 Balance tab
95 Horizontal stabiliser structure
96 De-icer boot
97 Trim tab
98 Aerials
99 Elevator
100 De-icer boot
101 Port fin
102 Rudder
103 Rear navigation light

104 Rudder tab
105 Tab hinge fairing
106 Rudder lower hinge
107 Fin spar attachment (outer face)
108 Tailboom/fin attachment butt
109 Tailboom structure
110 Tailboom joint
111 Wing/boom fairing fillet
112 Mainwheel well

113 Port outer wing fuel tank
114 Spar dihedral-break attachment bolts
115 Cooling gills
116 Port inner auxiliary tank
117 Four-bladed Curtiss Electric propeller
118 Propeller boss
119 Nacelle construction
120 Port mainwheel
121 Hydraulic and airbrake pressure lines
122 Port outer auxiliary tank
123 Mainwheel leg (hydraulic shock strut)
124 Drag strut

125 Intercooler and supercharger induction trunking
126 Mainwheel flap
127 Mainwheel door
128 Radio antenna (port and starboard booms)
129 Wing flap lock
130 Full-span flaps (Zapp type)
131 Retractable aileron (operable as spoiler)
132 Front spar
133 De-icer boot
134 Wing structure
135 Rear spar
136 Aileron tab
137 Port aileron
138 Port formation light
139 Port wingtip
140 Port navigation light

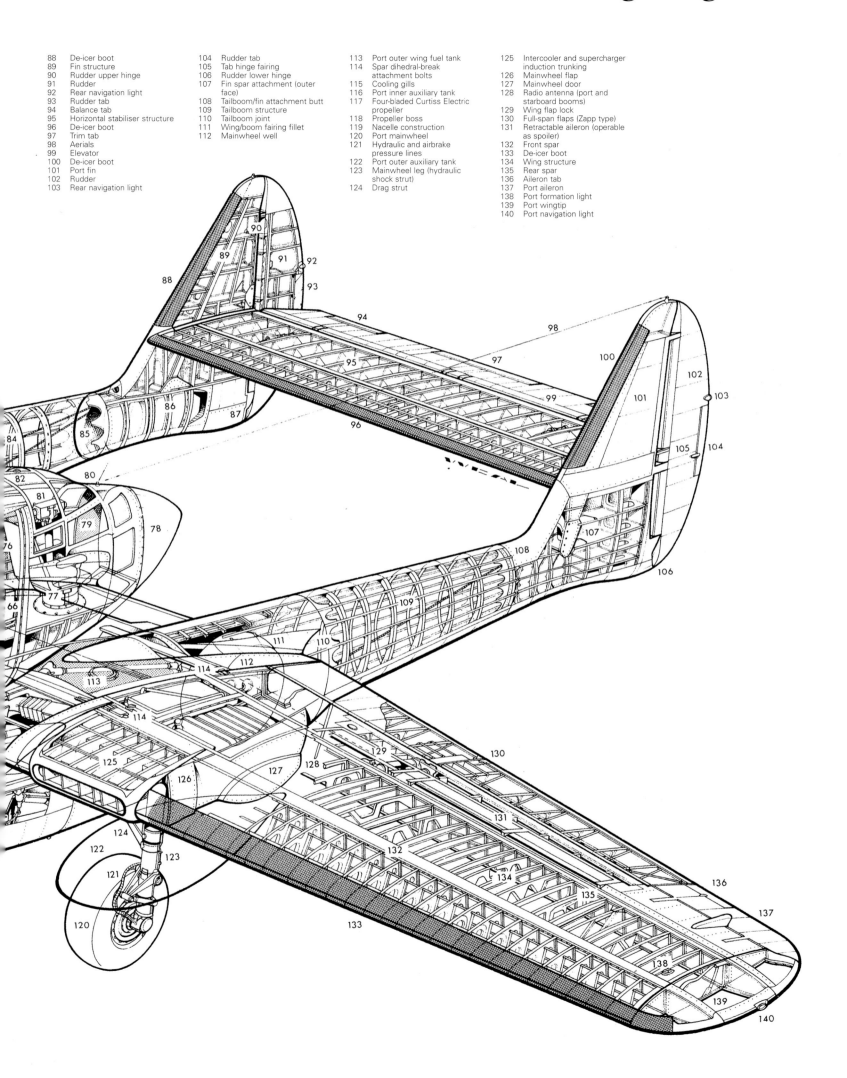

Northrop P-61 Black Widow

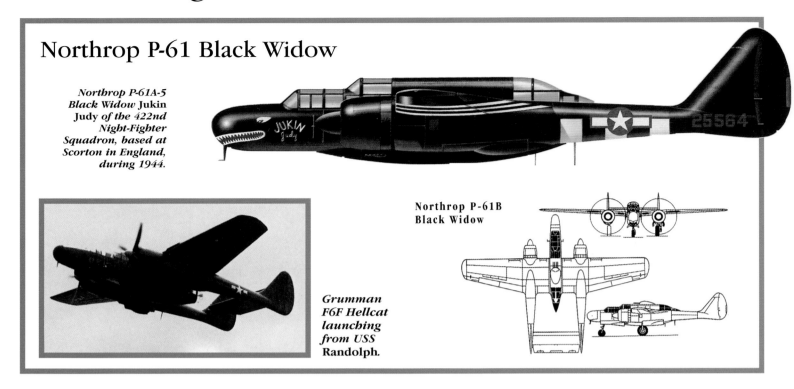

Northrop P-61A-5 Black Widow Jukin Judy *of the 422nd Night-Fighter Squadron, based at Scorton in England, during 1944.*

Grumman F6F Hellcat launching from USS Randolph.

Northrop P-61B Black Widow

Douglas P-70

This desperate attempt to make a night-fighter out of a good low-altitude attack bomber did not work. Radar and four 20-mm cannon were added, the aircraft was re-engined, and the performance went to hell. Operational early in 1943 as an interim type pending the arrival of P-61s, the P-70s themselves required a back-up in the form of field-modified P-38s. The P-70s were eventually used as trainers and, occasionally, as night intruders in the Southwest Pacific.

Northrop P-61 Black Widow

This was the first US aircraft designed specifically for night-fighting. Planned late in 1940 and ordered early in 1941,

Big, powerful and extremely complicated, the P-61 was the first aircraft designed from the outset as a radar-equipped night-fighter. Wearing invasion stripes, this trio is from the 9th Air Force's 422nd Night-Fighter Sqn based at Scorton.

the XP-61 first flew 21 May 1942. Production deliveries began in late 1943, and the Black Widow became operational in early summer 1944. The size of a medium bomber, it weighed twice as much as a loaded P-47. But it was the most manoeuvrable of any US night-fighter, and also operated as a very effective night intruder. Northrop delivered 682 by August 1945, and they cost about $190,000 each.

Navy night-fighters

The US Navy, with its well-established system of shipboard radar detection and fighter direction, extended that system for night operations. Adding short-range radar equipment to standard fighters provided 'fine-tuning' of the ship's control and enabled fighters to close to within lethal range of their guns.

Close relationships had been established with the British, and radar information was actively exchanged more than a year before the US went to war. British AI equipment

Night-Fighters

*Northrop P-61A-1
Black Widow Jap
Batty of the 6th Night-
Fighter Squadron
Saipan, 1944.*

*Northrop P-61B-15 Black
Widow of the 548th
Night-Fighter Squadron,
Ryukyu Islands, Japan,
August 1945.*

formed the basis for development of American systems, aimed at producing a small and lightweight unit that could be carried on a fighter without compromising performance.

Among the early night-fighting tactics used was the teaming of radar-equipped Grumman TBFs or Douglas SBDs with a pair of conventional fighters flown by skilled pilots. Called 'Bat Patrols', these trios were directed toward targets located by their carrier's radar The airborne equipment closed the Bats to gunnery range, and one of the two fighters made a visual sighting and attacked the target. Drawbacks of such a system were obvious. Team co-ordination was difficult, and depended of the rapid passing of accurate information among aircraft. Further,

dependence on visual sighting was, at best, a weak reed on which to base the whole offensive attack.

The first US Navy dedicated night-fighter squadron-VF (N)-75-began operating in October 1943 out of Munda, New Georgia, halfway up the Solomon Islands chain. On October 31, the squadron -flying Vought F4U-2 aircraft with AIA (Airborne Intercept radar type A)-logged its first night-time kill.

During the first half of 1944, the US Navy sent three more night-fighter squadrons to the Pacific and based them, in detachments, on nine carriers. Each detachment had a mixed complement of F6F-3E and F6F-3N Hellcats. The former carried search radar, and the latter carried the

*Left: The US Navy pioneered
the use of miniaturised radars
working on a wavelength of
3 cm for installation in single-
seaters. This Grumman F6F-5N
not only has the APS-6 pod on
its starboard wing, but also a
pair of 20-mm cannon (each
with flash eliminators), plus
four 0.50-in (12.7-mm) guns
and six zero-length rocket
launcher attachments.*

*Below: Two P-61As, probably of
the 548th NFS, prowl near
Saipan in January 1945. The
548th was soon joined by the
549th on Iwo Jima. The 548th
scored three kills and one
probable in June 1945, and the
549th notched up a single kill.*

Above: With SBDs and TBFs behind, F4U-2 night-fighters of VF(BN)-101 prepare to take off from USS Enterprise (CVE-6) for an operation against Truk in February 1944. This Marine squadron was the only one to fly F4U night-fighters from a wartime escort carrier.

Below: Grumman delivered 1,434 F6F-5N night-fighters for the US Navy as well as 80 similar Hellcat NF.Mk IIs for the Fleet Air Arm. The very useful F6F-5N is seen here aboard a US escort carrier in 1945. The fighters carried the 3-cm AN/APS-6 radar in a pod on the starboard wing leading edge.

Powered by two Double Wasp engines of over 2,000 hp (1491 kW) each, the Grumman F7F Tigercat was potentially a great fighter. This F7F-3N was a two-seat radar-equipped version of 1945, used by the Marines from shore bases.

interception radar. The aircraft worked as a team of one - 3E and one -3N.

But the US Navy found, in its early experimentation with night-fighting and radar, that it was hardly worth the trouble. Flying off carriers in those days involved much respotting of aircraft. The night-fighters had to be moved from the flight deck parking area, or up from the hangar deck, and room had to be made for their launch and recovery. The results obtained by the fighters were not, in many eyes, justifying the effort.

Dedicated night-fighter group

A dedicated night-fighter group was attached to the light carrier USS *Independence* between September 1944 and January 1945. Air Group 41 pioneered tactics and information processing that later became the foundation of the US Navy's night-fighter work. It marked the high point of the US Navy's wartime night-fighting effort. Six-aircraft detachments (generally four F6F-5N and two F6F-5E aircraft) served on board most of the carriers until the end of the war. But their kill record was not at all comparable with that of the daytime fighters.

Perhaps the brightest spot for the US Navy effort was the request from General Douglas MacArthur's headquarters. A US Marine night-fighter squadron – VMF(N)-541 – was requested to replace the P-61s on Tacloban early in December 1944. The P-61s were not able to fly the missions that MacArthur's air operations staff required, and the US

Marine night-fighter Corsairs were. But they found that they spent most of the time flying combat air patrols at dawn and dusk, rather than fighting at night. Nevertheless, they did what they were ordered to do, and became the only US Marine air unit to receive an Army Distinguished Unit Citation during the war.

Navy night-fighter sketches

Both the Grumman Hellcat and the Vought Corsair were produced in quantity in night-fighter models. The modification placed the radar equipment in a streamlined pod built into the outboard leading edge of the starboard wing. Performance was not greatly affected by the additional drag, although the stall could be a little tricky with that aerodynamic trigger sticking out in front of the wing. Early models of both aircraft carried the AN/APS-4 airborne search radar. Later models were equipped with AN/APS-6 airborne intercept radars of improved performance. Both aircraft often had new armament, a quartet of 20-mm cannon replacing the six 0.5-in (12.7-mm) machine-guns that were the standard battery.

Unable to afford the luxury of a purpose-developed night fighter, the US Navy resorted to modifying existing single-seat designs with wing-mounted radar for night-time operations. The ultimate expression of this philosophy was the postwar F4U-5N Corsair, development of which was begun in 1948. The type packed four 20-mm wing cannon, radar (note wingtip pod) and rocket launchers and had a distinguished combat record during the Korean War. Here a production -5N is seen on factory test over the Connecticut shore.

Non-Contenders

With fine aircraft in production, little thought was given to experimental types. But the US aircraft industry came up with some weird and wonderful prototypes throughout World War II; and then the jet engine led to massive new programmes.

The wartime environment bred new designs as well as special modifications. But none of the aircraft that entered development during World War II moved rapidly enough to serve in a combat theatre before the Japanese surrender. Several did survive the decimating cuts in production after VJ-Day, to become mainstays of the post-war fighter strength of both the US Army Air Forces and the US Navy. Let us look at the aircraft that first flew during the war years, and see what prompted them and what happened to them.

The Bell P-63 Kingcobra began as an improved P-39, redesigned around the new NACA laminar-flow wing, the basic aerofoil section used for the P-51 Mustang, and with a new Continental engine intended to replace the Allison. The wings were tested on three modified P-39Ds, results justified a go-ahead, and two prototype XP-63 aircraft were ordered on 27 June 1941. The first flew on 7 December 1942; production had been ordered the previous

September, and deliveries began in October 1943. The aircraft was rugged, with great firepower, but unwanted by the USAAF, which saw to it that 2,421 out of the total production of 3,303 went to the Russians. An additional 300 went to the Free French. The rest were converted to target aircraft with heavy armour, fired at by bomber gunners in training, using frangible bullets.

Better escort fighters

When the USAAF finally woke up to the crying need for escorts for its bomber fleets, a requirement surfaced in January 1944. The USAAF was still smarting from two disastrous raids on Schweinfurt the previous August and October, which consumed more than 25 per cent of the attacking bombers and, more importantly, their crews. North American Aviation proposed tying two Mustangs together for the job, and showed the USAAF the first drawings of the XP-82 Twin Mustang on 7 January 1944.

Left: The XP-67 'Bomber Destroyer' or 'Moonbat' emanated from the then little-known firm of McDonnell in St. Louis, Missouri. The XP-67 was a radical design featuring blended fuselage and engine nacelles. The aircraft was plagued by problems related to its troubled XI-1430 powerplant; although it handled well, every measure of performance fell short. By the time the first of two XP-67 prototypes flew on 6 January 1944, it had already been bypassed by history.

Below: The transfer of jet engine technology from Britian across the Atantic allowed the US to develop its first jet aircraft. The portly Bell P-59 Airacomet was designed around a pair of British turbojets, built under licence by General Electric as the GE 1-A (J31-GE-5). Although the type proved a disappointment, being slower and unable to outfight the supposedly inferior piston-engined types it was intended to replace, it did usher in a new era in flight.

Above: Though a reasonably adequate fighter, the Bell P-63 Kingcobra was never used in numbers by US forces and almost all the 3,303 production machines went to America's allies. The majority were delivered to the Soviet Union in whose service the P-63 proved the most popular and intensively used of all US combat types supplied to that country. This was the sixth production aircraft.

Above: The deeply curved belly of the P-63 and its 90° cornered rudder gave it a totally different appearance from the P-39 from which it was developed. Almost all productuion machines were various P-63A blocks. The dayglo orange paint scheme identifies these aircraft as RP-63C manned targets at which bomber or fighter gunners aimed with frangible bullets.

Right: Had it been designed in parallel with the P-51 in 1940, the P-82 Twin Mustang would have made a notable contribution to Allied victory. As it was only a modest number (270) was built, almost all post-war and with Allison engines.

The USAAF ordered three prototypes and 500 production aircraft. The first prototype flew 6 July 1945, but the order was cut back drastically at the war's end. Eventually, the Twin Mustang was used as a bomber escort and a night fighter. It got the first kill in the Korean conflict, where it saw limited combat action.

Too late the Tigercat

The US Navy had a new class of carrier coming, the 45,000-ton USS *Midway* and her sister ships, and wanted a long-range, twin-engined fighter to operate from them. Grumman developed one of the most elegant piston-engined aircraft ever. The F7F-1 Tigercat prototype made its first test flight on 2 December 1943, but it was later declared unsuitable for carrier use. Give it to the US

Marines, said the US Navy, and after 35 had been built, production switched to a night-fighter version. There were brief carrier trials of the new type in April 1945 aboard the USS *Antietam* and USS *Shangri-La*, and VMF(N)-533 took its new Tigercats to the Pacific, arriving on Okinawa the day before the Japanese surrender.

In autumn 1943, the US Navy needed a fast-climbing interceptor with limited range. Grumman started the design of the XF8F-1 Bearcat, a potent package of power. Two prototypes were ordered on 27 November 1943, and the first flew on 21 August 1944. By October, Grumman was sure it had a winner, a production order for 2,023 had come through, and Eastern Aircraft soon after received another massive order. The first US Navy acceptance of a production Bearcat took place in February 1945, and by

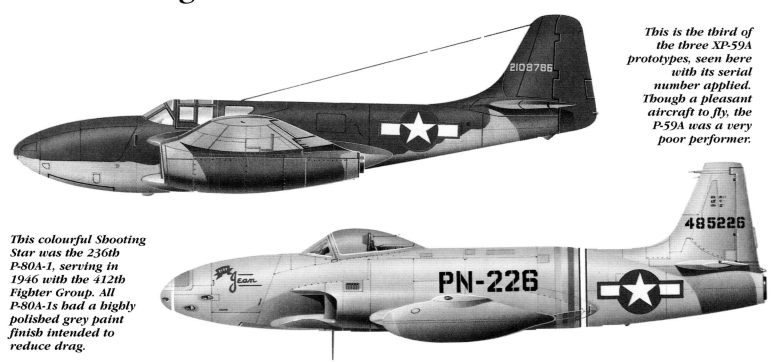

This is the third of the three XP-59A prototypes, seen here with its serial number applied. Though a pleasant aircraft to fly, the P-59A was a very poor performer.

This colourful Shooting Star was the 236th P-80A-1, serving in 1946 with the 412th Fighter Group. All P-80A-1s had a highly polished grey paint finish intended to reduce drag.

May F8F-1s were being delivered to Navy Fighting Squadron (VF) 19. The unit was working up for combat deployment aboard the USS *Boxer* when the war ended.

Enter the jet age

The greatest influence of the war years was jet propulsion. Germany flew a prototype fighter on 27 August 1939; the British duplicated the feat on 15 May 1941. On 5 September, the USAAF requested Bell Aircraft Corporation to design a fighter around General Electric jet engines and to build three prototypes. Construction began in early January 1942, and the first XP-59 Airacomet was shipped by rail to a remote airfield at Muroc, California (now part of the vast Edwards AFB complex). It flew on 1 October 1942, but only 15 flight hours were logged in the first five months. Thirteen service-test Airacomets were built. A few examples were evaluated in mock combat against a P-47D and a P-38J; the new jet proved disappointingly outclassed by the fighters it was supposed to replace. Only 34 reached USAAF fighter units. The USAAF suggested that the P-59 be used for research and training. Fifteen P-59As went to the 412th Fighter Group at Bakersfield, California, the first USAAF jet unit, while 19 P-

59Bs served only briefly as fighters with the same unit. The value of the entire project was that it provided a cadre of jet pilots for the newly-established US Air Force in 1947.

Lockheed P-80 Shooting Star

A new Lockheed pursuit, first built around a British jet engine, was begun in May 1943 and first flew on 8 January 1944, a remarkable accomplishment. Thirteen re-engined P-80 Shooting Stars entered service testing, which included four sent to the European and Mediterranean theatres of war, where they served until VE-Day. In January 1945, the USAAF assigned the P-80 programme the highest priority, placing it on a level with the Boeing B-29. By mid-1945, the 412th was re-equipping with Shooting Stars. The war ended before they got into action. But the P-80 became the foundation of the USAAF post-war fighter fleet and fought in the Korean conflict with distinction.

McDonnell Aircraft Corporation was asked to do the same thing for the US Navy in early 1943, but the design was tied to Westinghouse jet engines, powerplants that never lived up to their promise. It was the US Navy's first jet; almost two years elapsed between first drawings and first flight on 26 January 1945. Too late for the war, the type

By far the best US fighter flown during World War II, the Lockheed P-80 Shooting Star arrived too late to see action. This particular example was the 13th of 345 production P-80As, larger than the XP-80 prototype and powered by the J33-GE-9 turbojet engine.

served aboard post-war carriers as the FD-1. To avoid confusion with Douglas products, it was redesignated FH-1 and called the Phantom.

The US Navy, hedging its bets, had also ordered a mixed powerplant fighter, the Ryan FR-1 Fireball, in February 1943. It had a piston engine in the nose, and a single General Electric J31 turbojet in the tail. The FR-1 first flew on 25 June 1944, and production deliveries began in January 1945. First squadron deliveries were made in March 1945, and VF-66 became carrier-qualified on the type on 1 May 1945. The war ended with the Ryan still unblooded, and the type was withdrawn from service after the jets had proved their worth.

Above: The Republic XP-72 was the ultimate development of the proven P-47 Thunderbolt. Potentially the fastest piston-engined aircraft ever built, the second of two XP-72 prototypes had a 3,300-hp (2462-kW) R-4360-13 Wasp Major driving a massive Aeroproducts six-bladed contra-rotating propeller. The XP-72 could reach 20,000 ft (6096 m) in under five minutes, and with further development, would almost certainly have sustained speeds above 500 mph (805 km/h) in level flight. However, it had the misfortune to arrive at the end of the war when budgets were slashed overnight and the jet engine promised a quantum leap in performance.

Below: The XFD-1 flew in January 1945 and had the distinction of being the first McDonnell jet and the first jet designed to operate from aircraft carriers. The type itself was unremarkable, being underpowered and consequently lacking in performance. The St Louis company later delivered 60 production machines, redesignated FH-1.

American Fighters of World War II

Right: Unofficially called the Black Bullet, the Northrop XP-56 was a bold attempt to get the highest possible performance and was exotic in numerous respects. The powerplant originally intended for the XP-56 was Pratt & Whitney's experimental X-1800, but the prototype used the less powerful Double Wasp engine driving a contra-rotating pusher propeller. The design itself was strongly influenced by Northrop's pioneering work with flying wings; the airframe was built largely of magnesium.

Above: One of the numerous unconventional wartime prototypes was the Curtiss XP-55 Ascender. Three were built, with Allison engines and four 'fifty-cal' guns, but they proved markedly inferior to the P-51 Mustang.

Below: The bizarre-looking Fisher (General Motors) XP-75 was designed as a long-range escort and incorporated components from other existing aircraft. The first prototype had an Allison V-3420 double engine amidships, an SBD tail, F4U landing gears and P-40 outer wings. The production P-75 was redesigned as an uncompromised design but only five were ever completed. The end of the war at a stroke led to the cancellation of a further 2,495 aircraft.

Non-runnners

An even dozen prototypes of other, sometimes even more exotic, USAAF pursuits flew during the war years. (first flight date in parentheses):

Lockheed XP-49: (11 November 1942) an enlarged and re-engined P-38, but without better performance

Vultee XP-54: (15 January 1943) a twin-boomed pusher; it was intended as an interceptor, then as a bomber destroyer, neither of which roles was achieved

Curtiss XP-55: (13 July 1943) called the Ascender because it looked as if it flew tail-first. It had many serious problems

Northrop XP-56 'Black Bullet': (30 September 1943) a tiny flying wing; it flew poorly

Lockheed XP-58 Chain Lightning: (6 June 1944) a monstrous P-38; AAF never decided on an appropriate mission

Curtiss XP-62: (May 1943) intended as a competitor to the Republic P-47

McDonnell XP-67: (6 January 1944) an aerodynamic dream lost to a ground fire and cancelled

Republic XP-72: (2 February 1944) a huge P-47 derivative with twice the engine power and contra-rotating propellers, but the USAAF changed its requirements

Fisher XP-75 Eagle: (17 November 1943) an intended interceptor assembled, at first, from parts of other aircraft;

The Curtiss XP-62 was another unsuccessful monster. Designed as a high-altitude interceptor, it featured a pressurised cockpit, a turbocharged Duplex Cyclone driving contra-rotating propellers and either eight cannon or no less than 12 0.50-in (12.7-mm) guns. The ungainly type first flew in July 1943.

the concept was not pursued

Bell XP-77: (1 April 1944) a tiny all-wood fighter intended to manoeuvre with the Zeroes, there were not many Zeroes left by the time it flew

Vultee XP-81: (7 February 1945) was another composite powerplant design, intended for bomber escort; it was too late for service

Bell XP-83: (25 February 1945) an overblown P-59 with inherited characteristics.

The US Navy being somewhat more conservative, had fewer of these non-contenders. It flew the big Boeing XF8B-1 on 27 November 1944, after which Boeing sensibly stayed with transport and bomber design. The Curtiss XF14C-2, a second attempt to get a design right, flew in July 1944. The Curtiss XF15C-1 was a jet fighter design with a T-tail; it had good flying characteristics, according to reports, but was too late for the war and became outmoded very soon after by new developments.

And there they are, the good, the bad and the indifferent, the American fighters of World War II. There were two or three great ones, another half dozen that were not bad and

fought well, and a small galaxy of failures. The pattern was the same for every other belligerent's designs. We celebrate today the Spitfire and the Hurricane, the Bf 109 and the Fw 190, the Mustang, Hellcat, Thunderbolt and Lightning. Eight, out of dozens. It is a tough world, and only the fittest survive.

Graceful and beautifully engineered, the Convair XP-81 was an attempt to reconcile high performance with very long range. The type became the first turboprop-engined aircraft to fly in the US. The compound-engined XP-81 was designed to escort B-29 bombers in the Pacific but the war ended before production could begin.

Below: The XP-59A was first flown at Muroc on 1 October 1942. Although it offered only modest improvements in performance over the best propeller-driven US fighters of the early 1940s, US planners nevertheless recognised that jet power was the wave of the future. The wholesale transfer of German aerodynamic and jet technology gleaned by US forces at the end of the war, coupled with the experiences gained on the P-59 and P-80, combined to give the US an unassailable lead in jet fighters immediately after the war.

British Fighters

of

World War II

Early Fighters

Until the mid-1930s fighters were merely slightly more powerful versions of the fighting scouts of the Great War. Then engines, airframes, systems and armament changed dramatically.

When Germany invaded Poland at dawn on 1 September 1939 the latest Polish fighters were of a type designed in 1932 and flying in 1934. The United Kingdom's air capacity was in much the same situation, although the Royal Air Force (RAF) did have a substantial number of modern Hurricanes in service, thanks almost solely to the patriotism and guts of the directors of Hawker Aircraft. They had the nerve to go into mass-production with the Hurricane long before the Air Ministry ordered it, and this was one of the things that saved the UK when it faced Germany in the autumn of 1940.

The Hurricane was by far the most important British fighter in the first year of war, mainly because of Hawker's early start and the establishment of a massive manufacturing and repair organisation to support it on a large scale. The fighter's origins went back to mid-1933 when Hawker's chief designer, Sydney Camm, roughed out the design for a new monoplane fighter derived from the Fury biplane then in production for the RAF. Powered by the 660-hp (492-kW) steam-cooled Rolls-Royce Goshawk engine then in favour, it had double the Fury's armament: four instead of two machine-guns.

Had the Fury Monoplane been built the RAF would have been as outclassed as the Poles in 1939. Fortunately Camm decided to hold off, watching keenly as young Squadron Leader Ralph Sorley at the Air Ministry suggested fighters ought to have as many as eight guns, and Rolls-Royce switched effort from the Goshawk to a conventional liquid-cooled engine, similar to the Fury's Kestrel but of a larger capacity and designated PV.12.

Hawker's new bird

By early 1934 Camm was designing a completely new and slightly larger monoplane fighter, powered by the PV.12 engine (later named the Merlin) of about 900 hp (671 kW). For almost the first time in a British fighter, it had retractable landing gear, the main gears folding inwards to be housed in the rather thick wing centre-section. By the time the prototype was being built provision had been made for the unprecedented armament of eight machine-guns, in order to bring enough bullets on to the target in the expected brief shooting time available in future combat.

The Hawker High-Speed Monoplane, serial number K5083, made its first flight at Brooklands (Weybridge) on 6

Left: The night-time defence of the British Isles during the very early days of the war was entrusted to a bomber type – the Bristol Blenheim – converted to night-fighting duties. In addition, these aircraft flew in day-fighter and bombing roles. Having shown great early promise, the Blenheim suffered with the addition of more and more military equipment, which had a telling effect on its performance.

Below: Unmistakably a Hurricane, the Hawker High-Speed Monoplane (K5083) built to specification F.36/34 was just sufficiently modern to sustain an important fighter production programme until September 1944. Yet compared with the Messerschmitt Bf 109, which flew ahead of it, the larger Hurricane lacked stressed-skin structure, a variable-pitch propeller, slats and aerodynamically profiled radiators.

Above: The Fury II was the last of a distinguished line of Hawker biplane fighters, and though it looked much faster than the bluff two-bay Gloster Gauntlet, the latter could outrun and outclimb it at high altitude. The Fury II's range of 260 miles (418 km) was typical.

Left: The first Hurricane squadron, No. 111 Sqn, showing all nine aircraft. In 1938, this seemed the last word in modern defence; and indeed Britain would almost certainly have been defeated in 1940 without the Hurricane.

November 1935. It was larger than most existing fighters, with a span of 40 ft 0 in (12.19 m), and looked extremely modern. Structurally, however, it was somewhat dated, for instead of the new all-metal stressed-skin type of airframe, the High-Speed Monoplane was built by the traditional Hawker method of making a strong truss from metal tubes, with riveted and bolted joints, covered with fabric. No modern variable-pitch propellers were available in the UK,

so a traditional Watts propeller was fitted, with two blades carved from laminations of hardwood. And the chosen gun, the fast-firing belt-fed Colt-Browning, had been licensed to the UK only in July 1935, and few were available until 1937.

After numerous modifications, the Hurricane Mk I reached No. 111 Sqn in December 1937, with an unbraced tailplane, extra small ventral keel under the tail, modified

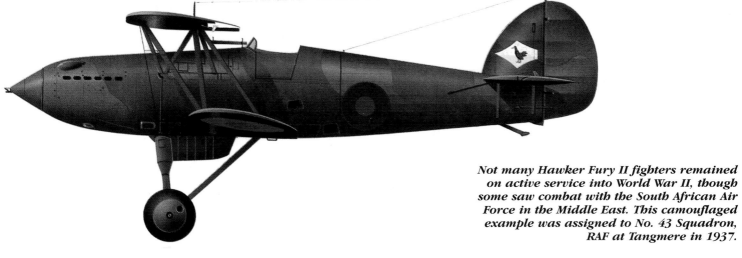

Not many Hawker Fury II fighters remained on active service into World War II, though some saw combat with the South African Air Force in the Middle East. This camouflaged example was assigned to No. 43 Squadron, RAF at Tangmere in 1937.

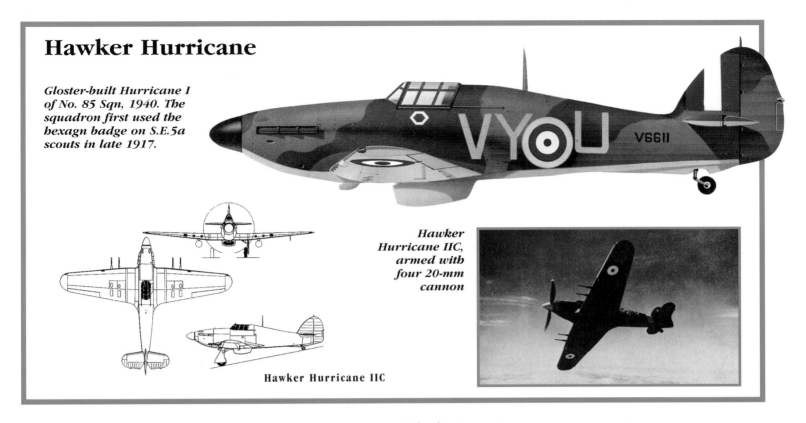

Hawker Hurricane

Gloster-built Hurricane I of No. 85 Sqn, 1940. The squadron first used the hexagn badge on S.E.5a scouts in late 1917.

Hawker Hurricane IIC, armed with four 20-mm cannon

Hawker Hurricane IIC

sliding cockpit canopy and ejector exhausts. Its armament comprised eight of the Browning guns, converted in the UK to fire 0.303-in (7.7-mm) rimmed ammunition and made under licence by the BSA Company. Boxes in the wings held 2,400 rounds, enough for about 20 seconds of continuous firing.

Hurricane co-production

Hawker brought in its sister-firm Gloster to help build Hurricanes, and also constructed a new factory at Langley, near Slough, so that 497 had been delivered by the time World War II began. In 1939 a few Hurricanes flew with licence-built American Hamilton-type propellers, and also with the British Rotol, but panic conversion from the fixed-pitch two-bladed unit did not happen until well into 1940. In April 1939 Hawker made a modern wing, with normal spars, ribs aligned fore/aft, and stressed-skin covering, and this later became standard along with a bullet-proof windscreen, pilot seat armour and self-sealing tanks.

Gladiator at war

Gloster could not begin making Hurricanes immediately because the company had only delivered its first Gladiator in February 1937 and had to continue building this biplane until April 1940. Though designed to a 1930 Air Ministry specification, the Gladiator was much delayed and by 1937 was becoming obsolete.

A fabric-covered metal-framed fighter, the Gladiator did at least have four guns; originally these comprised two 0.303-in (7.7-mm) Vickers machine-guns in the fuselage and two 0.303-in (7.7-mm) Lewis machine-guns under the lower wings, but later the new Brownings were fitted in all four locations. Like other biplanes the Gladiator was supremely agile, and very agreeable to fly, but in performance and firepower it was completely outclassed by Germany's Messerschmitt Bf 109E. Gladiators fought valiantly over France and Norway (and were used by the Finns and several other nations) but spent most of the war in the Mediterranean theatre.

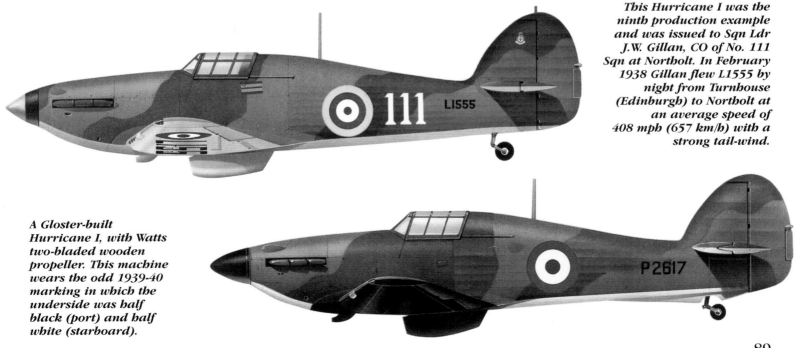

This Hurricane I was the ninth production example and was issued to Sqn Ldr J.W. Gillan, CO of No. 111 Sqn at Northolt. In February 1938 Gillan flew L1555 by night from Turnhouse (Edinburgh) to Northolt at an average speed of 408 mph (657 km/h) with a strong tail-wind.

A Gloster-built Hurricane I, with Watts two-bladed wooden propeller. This machine wears the odd 1939-40 marking in which the underside was half black (port) and half white (starboard).

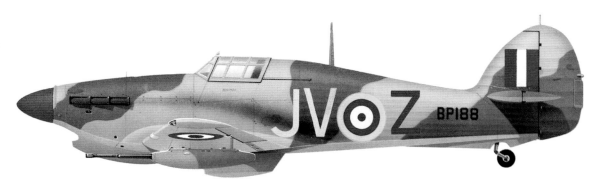

The Hurricane Mk IID tank-buster was the chief carrier of the Vickers S-Type 40-mm cannon. A pair was carried under the wings so that each shot depressed the nose of the aircraft noticeably. This Mk IID served with the most famous 'can openers' unit, No. 6 Sqn RAF.

Hawker Hurricane Mk IIC

1	Starboard navigation light	25	Starboard mainwheel	52	Oil system piping	84	Turnover reinforcement	97	Upward-firing recognition apparatus
2	Starboard wingtip	26	Low-pressure tyre	53	Pneumatic system air cylinder	85	Canopy track	98	Handhold
3	Aluminium alloy aileron	27	Brake drum (pneumatic brakes)	54	Wing centre-section/front spar girder construction	86	Fuselage framework cross-bracing	99	Diagonal support
4	Self-aligning ball-bearing aileron hinge	28	Manual-type inertia starter	55	Engine bearer support strut	87	Radio equipment (TR9D/TR133)	100	Fuselage fairing
5	Aft wing spar	29	Hydraulic system	56	Oil tank (port wingroot leading edge)	88	Support tray	101	Dorsal identification light
6	Aluminium alloy wing skinning	30	Bearer joint	57	Dowty undercarriage ram	89	Removable access panel	102	Aerial mast
7	Forward wing spar	31	Auxiliary intake	58	Port undercarriage shell	90	Aileron cable drum	103	Aerial lead-in
8	Starboard landing light	32	Carburettor air intake	59	Wing centre-section girder frame	91	Elevator control lever	104	Recognition-apparatus cover panel
9	Rotol three-bladed constant-speed propeller	33	Wingroot fillet	60	Pilot's oxygen cylinder	92	Cable adjusters	105	Mast support
10	Spinner	34	Engine oil drain collector/breather	61	Elevator trim tab control wheel	93	Aluminium alloy wing/fuselage fillet	106	Wire-braced upper truss
11	Propeller hub	35	Fuel pump drain	62	Radiator flap control lever	94	Ventral identification and formation-keeping lights	107	Wooden fuselage fairing formers
12	Pitch-control mechanism	36	Engine aft bearers	63	Entry footstep	95	Footstep retraction guide and support rail	108	Fabric covering
		37	Magneto	64	Fuselage tubular framework	96	Radio equipment (R3002)	109	Radio antenna
		38	Two-stage supercharger	65	Landing lamp control lever				
		39	Cowling panel attachments	66	Oxygen supply cock				
				67	Throttle lever				
				68	Safety harness				

13	Spinner back plate	40	Engine RPM indicator drive	69	Pilot's seat
14	Cowling fairings	41	External bead sight	70	Pilot's break-out exit panel
15	Coolant pipes	42	Removable aluminium alloy cowling panels	71	Map case
16	Rolls-Royce Merlin XX liquid-cooled 12-cylinder Vee engine	43	Engine coolant header tank	72	Instrument panel
17	Cowling panel fasteners	44	Engine firewall (armour-plated backing)	73	Cockpit ventilation inlet
18	'Fishtail' exhaust pipes	45	Fuselage (reserve) fuel tank, capacity 28 Imp gal (127 litres)	74	Reflector gunsight
19	Electric generator	46	Exhaust glare shield	75	Bullet-proof windscreen
20	Engine forward mounting feet	47	Control column	76	Rear-view mirror
21	Engine upper bearer tube	48	Engine bearer attachment	77	Rearward-sliding canopy
22	Engine forward mount	49	Rudder pedals	78	Canopy frame
23	Engine lower bearer tubes	50	Control linkage	79	Canopy handgrip
24	Starboard mainwheel fairing	51	Centre-section fuel tank	80	Plexiglas canopy panels
				81	Head/back armour plate
				82	Harness attachment
				83	Aluminium alloy decking

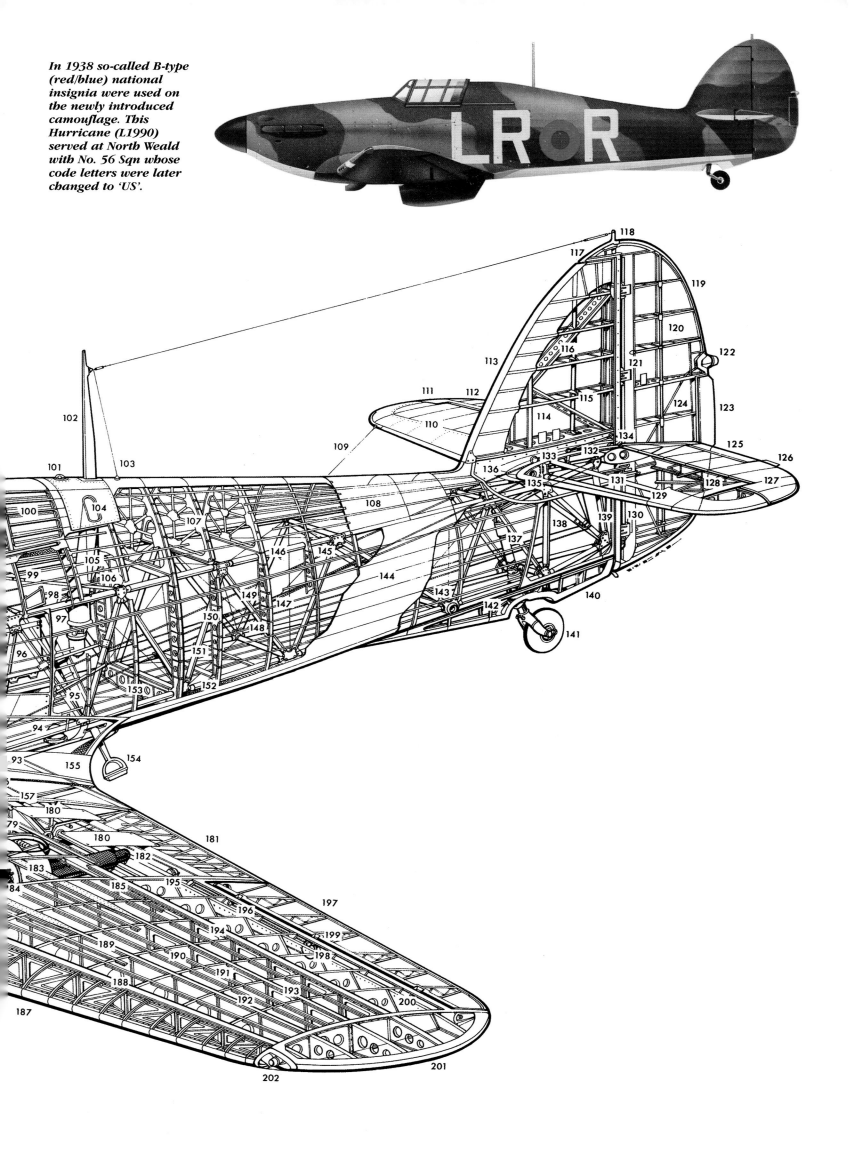

In 1938 so-called B-type (red/blue) national insignia were used on the newly introduced camouflage. This Hurricane (L1990) served at North Weald with No. 56 Sqn whose code letters were later changed to 'US'.

91

British Fighters of World War II

Hawker Hurricane

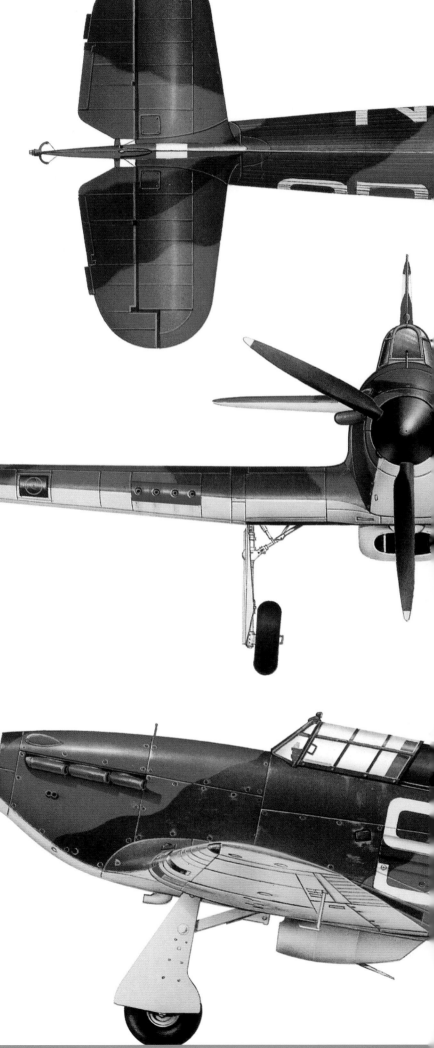

Throughout the war, the Hurricane was heavily committed to operations in support of the Allies in the Middle East and in North Africa. These Mk Is from No. 237 Sqn are seen departing from their base at Mosul, Iraq inMay 1942. At this time the squadron mainly flew tactical reconnaissance sorties in the defence of the Iraqi oilfields.

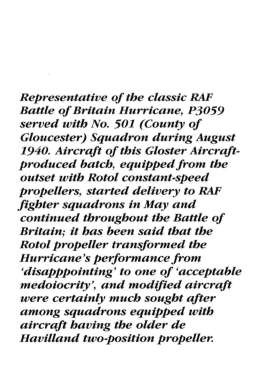

Representative of the classic RAF Battle of Britain Hurricane, P3059 served with No. 501 (County of Gloucester) Squadron during August 1940. Aircraft of this Gloster Aircraft-produced batch, equipped from the outset with Rotol constant-speed propellers, started delivery to RAF fighter squadrons in May and continued throughout the Battle of Britain; it has been said that the Rotol propeller transformed the Hurricane's performance from 'disapppointing' to one of 'acceptable medoiocrity', and modified aircraft were certainly much sought after among squadrons equipped with aircraft having the older de Havilland two-position propeller.

Hurricane Mk I
Type: single-seat fighter
Powerplant: one 1,030-hp (768-kW) Rolls-Royce Merlin II or III inline piston engine
Performance: maximum speed 318 mph (512 km/h); service ceiling 33,400 ft (10180 m); range 440 miles (708 km)
Weights: empty 4,670 lb (2118 kg); loaded 6,600 lb (2994 kg)
Dimensions: span 40 ft 0 in (12.19 m); length 31 ft 5 in (9.58 m); height 13 ft 1 in (3.99 m); wing area 258.00 sq ft (23.97 m²)
Armament: eight 0.303-in (7.7-mm) Browning machine-guns in outer wings

British Fighters of World War II

Enter the Spitfire

Best of all the pre-war designs was the Supermarine Spitfire, destined to be the only Allied fighter in production throughout the war. Designed by Reginald Mitchell, who had previously designed flying-boats and racing seaplanes of totally different construction, the Spitfire was, like the Hurricane, the result of enterprise by its designer. Again like the Hurricane, an official specification was later written around it. Though it used the same engine as the Hurricane, the Spitfire was smaller, and it had a modern stressed-skin airframe.

The elliptical-planform wing was most unusual, because it had curved leading and trailing edges leading to pointed tips, which were distinctive but did little for performance and were difficult to make. Structurally the wing was equally odd, because the strength lay in the thick leading-edge skin and single spar, forming a small box of D-section; and the spar was assembled from stacks of channel sections nesting one inside another. The engine radiator, which in the Hurricane was under the belly, was placed well back under the right wing on the Spitfire, with the oil cooler in a smaller duct under the left wing. The main landing gear

Gloster Gladiator

Gladiator Mk II
Type: single-seat biplane fighter
Powerplant: one 830-hp (619-kW) Bristol Mercury IX radial piston engine
Performance: maximum speed 257 mph (414 km/h) at 14,600 ft (4450 m); service ceiling 33,500 ft (10211 m); range 440 miles (708 km)
Weights: empty 3,444 lb (1562 kg); maximum take-off 4,864 lb (2206 kg)
Dimensions: span 32 ft 3 in (9.83 m); length 27 ft 5 in (8.36 m); height 11 ft 7 in (3.53 m); wing area 323 sq ft (30.01 m²)
Armament: four forward-firing 0.303-in (7.7-mm) machine-guns

Gladiators were doped in various colour schemes as well as the initial pre-war silver. The unusual three-shade camouflage applied to this Gladiator II was used by No. 615 (County of Surrey)) Squadron, AAF, in 1940, when the unit was defending its own county while based at Redhill, after returning from France.

Gloster Gladiator Mk II

Gloster Gladiators equipped for desert operations.

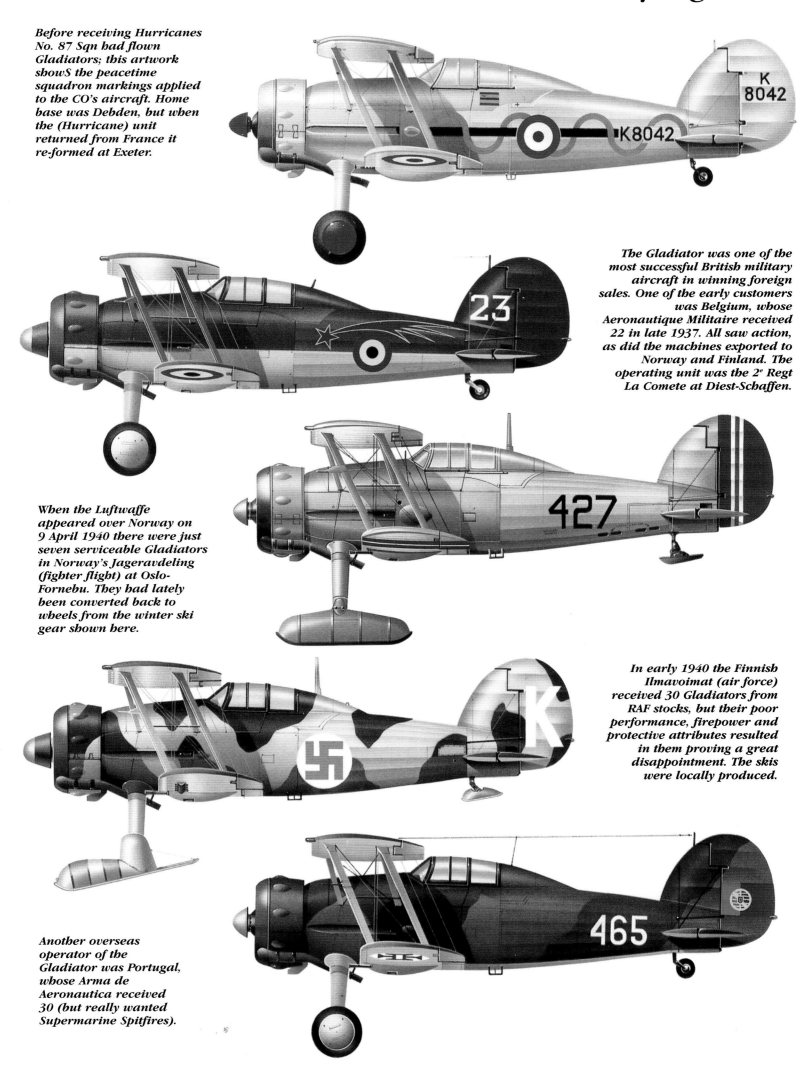

Before receiving Hurricanes No. 87 Sqn had flown Gladiators; this artwork shows the peacetime squadron markings applied to the CO's aircraft. Home base was Debden, but when the (Hurricane) unit returned from France it re-formed at Exeter.

The Gladiator was one of the most successful British military aircraft in winning foreign sales. One of the early customers was Belgium, whose Aeronautique Militaire received 22 in late 1937. All saw action, as did the machines exported to Norway and Finland. The operating unit was the 2e Regt La Comete at Diest-Schaffen.

When the Luftwaffe appeared over Norway on 9 April 1940 there were just seven serviceable Gladiators in Norway's Jageravdeling (fighter flight) at Oslo-Fornebu. They had lately been converted back to wheels from the winter ski gear shown here.

In early 1940 the Finnish Ilmavoimat (air force) received 30 Gladiators from RAF stocks, but their poor performance, firepower and protective attributes resulted in them proving a great disappointment. The skis were locally produced.

Another overseas operator of the Gladiator was Portugal, whose Arma de Aeronautica received 30 (but really wanted Supermarine Spitfires).

British Fighters of World War II

Supermarine Spitfire Mk I/II

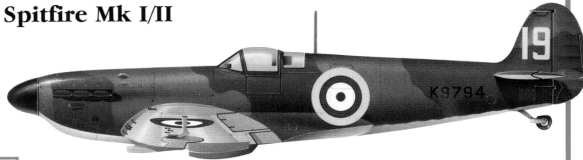

Spitfire Mk I
Type: single-seat fighter
Powerplant: one 1,030-hp (768-kW)
Rolls-Royce Merlin II inline piston
engine
Performance: maximum speed
364 mph (586 km/h) at 18,500 ft
(5639 m); service ceiling 31,500 ft
(9601 m); normal range 395 miles
(636 km)
Weights: empty 4,341 lb (1969 kg);
loaded 5,800 lb (2631 kg)
Dimensions: span 36 ft 10 in
(11.23 m); length 29 ft 11 in
(9.10 m); height 11 ft 5 in (3.48
m); wing area 242 sq ft (22.48 m²)
Armament: eight 0.303-in
(7.7-mm) machine-guns in wings

In October 1938, No. 19 Sqn at Duxford became the first unit to receive the new Spitfire fighter. K9794 was the eighth production Spitfire I and was assigned to Sqn Ldr Henry Cozens, CO of the unit.

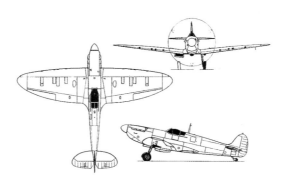

Supermarine Spitfire Mk IIA

Spitfire Mk Is of No. 19 Sqn, RAF.

Left: No. 92 Sqn received Spitfire Mk Is in March 1940 at Tangmere and flew patrols over France before being sent to south Wales for defensive duties. In early September the unit transferred to Biggin Hill within No. 11 Group, to play a part in the aerial battles raging over Kent.

Below: Pilots of No. 601 Sqn at RAF Northolt race to their Hurricanes in January 1941. The part played by the type during the Battle of Britain can not be overstated - it destroyed more enemy aircraft than all the rest of the RAF's fighters combined.

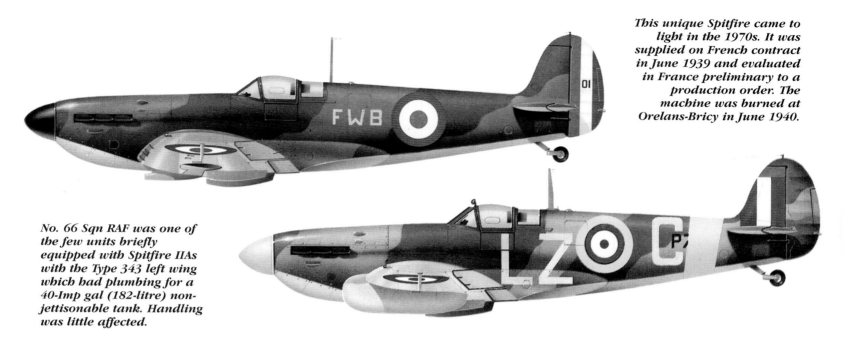

This unique Spitfire came to light in the 1970s. It was supplied on French contract in June 1939 and evaluated in France preliminary to a production order. The machine was burned at Orelans-Bricy in June 1940.

No. 66 Sqn RAF was one of the few units briefly equipped with Spitfire IIAs with the Type 343 left wing which had plumbing for a 40-Imp gal (182-litre) non-jettisonable tank. Handling was little affected.

legs were like those of the Messerschmitt Bf 109, hinged near the root of the wing and retracting outwards.

Best all-round fighter in the world

The prototype (K5054) of what was originally called the Supermarine Type 300, was flown at Eastleigh (today Southampton Airport) on 5 March 1936. It handled superbly, and despite the narrow track and relatively huge engine was found to be simple to taxi on the ground. On take-off, engine torque tended to swing the nose to the left and had to be countered by a 'bootful of right rudder'. In the air the 'Spit' was superb, and after provision of self-sealing tanks, armour and the missing four guns (absent from early examples) to make up the full octet, was arguably the best all-round fighter in the world when it reached No. 19 Sqn at Duxford in June 1938. By that time the pathetic out-

put of the parent firm, which only managed to complete five aircraft by the time of the Munich Crisis in September 1938, was being rapidly accelerated, and plans were in hand to build Spitfires at a much faster rate at a giant Shadow Factory built by the Nuffield organisation at Castle Bromwich, east of Birmingham. Mitchell died of tuberculosis in June 1937 and was succeeded by the equally brilliant and dedicated Joe Smith who was to develop the Spitfire out of all recognition.

This pre-war picture is believed to show No. 19 or No. 66 Sqn Spitfire Mk Is peeling off behind a Blenheim. Before the war the number of Spitfires available was insignificant. In the Battle of Britain RAF fighters inevitably had to climb to meet the enemy, and seldom had the height advantage. Experience over France led to a revision of tactics, which intensified during the Battle of Britain.

1940 and Beyond

For all practical purposes the RAF relied totally upon the Hawker Hurricane and the rather better, but scarcer, Supermarine Spitfire in the crucial first year of the war. In armament and combat tactics it had to make up for years of neglect.

The UK's need for fighters in 1940 was desperate. Had this been foreseen some of the pre-war prototypes might have gone into production, an outstanding example being the Martin-Baker M.B.2 which was almost exactly as fast as a Spitfire despite having fixed landing gear! This machine had numerous engineering features officially described as 'far in advance of existing practice', but its flight stability needed perfecting and in 1938 the need for such serviceable machines was not so pressing. Another fighter of the 1937-38 period, the Gloster F.5/34, was startlingly similar in almost all respects to the Japanese Mitsubishi A6M Zero, but it, too, was rejected.

One fighter which was accepted for production, but turned out to be a disappointment, was the Westland Whirlwind. This was the most radical of seven proposals to meet Air Ministry specification F.37/35 for a fighter carrying the very heavy armament of four 20-mm cannon. Though only fractionally larger than the Hurricane, it had twin engines, the chosen Rolls-Royce Peregrine of 885 hp (660 kW) being a development of the familiar Kestrel. It had coolant radiators inside the wing centre section, offering minimal drag (later designers found such radiators could actually provide propulsive thrust); the guns were grouped in the short nose, and the tailplane was mounted very high on the tall fin to keep it clear of the wake from the powerful Fowler-type flaps.

Unreliable Whirlwind

Despite these flaps, the Whirlwind had what was then considered a very high landing speed, making it difficult to operate from short grass fields. Wing loading (weight supported by unit area of wing) was high, being almost twice that of a Hurricane Mk I, which made manoeuvrability poor. Worst of all, the Peregrine was very unreliable, and only two squadrons operated with Whirlwinds, flying almost all of their missions in the role of attack bombers. With Merlins, operating from the 6,000-ft (1830-m) long runways that by 1942 were common, the Whirlwind might have been a most formidable fighter, but such a machine was never built.

Another disappointment was the Boulton Paul Defiant. This was the successful design to meet a 1935 specification for a two-seat fighter armed with a four-gun turret. The Defiant was a pleasant aircraft to fly, rather like a Hawker

The turret-armed Boulton Paul Defiant was found wanting during daylight operations and found greater success as a night-fighter. This is a line-up of aircraft from No. 264 Sqn, which became operational with the type on 22 March 1940.

No. 303 (Polish) Sqn, RAF had flown Hurricanes during the Battle of Britain but began conversion to Spitfire Mk IIAs late in 1940. The unit subsequently re-equiped with Spitfire VBs in 1941. This is the CO's Mk VB.

British Fighters of World War II

Westland Whirlwind

Whirlwind Mk I
Type: single-seat long-range
fighter-bomber
Powerplant: two 885-hp (660-kW)
Rolls-Royce Peregrine inline piston
engines
Performance: maximum speed 360
mph (579 km/h) at 15,000 ft (4572
m); service ceiling 30,300 ft (9235 m);
range 800 miles (1287 km)
Weights: empty 8,310lb (3769 kg);
maximum take-off 11,388 lb (5166 kg)
Dimensions: span 45 ft 0 in (13.72 m);
length 32 ft 9 in (9.98 m); height
11 ft 7 in (3.53 m); wing area 250 sq ft
(23.23 m2)
Armament: four 20-mm cannon in
nose, plus up to 1,000 lb (454 kg) of
bombs

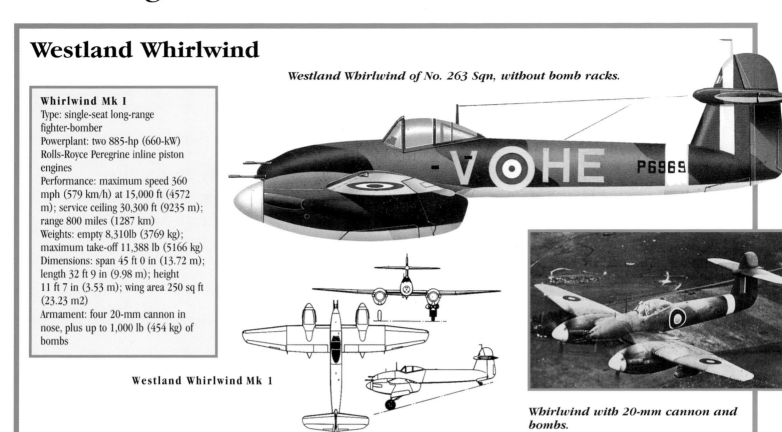

Westland Whirlwind of No. 263 Sqn, without bomb racks.

Westland Whirlwind Mk 1

Whirlwind with 20-mm cannon and bombs.

P7110 was from one of the last batch of Whirlwinds, delivered in December 1941. In many ways an outstanding aircraft, the Whirlwind was crippled by low-power engines with poor reliability. A high landing speed was also held against it, but in fact it landed slower than the Fw 190 which was used from every kind of rough front-line strip.

Westland produced a total of 114 Whirlwind Mk Is. The aircraft saw action chiefly as fighter-bombers against targets of opportunity over northern Europe in 1941-42. The Whirlwind was also found to have excellent performance at low level, and with their long-range capability proved to be excellent bomber escorts. This aircraft was retained by Westland Aircraft and registered as G-AGOI in late 1945.

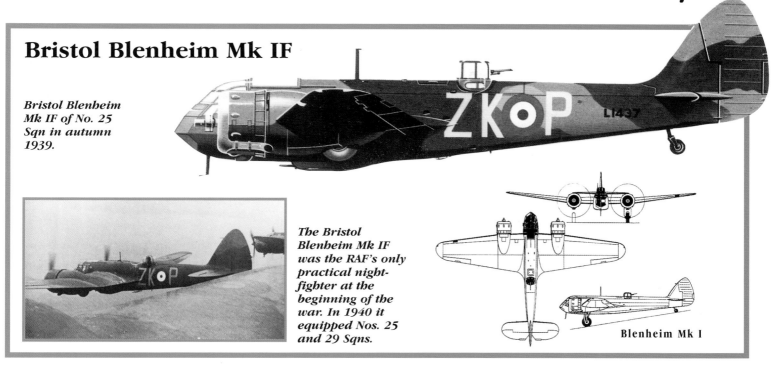

Bristol Blenheim Mk IF

Bristol Blenheim Mk IF of No. 25 Sqn in autumn 1939.

The Bristol Blenheim Mk IF was the RAF's only practical night-fighter at the beginning of the war. In 1940 it equipped Nos. 25 and 29 Sqns.

Blenheim Mk I

Hurricane but with modern stressed-skin construction, but the concept of putting the guns in a turret proved mistaken. Inevitably, with the same engine as a Hurricane but greater weight and a slightly smaller wing, the Defiant was poor in manoeuvrability as well as in flight performance and firepower, and was soon relegated to such duties as air/sea rescue and target towing. Some became quite successful night-fighters, but it was surely a waste of resources to go on making Defiants into 1943, to a total well in excess of 1,000.

Boulton Paul P92 heavy fighter

When the idea of a turret-armed fighter was still exciting, a far more ambitious specification was written, F.11/37, for a fighter with a turret armed with four 20-mm cannon. Unlike those of the Defiant, these guns were to be able to fire straight ahead, aimed by the pilot in the usual way, as well as trained by the gunner right round 360°. The winning design was again by Boulton Paul, the P.92 being a very fast and powerful machine with two Rolls-Royce Vulture or Napier Sabre engines each of some 2,000 hp

(1492 kW). The P92 was cancelled before it flew, in 1940, but a low-powered scale model, the P.92/2, was flown to test the basic idea.

In fact the RAF had rather overlooked the need for a long-range escort fighter, and the gap was expected to be filled by an attractive single-seat twin-engined fighter by Gloster, the G.39 to specification F.9/37. Though this handled well and was almost as fast as a Spitfire (despite its large fuel capacity and armament of two cannon and four machine-guns), it was abandoned. The only long-range fighters at the start of the war were about 200 Bristol Blenheim light bombers which had hastily been fitted with a belly installation of four machine-guns. These became the first radar-equipped night-fighters.

In 1940-41 the tough and easily repaired Hurricane continued to be the most important RAF fighter, developed in several improved versions with metal-skinned wings and the more powerful Merlin XX driving the excellent Rotol

This dramatic photograph shows trials on Salisbury Plain of the Hurricane IID mounting two 40-mm cannon.

Bristol Blenheim

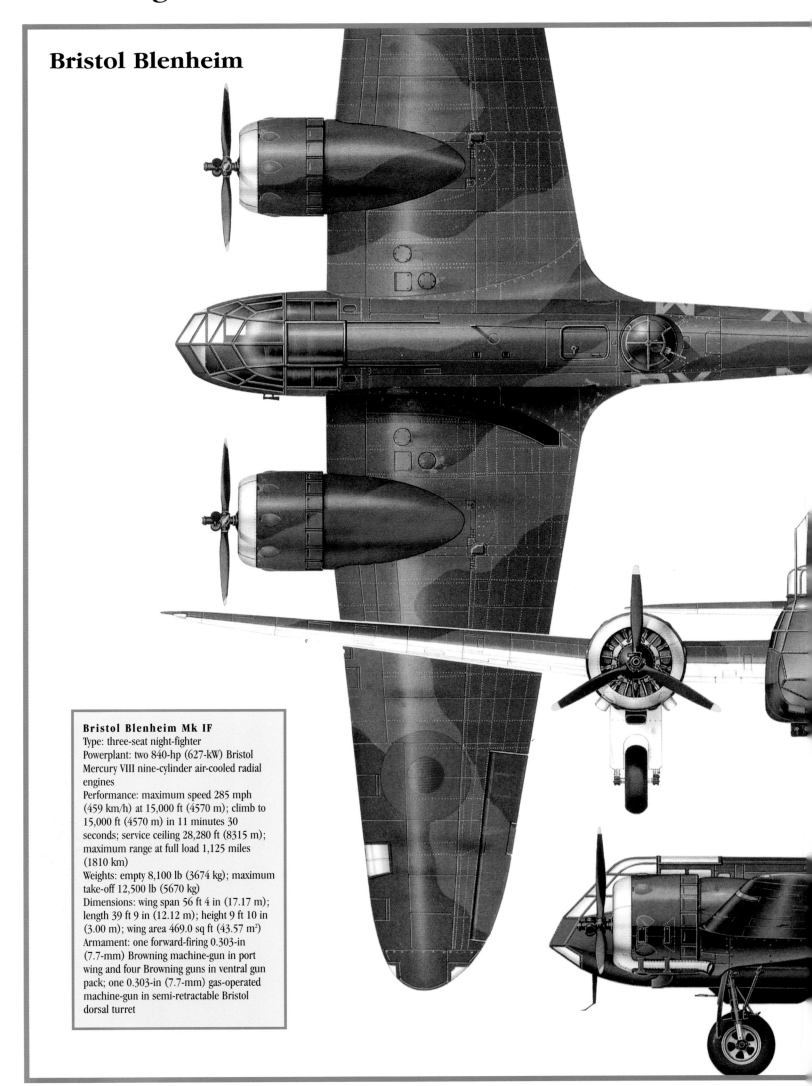

Bristol Blenheim Mk IF
Type: three-seat night-fighter
Powerplant: two 840-hp (627-kW) Bristol
Mercury VIII nine-cylinder air-cooled radial
engines
Performance: maximum speed 285 mph
(459 km/h) at 15,000 ft (4570 m); climb to
15,000 ft (4570 m) in 11 minutes 30
seconds; service ceiling 28,280 ft (8315 m);
maximum range at full load 1,125 miles
(1810 km)
Weights: empty 8,100 lb (3674 kg); maximum
take-off 12,500 lb (5670 kg)
Dimensions: wing span 56 ft 4 in (17.17 m);
length 39 ft 9 in (12.12 m); height 9 ft 10 in
(3.00 m); wing area 469.0 sq ft (43.57 m²)
Armament: one forward-firing 0.303-in
(7.7-mm) Browning machine-gun in port
wing and four Browning guns in ventral gun
pack; one 0.303-in (7.7-mm) gas-operated
machine-gun in semi-retractable Bristol
dorsal turret

No. 25 Sqn was the first Blenheim Mk IF fighter unit but it was soon followed by No. 604 'County of Middlesex' Squadron at Northolt, whose aircraft are seen here in summer 1939. They were soon afterwards pioneering the use of Mk II AI (airborne interception) radar.

This Blenheim Mk IF of No. 25 (Fighter) Squadron was based at Hawkinge in Kent immediately prior to the outbreak of World War II. Points of interest include the black-and-white undersurfaces, the squadron codes 'RX' (changed to 'ZK' in September 1939) and the squadron badge (obliterated when hostilities started) on the fin. The four-gun belly pack was a feature of most Blenheim fighters (including the Mk IVF), but the single gas-operated Lewis gun in the semi-retractable dorsal turret was a relic of the inter-war conviction that single dorsal gun armament constituted adequate tail protection for 'fast' aircraft.

Left: The Hillson F.H.40 bi-mono experiment was one of the more bizarre schemes concoted by the British during World War II. It began as a standard Hawker-built Hurricane I (L1884) that was shipped to Canada. The aircraft returned to Britain where it underwent trials with a jettisonable upper wing, intended to provide extra lift to enable the aircraft to be flown out of small airfields; the wing could also be used to house fuel for ferry flights. The scheme was abandoned in 1943.

Below: An echelon of tropicalised Hurricane IIB fighter-bombers over the Tunisian front around December 1942. Some Hurricanes were hard-pressed to reach 300 mph (483 km/h) but even with the tropical filter the Mk IIB was able to attain 330 mph (531 km/h); this performance allowed it to take care of most enemy aircraft over Tunisia apart from the Messerschmitt Bf 109.

RX5/2 constant-speed propeller. The improved wings could carry heavier armament: by 1941 the RAF thus had the choice of eight machine-guns (Hurricane Mk IIA), 12 machine-guns (Mk IIB) or four 20-mm cannon (Mk IIC). Further options included drop tanks (extra fuel tanks, jettisoned when empty) or two bombs, initially of the 250 lb (113 kg) size but later of double this weight.

Hurricane tank-buster

In 1942 the Hurricane Mk IID began a career of tankbusting with two 40-mm high-velocity cannon, and a year later Hurricanes went into action with eight 60-lb (27-kg) rockets. From 1940 Hurricanes were also made by Cancar (Canadian Car and Foundry) at Fort William, Ontario, and the final variant in 1943 was the versatile Mk IV with a 1,620-hp (1209-kW) Merlin driving a four-bladed propeller, and with a Universal Wing able to carry any of the wide range of guns or underwing loads. Total production of Hurricanes was 14,231 examples.

Biplane Hurricane

One odd Hurricane version not built in quantity was the Slip-Wing or Bi-Mono Hurricane, built by Hillson in Manchester in 1940. Range was increased by the carriage of extra fuel in a new upper wing, slightly larger than the original, which effectively turned the Hurricane into a biplane. When the top wing tanks were empty the pilot jettisoned this wing complete with its struts, leaving a normal Hurricane to do battle. As described later, many Hurricanes fought at sea, but plans for a seaplane version were not realised. Seaplane fighters were suddenly thought of in April 1940 to fight in Norway, and from 1941 four Spitfires were actually flown as seaplanes. They were extremely good seaplanes, but the RAF dropped the idea and never had a fighter seaplane in World War II.

The Spitfire itself, however, developed in an ever-increasing number of versions. After the very similar Mks I and II that fought in the Battle of Britain, the next mass-produced version was the Mk V with a strengthened fuse-

Soon after the German invasion of the USSR in June 1941 the RAF sent No. 151 Wing to help counter the Luftwaffe. This Hurricane IIB of No.81 Sqn was based at Vaenga in September 1941, and has a Soviet number code in place of the individual aircraft letter. Some Hurricanes were fitted with skis and even converted as two-seaters.

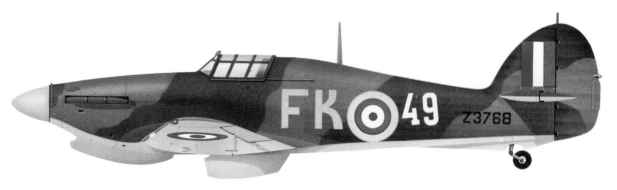

No. 30 Sqn was one of the RAF's more isolated Hurricane units, being based on Ceylon (mainly at Negombo for local defence) in late 1942, at a time when even that island did not appear safe from invasion. BG827 was a Gloster-built Hurricane Mk IIB.

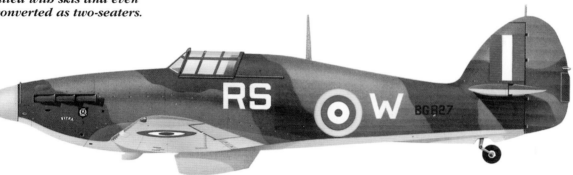

One of the RAF squadrons that sought to retain its pre-war insignia on the fuselage was No. 73 Sqn, which on this Langley-built Hurricane Mk IIB overlapped the yellow ring on the fuselage roundel. The 'TP' code letters were omitted in consequence.

When Yugoslavia was invaded by the Germans in April 1941 its chief fighters included the Hawker Fury and Hurricane. This aircraft was one of a batch of Mk Is made under licence at Zemun. Several escaped to Paramythia in Greece only to be destroyed there by bombing.

This Hurricane IIC of No. 1 Sqn features a new camoufalge scheme introduced on British military aircraft from September 1941. The Air Ministry directive replaced Dark Earth (brown) by Ocean Grey in the upper-surface camouflage. Modified national insignia were introduced from June 1942, with narrower yellow and white rings in the roundel, a white band in the fin flash and a yellow stripe along the wing leading edge.

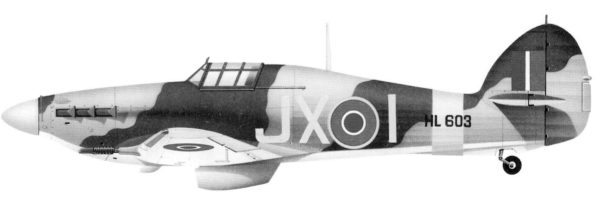

Believed to be the sole Hurricane in Australia during World War II, V7476 (the hyphen was added 'down under') was one of the first Hurricane Mk Is to have stressed-skin wings. It served the Royal Australian Air Force on communications duties.

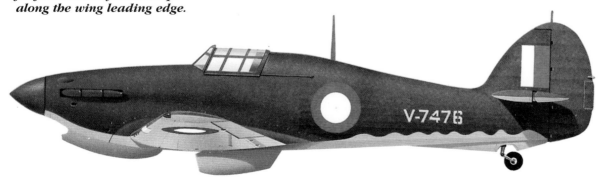

British Fighters of World War II

Supermarine Spitfire Mk V

This Mk VA was the personal aircraft of Wing Commander Douglas Bader when he commanded the TangmereWing in 1941. The aircraft was one of the last built without cannon armament, which was distrusted by Bader. It was one of a batch of 450 Mk 1s ordered from Vickers-Armstrong (Supermarine) on 22 March 1940. The order was subsequently amended to cover Mk V aircraft; most were Spitfire Vbs, but a small batch of Spitfire Vas was also built. Bader was flying this aircraft when he collided with a Messerschmitt Bf 109 over France and baled out to captivity on 7 August 1941.

Supermarine Spitfire Mk V
Type: single-seat fighter
Powerplant: one 1,478-hp (1103-kW)
Rolls-Royce Merlin 45 Vee piston engine
Performance: maximum speed 369 mph
(594 km/h) at 19,500 ft (5945 m); initial climb
rate 4,740 ft (1445 m) per minute; service
ceiling 36,500 ft (11125 m); maximum range
1,135 miles (1827 km)
Weights: empty 4,998 lb (2267 kg); maximum
take-off 6,417 lb (2911 kg)
Dimensions: wing span 36 ft 10 in (11.23 m);
length 29 ft 11 in (9.12 m); height 9 ft 11 in
(3.02 m); wing area 242.00 sq ft (22.48 m²)
Armament: eight 0.303-in (7.7-mm) Browning
machine-guns in wings with 350 rounds per gun

106

British Fighters of World War II
Supermarine Spitfire Vb

1   Aerial stub attachment
2   Rudder upper hinge
3   Fabric-covered rudder
4   Rudder tab
5   Sternpost
6   Rudder tab hinge
7   Rear navigation light
8   Starboard elevator tab
9   Starboard elevator structure
10 Elevator balance
11 Tailplane front spar
12 IFF aerial

41 HF aerial
42 Aerial mast
43 Cockpit aft glazing
44 Voltage regulator
45 Canopy track
46 Structural bulkhead
47 Headrest
48 Plexiglas canopy
49 Rear-view mirror
50 Entry flap (port)
51 Air bottles (alternative rear
    fuselage stowage)

74 Magneto
75 "Fishtail" exhaust manifold
76 Gun heating "intensifier"
77 Hydraulic tank
78 Fuel filler cap
79 Air compressor intake
80 Air compressor
81 Rolls-Royce Merlin 45 engine
82 Coolant piping
83 Port cannon wing fairing
84 Flaps
85 Aileron control cables
86 Aileron push tube
87 Bellcrank

103 Engine bearers
104 Main engine support member
105 Coolant pipe
106 Exposed oil tank
107 Port mainwheel
108 Mainwheel fairing
109 Carburettor air intake
110 Stub/spar attachment
111 Mainwheel leg pivotpoint
112 Main spar
113 Leading-edge ribs (diagonals
    deleted for clarity)
114 Mainwheel leg shock-absorber
115 Mainwheel fairing
116 Starboard mainwheel
117 Angled axle

118 Cannon barrel support fairing
119 Spar cut-out
120 Mainwheel well
121 Gun heating pipe
122 Flap structure
123 Cannon wing fairing
124 Cannon magazine drum
    (120 rounds)
125 Machine-gun support brackets
126 Gun access panels
127 0.303-in (7.7-mm)
    machine-gun barrels
128 Machine-gun ports
129 Ammunition boxes (350 rpg)
130 Starboard aileron construction
131 Wing ribs
132 Single-tube outer spar section
133 Wingtip structure
134 Starboard navigation light

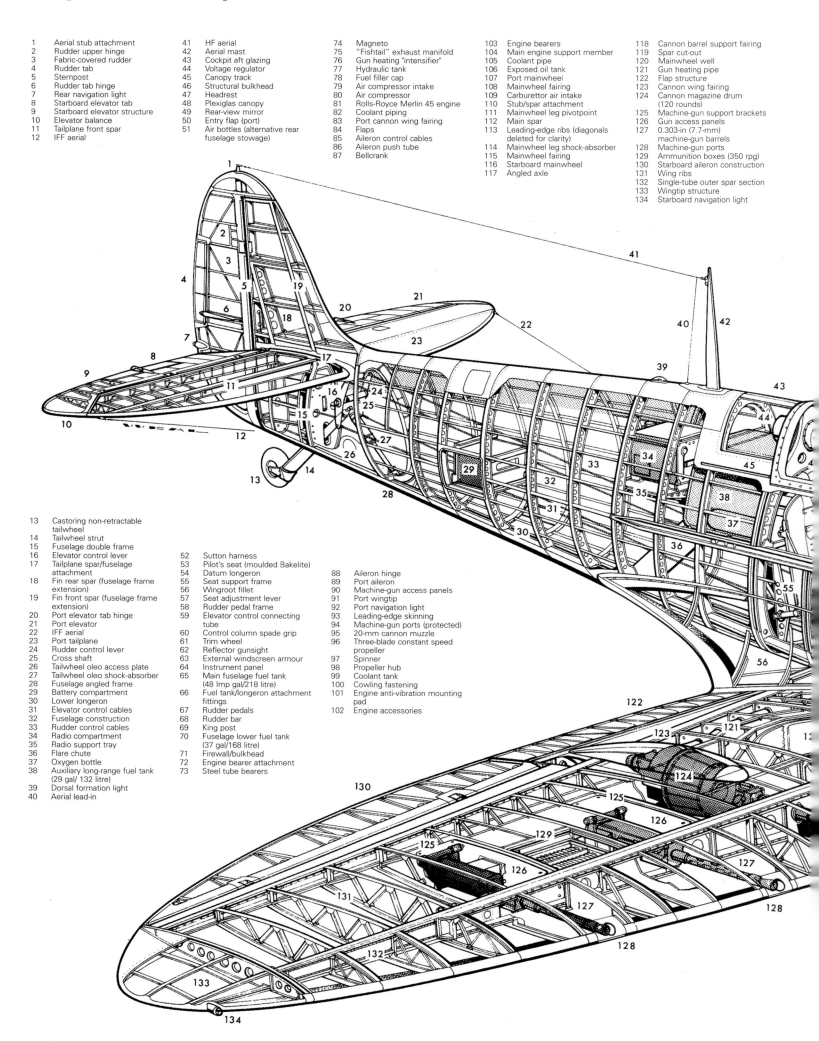

13 Castoring non-retractable
    tailwheel
14 Tailwheel strut
15 Fuselage double frame
16 Elevator control lever
17 Tailplane spar/fuselage
    attachment
18 Fin rear spar (fuselage frame
    extension)
19 Fin front spar (fuselage frame
    extension)
20 Port elevator tab hinge
21 Port elevator
22 IFF aerial
23 Port tailplane
24 Rudder control lever
25 Cross shaft
26 Tailwheel oleo access plate
27 Tailwheel oleo shock-absorber
28 Fuselage angled frame
29 Battery compartment
30 Lower longeron
31 Elevator control cables
32 Fuselage construction
33 Rudder control cables
34 Radio compartment
35 Radio support tray
36 Flare chute
37 Oxygen bottle
38 Auxiliary long-range fuel tank
    (29 gal/ 132 litre)
39 Dorsal formation light
40 Aerial lead-in

52 Sutton harness
53 Pilot's seat (moulded Bakelite)
54 Datum longeron
55 Seat support frame
56 Wingroot fillet
57 Seat adjustment lever
58 Rudder pedal frame
59 Elevator control connecting
    tube
60 Control column spade grip
61 Trim wheel
62 Reflector gunsight
63 External windscreen armour
64 Instrument panel
65 Main fuselage fuel tank
    (48 Imp gal/218 litre)
66 Fuel tank/longeron attachment
    fittings
67 Rudder pedals
68 Rudder bar
69 King post
70 Fuselage lower fuel tank
    (37 gal/168 litre)
71 Firewall/bulkhead
72 Engine bearer attachment
73 Steel tube bearers

88 Aileron hinge
89 Port aileron
90 Machine-gun access panels
91 Port wingtip
92 Port navigation light
93 Leading-edge skinning
94 Machine-gun ports (protected)
95 20-mm cannon muzzle
96 Three-blade constant speed
    propeller
97 Spinner
98 Propeller hub
99 Coolant tank
100 Cowling fastening
101 Engine anti-vibration mounting
    pad
102 Engine accessories

'WZ', the 1938 code of No. 19 Sqn, was later worn by the USAAF 78th Fighter Group, though this particular 'Spit', a Mk VB, was actually on the strength of the famed 4th FG formed from the four RAF Eagle squadrons.

P7666 was a Spitfire Mk IIA presentation aircraft that had been paid for by donations from the Observer Corps {later Royal Observer Corps). The aircraft was flown from Hornchurch by the CO of No. 41 Sqn, Sqn Ldr Don Finlay, a pre-war Olympic hurdler.

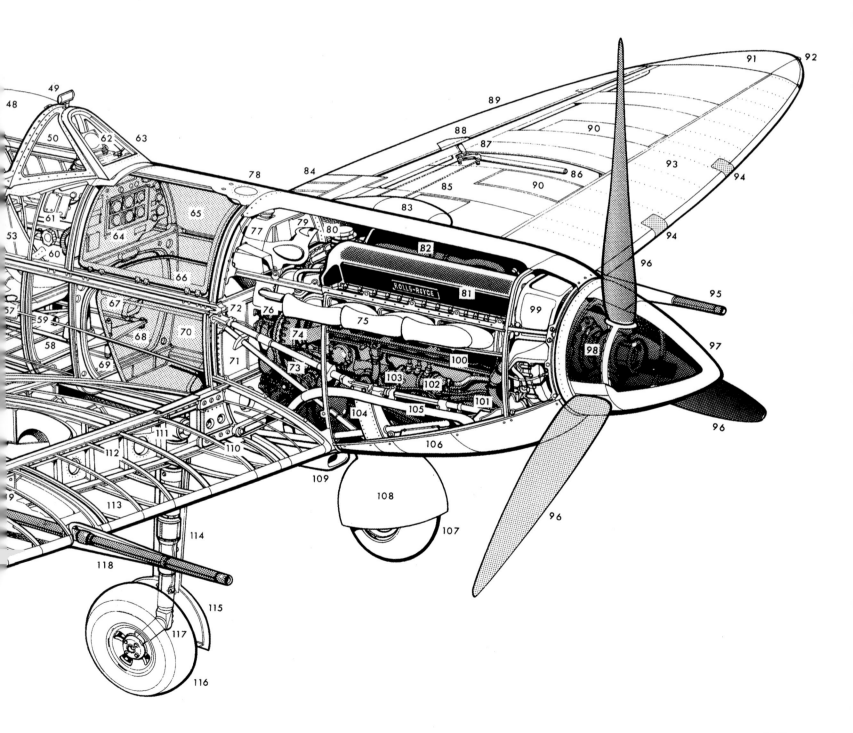

Left: In many ways the wooden Miles M.20 was a remarkably fine fighter, and it was a pity that the type ran up against totally negative thinking on the part of the Air Staff. This example, the M.20/4, was built to Naval specification N.1/41, later becoming DR616.

Right: According to test pilots the Gloster F.9/37 long-range, single-seat twin-engined fighter prototype was an outstanding aircraft, and many observers thought that it should have gone into production. This photograph shows an example powered by Bristol Taurus radial engines, the other prototype having Rolls-Royce Peregrine V-12 inline engines.

lage to take the more powerful 1,470-hp (1097-kW) Merlin 45 and related engines, driving better constant-speed propellers. No fewer than 6,479 Spitfire Mk Vs were made, in three major sub-types: the Mk VA with the original eight machine-guns, the Mk VB with two 20-mm cannon and four machine-guns, and the Mk VC with four cannon. Like the Hurricane, the Spitfire was developed to carry bombs and drop tanks, though at first these loads were on the centreline instead of under the wings. Joe Smith's engineers also developed something Camm never did for the Hurricane: a range of different wings with the normal span of 36-ft 10-in (11.23-m), a clipped wing of 32-ft 2-in (9.80-m) and a long pointed wing of 40-ft 2-in (12.24-m) span. The clipped wing gave more rapid roll and in most

Below: A line-up of tropicalised Spitfire Mk VC fighter-bombers of No. 417 (RCAF) Sqn, on the dusty Italian front in early 1943. At this time, No. 417 Sqn was converting to the high-altitude Mks VII and VIII.

respects improved performance at low altitudes, and in 1941-42 the clipped Mk VB was the best the RAF could offer to match the Focke-Wulf Fw 190. The long pointed wing was for ultra-high altitude work.

In the summer of 1940 the need for fighters was so urgent that there were even plans for fitting guns in light-planes, and in the tiny Percival Mew Gull racer, proposed in a fractionally enlarged form with retractable landing gear. One company, Miles Aircraft, even designed and built a fighter from scratch and flew it in much less than three months. This M.20 was an outstanding machine, the first fighter to have the teardrop type of canopy giving all-round view (and soon universal on almost all fighters) and despite fixed landing gear having a speed near that of a Spitfire and much higher than a Hurricane. It was highly manoeuvrable, and in range and ammunition capacity was superior to all other British single-seat fighters, but the crisis passed and the M.20 never went into production.

A Spitfire Mk IIB in service with No. 304 (Polish) Sqn, RAF, based at Northolt in mid-1941. Built at Castle Bromwich, this mark was was one of the first cannon-armed versions. Note the Polish air force insignia behind the roundel and badge of the Torun squadron on the nose.

The tropicalised Mk Vc was one of the slowest marks of the 'Spit'. This example served on the North African front in 1942. Not all Mk Vc aircraft were fitted with all four cannon.

Clipped wing Spitfire Mk Vb (built at Castle Bromwich) of No. 40 Sqn SAAF, on the Italian front in 1943. Note the enlarged 'Aboukir' carburettor-air filter and the reconnaissance camera behind the cockpit.

Hundreds of Spitfires served with US units. The 'XR' code on this Castle Bromwich-built Mk Vb was originally allocated to No. 71 (Eagle) Sqn, RAF, whose pilots were all freelance Americans. EN783 is depicated just after the unit became the 334th Sqn of the USAAF in September 1942.

JK226 was another of the 'reverse Lend-Lease' Spitfires. Built at Castle Bromwich, it was a tropicalised Mk Vc and was assigned to the 308th Fighter Squadron, 31st Fighter Group, of the US 12th Air Force in Tunisia.

By February 1943 No. 54 Sqn was in business with tropical Spitfire Vcs defending Darwin alongside Nos 452 and 457 Sqns of the RAAF, all under the command of Wing Cdr 'Killer' Caldwell. The unit disbanded in 1945, but No. 183 Sqn subsequently renumbered as No. 54 Sqn.

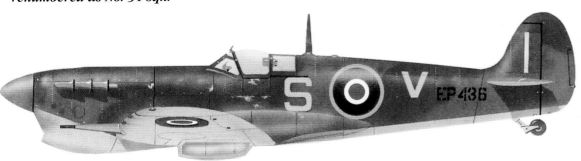

This Castle Bromwich Spitfire Mk Vc (note with only two cannon fitted) featured a tropical filter and a naval paint scheme and is depicted after transfer to the Fleet Air Arm as a non-navalised Seafire Mk I for airfield training. No Seafire Mk I aircraft were built as such; all were conversions.

Fierce Storms from Hawker

Famed designer Sydney Camm built fighters that were tough (with a few rare exceptions) and eminently serviceable. The very important Typhoon initially proved such a disappointment that it was almost cancelled, but it later found its true niche as a ground-attack aircraft.

Though the evergreen Hurricane remained in production well into 1944, Camm recognised even before the war that in many respects it was of an obsolescent character. By 1937 he was drafting a new fighter with all stressed-skin construction, to be powered by one of the new engines in the 2,000 hp (1492 kW) class. Experience showed that the best engine was an air-cooled radial, the Bristol Centaurus, but the official view was almost to ignore such engines until an example of the superb radial-engined Focke-Wulf Fw 190 was captured in 1942. So Camm concentrated on the Rolls-Royce Vulture, with 24 cylinders in X-arrangement, and the Napier Sabre, with 24 much smaller cylinders in a unique configuration resembling two horizontally opposed 12-cylinder units with the upper and lower crankshafts geared to a single front output pinion. The result was the F.18/37 specification to cover the Hawker Tornado (Vulture) and Typhoon (Sabre).

Almost the same size as the Hurricane, these fighters looked much more impressive. The first Tornado flew on 6 October 1939, and the first Typhoon (distinguished by having only one row of exhaust stacks on each side instead of two) followed on 24 February 1940. Eventually the Vulture had to be abandoned, and the Tornado was abandoned with it. This was tragic, because in October 1941 a Tornado had flown with a Centaurus, a splendid 18-cylinder sleeve-valve radial, and although the installation was a bit of a lash-up, it did reach 421 mph (678 km/h), faster than any other fighter in the world at that time.

Centaurus engine

The Centaurus continued to be ignored, and every effort was put behind the Typhoon; but the Sabre suffered from such severe troubles that it was officially called 'one of the Second World War's most melancholy stories', and the Centaurus would not fit in the Typhoon airframe.

Though the Typhoon had a modern wing structure, its wing was relatively thick, and aerodynamically it was nothing like as good at high speeds as the wing of the Spitfire. This caused high drag, which combined with the high wing-loading to give performance far below the predicted

Left: Though a disappointing fighter, the Typhoon eventually proved to be an outstanding ground-attack aircraft armed with bombs and rockets. Although the machine-gun-armed Mk IA was the first to enter service, it was the four-cannon-armed Mk IB which became the definitive model.

This photograph shows a Typhoon Mk IB of No. 175 Sqn being bombed up for a 'Rhubarb' attack sortie with two 500-lb (227-kg) bombs. Although still fitted with the 'car door' style cockpit canopy, it does have the smoothly faired cannon barrels which gave a welcome increase in maximum speed.

British Fighters of World War II

Hawker Typhoon

Typhoon Mk Ib MN235, was one of the fifth production batch of 800 Typhoons built by Gloster.

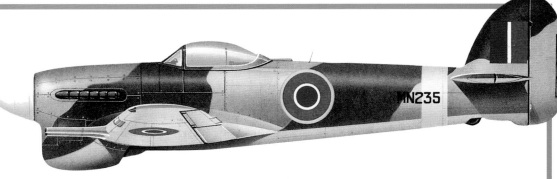

Typhoon Mk IB armed with four 20-mm cannon and wearing invasion stripes.

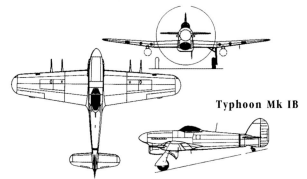

Typhoon Mk IB

This is an early Typhoon IB with car-type doors and fixed canopy, which obstructed the pilot's view to some degree. R7684 carries the initials of the pilot, John Grandy, commander of the Duxford Wing in June 1942 (and 20 years later Chief of the Air Staff, retiring as a Marshal of the Royal Air Force).

Typhoon Mk IB DN406 belonged to No. 609 Sqn; on 12 March 1943 it caught and destroyed a lone Fw 190 over Kent. The 18 small white locomotive markings record confirmed train 'kills' in France.

Despite its late serial number, this Typhoon Mk IB has unfaired gun barrels, as well as the original form of cockpit. It is was assigned to No. 3 Sqn at West Malling, from where it made its last mission on 18 May 1043, being shot down by I./JG 27 over Poix airfield.

The serial on this Typhoon Mk IB (MN363) has been obscured by invasion stripes applied in June 1944. The aircraft was flown by No. 247 Sqn which later became the first unit to receive de Havilland Vampires.

This brace of illustrations depicts two late-model Typhoon Mk Ibs; fitted with underwing 60-lb (27-kg) rocket projectiles, the upper aircraft was from the final production batch and served with No. 175 Sqn. The lower aircraft (RB389) served with No. 440 Sqn of the RCAF and carries two 1,000-lb (454-kg) bombs.

values, together with poor manoeuvrability. The cockpit had unusual car-type doors on each side, and in high-speed dives these tended to unlock and try to open because of suction on the external hand-lever. Worse, elevator flutter caused persistent failure of the rear fuselage, which added to the casualties from frequent engine failure. Though a few Typhoons reached No.56 Squadron and the Air Fighting Development Unit before the end of 1941, there were so many problems that for much of 1942 the whole programme was under threat of cancellation. It was only the tenacity and personal example of R. P. Beamont (then CO of No.609 Sqn and later a famed test pilot) that just saved this potentially valuable aircraft.

Beamont, who had played a major role in the Hawker flight-test programme, could do nothing to give the Typhoon the hoped-for speed or performance at high altitude, but he was convinced that at low levels it was as good as any other fighter and much better than most. In particular he was interested in its performance in the ground-attack role, but first he managed to show its worth as a low-level interceptor of Luftwaffe hit-and-run raiders, mainly Fw 190s, which no other RAF fighter could easily catch. From November 1942 increasing numbers of Typhoons roamed over Europe by day and night with four 20-mm

This is one of the Typhoon development aircraft with the original canopy, long-barrel cannon with fairings, four-bladed propeller and several non-standard details. The great effort put into Typhoon development was nullified by inherent shortcomings in the type's performance at altitude and its poor reliability during its four year gestation period.

Hawker Typhoon

This aircraft represents the ultimate standard of build of the Typhoon Mk IB, which accounted for all but 105 of the entire production run. The four-bladed propeller was introduced in 1943 but did not completely supplant the original unit. The rocket-armed aircraft shown flew with No. 181 Squadron, 2nd Tactical Air Force, and served in France during June 1944.

Typhoon Mk F.Mk IB (early production)
Type: single-seat fighter-bomber
Powerplant: one 2,180-hp (1626-kW) Napier Sabre IIA horizontal H piston engine
Performance: maximum speed (clean) 405 mph (652 km/h) at 18,000 ft (5486 m); cruising speed 254 mph (1409 km/h); time to 15,000 ft (4570 m) from sea level, 5 minutes 55 seconds; service ceiling 34,000 ft (10363 m); range with 2,000-lb (907-kg) bombload 510 miles (821 km)
Weights: empty 8,800 lb (3992 kg); maximum take-off 13,250 lb (6010 kg)
Dimensions: wing span 41 ft 7 in (12.67 m); length 31 ft 11 in (9.73 m); height 14 ft 10 in (4.52 m); wing area 279.0 sq ft (25.92 m²)
Armament: four 20-mm cannon in wings, plus up to eight 60-lb (27-kg) rocket projectiles or two 250-lb (113-kg), 500-lb (227-kg) or 1,000-lb (454-kg) bombs on underwing racks

JR371 was one of the last Typhoons to be fitted with side doors and a fixed canopy. It was assigned to No. 198 Sqn, a major constituent unit of the Second Tactical Air Force in 1944.

28	Exhaust stubs	43	Control column handgrip	65	Fabric-covered rudder construction
29	Napier Sabre II, 24-cylinder flat H engine	44	Engine throttle controls	66	Rudder trim tab
30	Engine cowlings	45	Trim handwheels	67	Tail navigation light
31	Cartridge starter	46	Emergency hydraulic handpump	68	Elevator trim tab
32	Engine compartment fireproof bulkhead	47	Forward fuselage steel tube construction	69	Port tailplane construction
33	Oxygen bottle	48	Pilot's seat	70	Tailplane spar attachments
34	Gun heating air duct	49	Safety harness	71	Tailwheel hydraulic jack
35	Hydraulic reservoir	50	Back and head armour plate	72	Forward-retracting tailwheel
		51	Pneumatic system air bottle	73	Dowty oleo-pneumatic tailwheel strut
		52	Rearward-sliding canopy cover	74	Tailplane spar fixing double bulkhead
		53	Aft fuselage joint	75	Tailplane attachment joint strap
		54	Canopy rails	76	External strengthening fishplates
		55	Radio transmitter/receiver		
		56	Fuselage double frame		

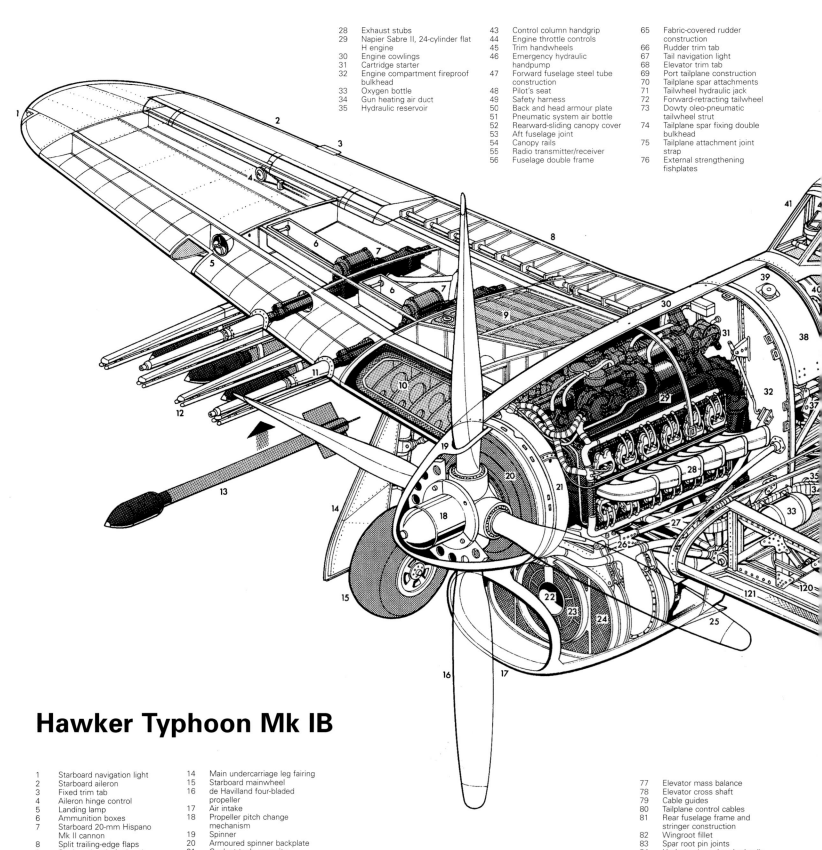

Hawker Typhoon Mk IB

1	Starboard navigation light	14	Main undercarriage leg fairing			
2	Starboard aileron	15	Starboard mainwheel			
3	Fixed trim tab	16	de Havilland four-bladed propeller			
4	Aileron hinge control	17	Air intake			
5	Landing lamp	18	Propeller pitch change mechanism			77 Elevator mass balance
6	Ammunition boxes	19	Spinner			78 Elevator cross shaft
7	Starboard 20-mm Hispano Mk II cannon	20	Armoured spinner backplate			79 Cable guides
8	Split trailing-edge flaps	21	Coolant tank, capacity 7.25 Imp gal (33 litres)	36	Footboards	57 Whip aerial	80 Tailplane control cables
9	Starboard main fuel tank, capacity 40 Imp gal (182 litres)	22	Supercharger ram air intake	37	Rudder pedals	58 Fuselage skinning	81 Rear fuselage frame and stringer construction
10	Self-sealing leading-edge fuel tank, capacity 35 Imp gal (159 litres)	23	Oil radiator	38	Oil tank, capacity 18 Imp gal (82 litres)	59 Starboard tailplane	82 Wingroot fillet
		24	Coolant radiator	39	Oil tank filler cap	60 Starboard elevator	83 Spar root pin joints
11	Cannon barrel fairings	25	Radiator shutter	40	Instrument panel	61 Elevator trim tab	84 Undercarriage door hydraulic jack
12	Rocket launcher rails	26	Engine mounting block	41	Bullet-proof windscreen	62 Fin leading edge	85 Mainwheel door
13	60-lb (27-kg) ground-attack rockets	27	Tubular steel engine support framework	42	Reflector sight	63 Fin construction	86 Main undercarriage bay
						64 Rudder sternpost	87 Rear spar
							88 Port main fuel tank, capacity 40 Imp gal (182 litres)
							89 Flap shroud construction
							90 Port split trailing-edge flaps

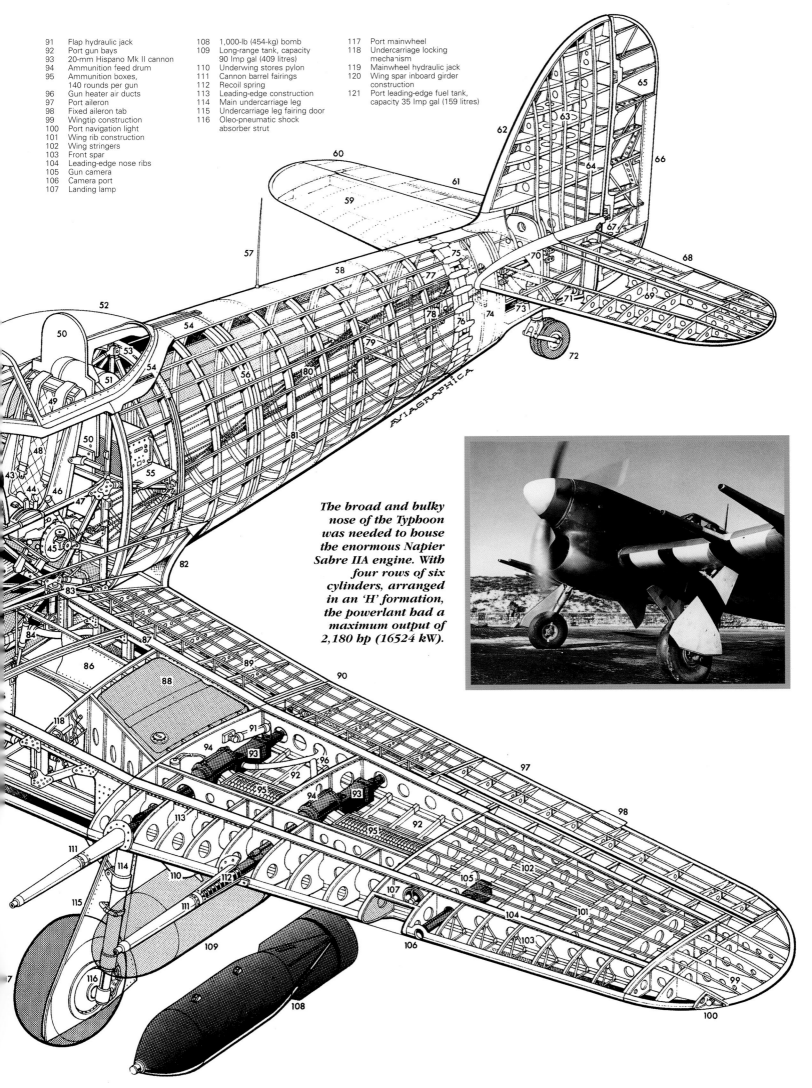

91 Flap hydraulic jack
92 Port gun bays
93 20-mm Hispano Mk II cannon
94 Ammunition feed drum
95 Ammunition boxes,
    140 rounds per gun
96 Gun heater air ducts
97 Port aileron
98 Fixed aileron tab
99 Wingtip construction
100 Port navigation light
101 Wing rib construction
102 Wing stringers
103 Front spar
104 Leading-edge nose ribs
105 Gun camera
106 Camera port
107 Landing lamp

108 1,000-lb (454-kg) bomb
109 Long-range tank, capacity
    90 Imp gal (409 litres)
110 Underwing stores pylon
111 Cannon barrel fairings
112 Recoil spring
113 Leading-edge construction
114 Main undercarriage leg
115 Undercarriage leg fairing door
116 Oleo-pneumatic shock
    absorber strut

117 Port mainwheel
118 Undercarriage locking
    mechanism
119 Mainwheel hydraulic jack
120 Wing spar inboard girder
    construction
121 Port leading-edge fuel tank,
    capacity 35 Imp gal (159 litres)

The broad and bulky nose of the Typhoon was needed to house the enormous Napier Sabre IIA engine. With four rows of six cylinders, arranged in an 'H' formation, the powerlant had a maximum output of 2,180 hp (16524 kW).

The bulk of the 800 production Tempest Vs were of the Series 2 model with guns that did not have protruding barrels. This example from No. 501 Sqn (County of Gloucester) AAF Squadron has 45-Imp gal (205-litre) drop tanks.

The first Tempests to go into action flew with R. P. Beamont's Newchurch (Kent) Wing, comprising Nos 3 and 486 Sqns from April 1944, with No. 56 Sqn completing the wing in July. From mid-June the wing was the top scoring unit in intercepting V-1 flying bombs; this No. 486 Sqn machine has two kills.

guns, two 1,000-lb (454-kg) bombs and, from 1943, eight 60-lb (27-kg) rockets. In this role the bluff but capable Typhoon at least found its forte.

Altogether the RAF received 3,300 Typhoons built by Gloster plus a handful of the 15 production machines from the parent firm. A few early examples were Mk IAs with 12 machine-guns, but the standard model was the Mk IB with four cannon. During the course of production the original cockpit was replaced by a superior cockpit without doors but with one of the new sliding teardrop canopies. The cannon barrels were covered by neat fairings and the de Havilland three-bladed propeller was replaced by a unit with four blades. In service Typhoons were painted with distinctive black/white stripes to prevent 'confusion with an Fw 190'. By late 1944 Typhoons equipped 23 squadrons in the 2nd Tactical Air Force operating from newly liberated bases on the continent, and they did more than any other single type to smash the German army in the west.

Left: No. 193 Sqn was one of the intensively active wartime units; it had an existence of only three years and flew only Typhoon Mk IBs. Under Wing Cdr Baldwin several of its aircraft shot up Rommel's staff car in 17 July 1944, wounding the German C-in-C West. These nine aircraft were funded by the 'Fellowship of the Bellows of Brazil' and were handed over to the squadron by the Brazilian Ambassador.

Below: This beautiful air-to-air portrait of a Hawker Typhoon Mk IB with bubble canopy was captured during a flight test sortie from the Gloster factory.

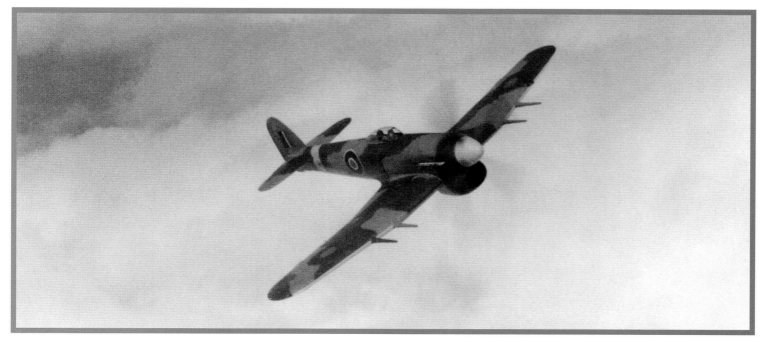

Some Tempests carried the identification stripes that were applied to early Typhoons, and, like all Allied aircraft from 6 June 1944 onwards, the Tempest wore D-Day invasion markings. This example, from No. 274 Sqn, RAF, carried them on the fuselage underside only.

The first Tempests to go into action flew with R. P. Beamont's Newchurch (Kent) Wing, comprising Nos 3 and 486 Sqns from April 1944, with No. 56 Sqn completing the wing in July. From mid-June the wing was the top scoring unit in intercepting V-1 flying bombs; this No. 486 Sqn machine has two kills.

Improving the breed

In 1941 Camm had schemed a Typhoon Mk II with a thinner wing to try to recover some of the lost performance. It was arranged to house four cannon installed farther back, with shorter barrels wholly inside the wing, and this led to a curious elliptical wing plan rather like that of the Spitfire. There was at this time an amazingly powerful prejudice against fighters that did not look like a Spitfire (to the extent that early Typhoon squadrons had to be based at airfields without Spitfire squadrons), and Camm admitted this played a part in deciding the new wing shape! Wisely the Typhoon Mk II was planned to have the Centaurus or Griffon as alternatives to the Sabre, but the first examples had Sabres. The first to fly, HM595 on 2 September 1942, had a Typhoon engine installation with radiator in the chin position, but the next machine, in February 1943, had wing leading-edge radiators and achieved 466 mph (750 km/h). Eventually the aircraft was renamed Tempest and put into production with the original engine installation as the Mk V. Even so, it was not only much faster than a Typhoon but more manoeuvrable, and a most formidable fighter except at high altitude.

Both Hawker and Gloster made Tempests, and the aircraft were the top scoring killers of V-1 flying bombs in the summer and autumn of 1944, besides establishing complete superiority over the Luftwaffe – to a remarkable degree this even extended to the Messerschmitt Me 262 jet, though the Me 262 was almost 100 mph (161 km/h) faster. The Tempest Mk V series 2 had slightly more power, spring-tab ailerons for faster rate of roll and short barrel Mk V cannon wholly buried in the wings.

Two even better Tempests failed to reach the RAF until after the war. One was the Mk VI, with a more powerful version of the Sabre and the oil cooler displaced to the right wing, with small inlet ducts at the root on each side

Scramble by Typhoons of No. 56 Sqn, which had converted to the type with some misgivings as early as December 1941. Eventually this powerful machine was to make good; 13 years later No. 56 introduced another new fighter, the Supermarine Swift, which did not.

Above: These Tempests were photographed returning from targets to the east of the Rhine, although the fact that they still have drop tanks suggests that no combat took place.

Left: This is one of the first production Tempests (the first was JN729) on test from Langley in June 1943. The initial batches were called Tempest V Series 1; the main run of Series 2 had Hispano Mk V cannon with short barrels which did not project ahead of the leading edge, and rate of roll was improved by fitting spring-tab ailerons.

Below: This regular production Tempest was one of a batch of 130 Mk V Series 2 aircraft with spring-tab ailerons and gun barrels wholly within the wings.

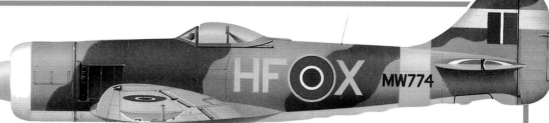

Hawker Tempest

Tempest Mk V
Type: single-seat
fighter/fighter-bomber
Powerplant: one 2,180-hp
(1626-kW) Napier Sabre IIA
inline piston engine
Performance: maximum speed
426 mph (686 km/h) at 18,500
ft (5639 m); service ceiling
36,500 ft (11125 m); maximum
range 1,530 miles (2462 km)
Weights: empty 9,000 lb (4082
kg); maximum take-off 13,540
lb (6142 kg)
Dimensions: span 41 ft 0 in
(12.50 m); length 33 ft 8 in
(10.26 m); height
16 ft 1 in (4.90 m); wing area
302 sq ft (28.06 m2)
Armament: four 20-mm
cannon, plus two 500-lb
(227-kg) or two 1,000-lb
(454-kg) bombs, or rocket
projectiles

This Tempest Mk II is illustrated as it appeared when serving with the type's first squadron, No. 183. The unit was renumbered No. 54 Sqn before being declared operational.

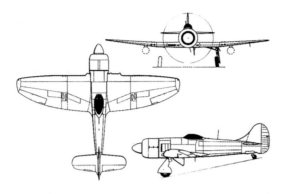

Hawker Tempest Mk II

Hawker Tempest Mk V.

---

to serve the engine's injection carburettor. Napier tested lower-drag Sabre installations with annular radiators, either with a conventional propeller or with a large ducted spinner giving an appearance like a jet aircraft, but these did not go into production.

Tempest II

The best Tempest of all was powered by the shamefully neglected Centaurus radial. This Mk II aircraft flew as a prototype at Langley on 28 June 1943. It was also ordered from Gloster in 1942 but was severely delayed by Gloster's overwork; eventually the programme was moved to the Bristol Aeroplane Company, where at last a Tempest Mk II flew on 4 October 1944. The programme was then moved back to Hawker, so that this first-class fighter-bomber

missed the war, Bristol actually making 50 of the total of 452. Quieter and less-tiring to fly than the Sabre versions, the Mk II was the only mark to remain in the RAF as a fighter after the war. From it Hawker derived the superlative Fury and Sea Fury, arguably the pinnacle of piston-engine fighter development.

PR533 was one of the first 332 Tempest Mk II fighters built by Hawker at Langley. Certainly the best of all the wartime Hawker fighters, the Mk II was tragically subjected to prolonged delays, mainly because of official disbelief that an air-cooled engine could prove suitable. When a Centaurus was installed by Camm in the prototype Typhoon Mk II (later named Tempest) in August 1942, Air Marshall Freeman ordered the engine removed. This aircraft was therby delayed a full year.

Later Spitfires

Under Joe Smith's direction the Spitfire was developed to such a degree that the later Griffon-engined versions had practically nothing in common with the Mk I. They were among the best piston-engined fighters ever built.

Though the Spitfire ran up a string of mark numbers as high as 24, virtually all were production types. There were remarkably few oddities or unsuccessful versions, or even experimental fits of equipment or armament. Amazingly, though there were schemes for several others, no engine was fitted except the regular Merlin or Griffon (apart from two trial installations of the Daimler Benz DB 601 and 605 on Spitfires captured by the Germans). The only markedly different proposal was for a so-called 'Plastic Spitfire' with a high proportion of resin-bonded flax and wood construction, and though it would have achieved its objective of conserving imported aluminium it was never built.

The mass-produced Mk V has already been described, as a Mk I or II with more power. The Mk III would have introduced further improvements, including wheels set further forward to avoid nosing-over, the bullet-proof windscreen inside instead of outside, better armour protection and a retractable tailwheel, but only two were made. The mark number IV was confusingly used twice. The PR. IV was just an unarmed photo-reconnaissance Mk V, but the true Mk IV was the first of a completely different family with the larger Griffon engine. The Mk IV, DP845, was a frequently modified aircraft with four-bladed propeller and retractable tailwheel, and it had six cannon.

The Mk VI was the first special high-altitude model, with a pressurised cockpit without side access flaps and with a special non-sliding hood. Long-span pointed wings were fitted, and the engine was a Merlin 47 driving a four-bladed propeller; otherwise the 100 delivered were like Mk Vs.

Left: If the Spitfire had a serious shortcoming it was inadequate fuel capacity, but the dedicated photo-reconnaissance (PR) marks went some way to rectifying this. The PR.Mk XI was by far the most important PR version, which covered targets east of Berlin and in Poland and Czechoslovakia; this example carries full invasion stripes.

This rare wartime air-to-air colour photograph features a Spitfire Mk Vb. This aircraft was the personal mount of the commander of No. 222 Squadron, some time in late 1941/ early 1942 while based at North Weald. Although improved variants were trialled, the Mk V remained the standard production variant of Spitfire during the middle of the war.

British Fighters of World War II

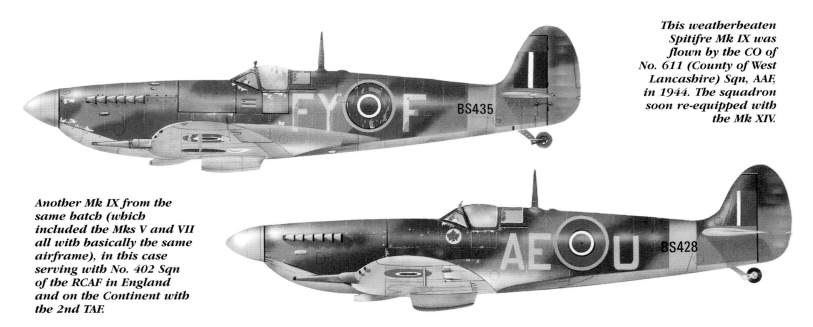

This weatherbeaten Spitfire Mk IX was flown by the CO of No. 611 (County of West Lancashire) Sqn, AAF, in 1944. The squadron soon re-equipped with the Mk XIV.

Another Mk IX from the same batch (which included the Mks V and VII all with basically the same airframe), in this case serving with No. 402 Sqn of the RCAF in England and on the Continent with the 2nd TAF.

The slightly improved engine and extended tips raised service ceiling considerably, but a far greater improvement came with the Merlin 60-series engine, which had two superchargers in series and an intercooler. Installation of this new family of engines was signalled by a longer nose, six exhaust stubs on each side, four-bladed propeller and symmetrical cooling radiators, one under each wing. The first Spitfire to have one of these engines, which doubled the power available above 30,000 ft (9145 m), was the Mk VII. This was a most effective high-altitude fighter, with pointed wings, retractable tailwheel, pressurised cockpit and a broad pointed rudder also flown at this time (April 1942) on the Mk XII.

Just as the 6,479 Mk Vs were essentially re-engined lash-ups of the original Spitfire, so was the next most numerous

While the Spitfire Mk V was basically a strengthened Mk I with a more powerful Merlin engine, the Mk IX was just a hasty lash-up of the Mk V with the new 60-series Merlin giving much greater high-altitude performance, yet it was kept in production until 5,739 had been built. These Mk IXs from No. 241 Sqn are patrolling over Cassino in March 1944.

mark, the 5,739 Mk IXs, ostensibly a hasty re-engined lash-up of the Mk V. There has never been any attempt to explain why the Mk IX was kept in production almost to the end of the war in preference to the intended model, the Mk VIII. The Mk IX was rushed through to meet the severe challenge of the Fw 190 in 1942.

Spitfire Mk IX

It was basically a Mk V with the Merlin 61; indeed hundreds began life as the earlier version and were fitted with the new engine either on the assembly line or after delivery. Though unpressurised, some Mk IXs had the long-span pointed wing, while a much larger number had the LF (low-altitude fighter) clipped wing. Most had the B-wing with two cannon. By 1944 the E-wing was also common, with two cannon and two 0.5-in (12.7-mm) heavy machine-guns. As on the other marks a flush-fitting slipper drop tank of 45, 90 or (rarely) 170 Imp gal (205, 409 or 773 litres) could be fitted under the belly; alternatively a 500-lb (227-kg) bomb could be hung here, plus two 250-lb (113-kg) bombs under the wings. Other features included a

Supermarine Spitfire Mk IX

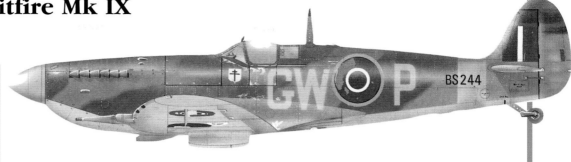

Supermarine Spitfire Mk IX
Type: single-seat day fighter-bomber
Powerplant: one 1,515-hp (1130-kW) Rolls-Royce Merlin 61 or 1,710-hp (1276-kW) Merlin 63 or 63A Vee-12 piston engine
Performance: maximum speed 408 mph (657 km/h) at 25,000 ft (7620 m); service ceiling 44,000 ft (134 10 m); range on internal fuel 434 miles (698 km)
Weights: empty 5,610 lb, (2545 kg), maximum take-off 7,500 lb (3402 kg)
Dimensions: wing span (normal) 36 ft 10 in (11.23 m), (clipped) 32 ft 2 in or 32 ft 7 in (9.93 m); length 31 ft 3½ in (9.54 m); height 11 ft 9 in (3.58 m); wing area (normal) 242.0 sq ft (22.48 m²), (clipped) 231.0 sq ft (21.46 m²)

Spitfire F.Mk IX of No. 340 (Free French) Sqn, RAF. Note the Cross of Lorraine, the insignia of the Free French forces.

Armament: two 20-mm Hispano cannon and either four 0.303-in (7.7-mm) machine guns or (E-type wing) two 20-min and two 0.50-in (12.7-mm) and provision for up to 1,000-1b (454-kg) bombload (two 250-lb/113-kg) under wings and one 500-lb/227-kg under fuselage)

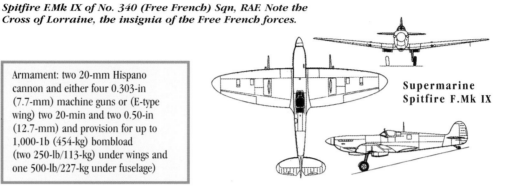

Supermarine Spitfire F.Mk IX

Left: A Spitfire PR.Mk XI of No. 541 Squadron from RAF Benson cavorts for the camera. Mission-specific equipment comprised a range of cameras peering through the two windows in the underside of the mid-fuselage. PR.Mk XIs had the 'U' (Universal) camera installation allowing a variety of sensors to be fitted.

Below: The RAF and Royal Navy never had a water-based fighter in World War II, though Folland Aircraft tested a seaplane conversion of a Spitfire Mk VB in 1942 and this broadly similar conversion of a Mk IX in 1943. Note the extra fin area needed by this rebuild, which was successful but never put into production.

British Fighters of World War II

Supermarine Spitfire Mk VII

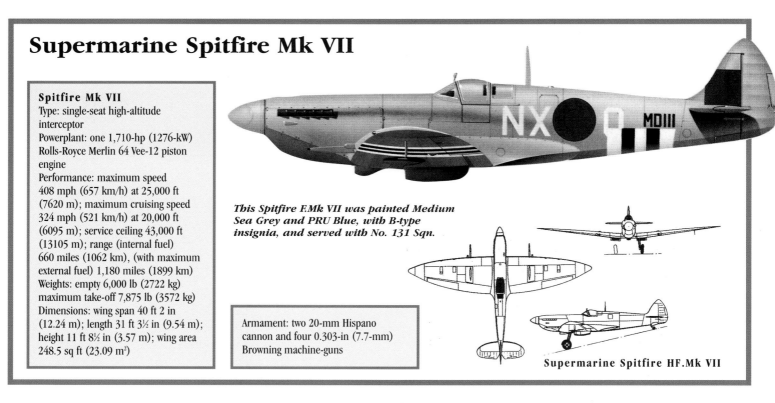

Spitfire Mk VII
Type: single-seat high-altitude interceptor
Powerplant: one 1,710-hp (1276-kW) Rolls-Royce Merlin 64 Vee-12 piston engine
Performance: maximum speed 408 mph (657 km/h) at 25,000 ft (7620 m); maximum cruising speed 324 mph (521 km/h) at 20,000 ft (6095 m); service ceiling 43,000 ft (13105 m); range (internal fuel) 660 miles (1062 km), (with maximum external fuel) 1,180 miles (1899 km)
Weights: empty 6,000 lb (2722 kg) maximum take-off 7,875 lb (3572 kg)
Dimensions: wing span 40 ft 2 in (12.24 m); length 31 ft 3½ in (9.54 m); height 11 ft 8½ in (3.57 m); wing area 248.5 sq ft (23.09 m²)

This Spitfire F.Mk VII was painted Medium Sea Grey and PRU Blue, with B-type insignia, and served with No. 131 Sqn.

Armament: two 20-mm Hispano cannon and four 0.303-in (7.7-mm) Browning machine-guns

Supermarine Spitfire HF.Mk VII

---

broader rudder, sometimes with the pointed top, and metal-skinned ailerons.

The very last batches of Mk IXs had a teardrop hood, and this was also a feature of the Mk XVI, mass-produced from 1944 at Castle Bromwich as a Mk IX with the American-made Packard Merlin 266. Most of this series were of the LF.XVIE type, with clipped wings and E-type guns. After the war they were redesignated Mk 16.

Sptifire Mk VIII

Thus, while floods of lash-up Mk IX and Mk XVI Spitfires were made, the parent firm slowly proceeded with the intended variant with the Merlin 60-series engine, the Mk VIII. This had many refinements such as all those introduced on the Mk VII except pressurisation, and a Universal wing able to take any armament and have any span, with short-span metal ailerons. The Mk VIII was certainly the nicest of all marks to fly, but Supermarine got into real production only in mid-1943 and a mere 1,658 were built, all being tropicalised and sent overseas. The Mk VIII was the chief variant in the Pacific theatre.

Photo-recce variants

By far the best of many photo-reconnaissance versions was the PR.Mk X, basically a Mk VIII with guns removed, leading-edge fuel tanks, an enlarged oil tank (resulting in a characteristically deep underside to the cowling) for missions lasting up to 10 hours, and comprehensive camera installations. The Mk XI frequently went on lone missions to places as distant as Berlin and Prague, with no special navigation aids or electronic defence. The PR.XII was a low-level reconnaissance rebuild of the Mk V, 18 being converted with a Merlin 32 and four-bladed propeller; unusually among PR variants, they had four machine-guns.

Griffon powerplant

DP845, the Mk IV already mentioned, was redesignated Mk XX and finally, in early 1942, became the basis for the Mk XII, the first production Spitfire with the larger Griffon engine. The Mk XII was, like the Mk V and MK IX, a hasty lash-up, in this case to chase low-level Fw 190s bombing southern England. The low-rated Griffon III or VI, with four-bladed propeller, was ideal to pull what was otherwise

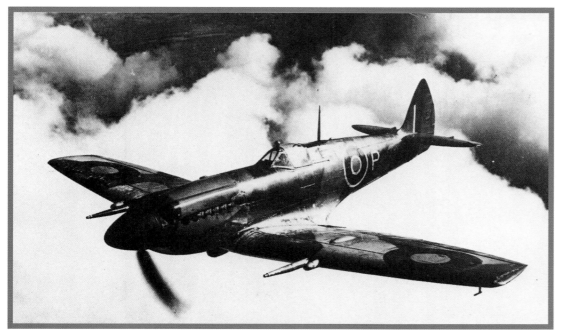

This aircraft, DP845, was retained by Supermarine and Rolls-Royce for prolonged research and passed through numerous configurations. It is seen here as the first 'Spit' with a Griffon engine, and after being designated Mk IV (there was already a PR.Mk IV with a Merlin engine) was redesignated Spitfire Mk XX. Chief test pilot Jeffrey Quill thought it the best Spitfire to fly, though pilots had to remember that the propeller rotated in the opposite direction, so swing on take-off was not to the left as with the Merlin, but to the right.

Generally agreed to be the nicest of all marks to fly, the Mk VIII was intended to be the standard production model from late 1942, but was delayed by repeated re-orders for the Mk IX. This Mk VIII served with the USAAAF 31st Fighter Group on the Italian front in 1944.

This extremely rare bird was originally one of the earliest Spitfire Mk I fighters delivered just after the outbreak of war. It is shown as a Type C photo-recce conversion, assigned to Photo Reconnaissance Unit Detachment E (Experimental) under Flt Lt 'Shorty' Longbottom in August 1940. One of the unit's tasks was selecting a colour scheme for low and high photo missions.

The Soviet Union received 1,188 Mk IX Spitfires, though like most supplies from Western Allies they appear to have been under-utilised. Some, such as this black-painted example, were locally converted as high-speed liaison aircraft without guns. Others were dual trainers, a type missing from the RAF.

Named for a dangerous type of shark, this Mk VIII was flown by WC Glenn Cooper, CO of No. 457 Sqn, RAAF. As a newly re-formed unit with totally raw pilots it helped defend Darwin in 1942-43 but later, with the Spitfire Mk VIII, it became highly offensive.

The Mk XI was by far the most important reconnaissance Spitfire. It was designed from the outset for such duty and featured extra fuel in the wing in place of guns. The longer duration of flights as far as Berlin and Prague demanded more engine oil, hence the deeper cowling.

TZ214 was an FR.Mk XVIII serving in the Middle East with No. 32 Sqn. This mark resembled the FR.Mk XIV with a teardrop hood but had a stronger wing and landing gear, extra fuel (both in the wings and rear fuselage) and normal, instead of clipped, wingtips.

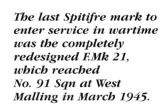

The last Spitfre mark to enter service in wartime was the completely redesigned F.Mk 21, which reached No. 91 Sqn at West Malling in March 1945.

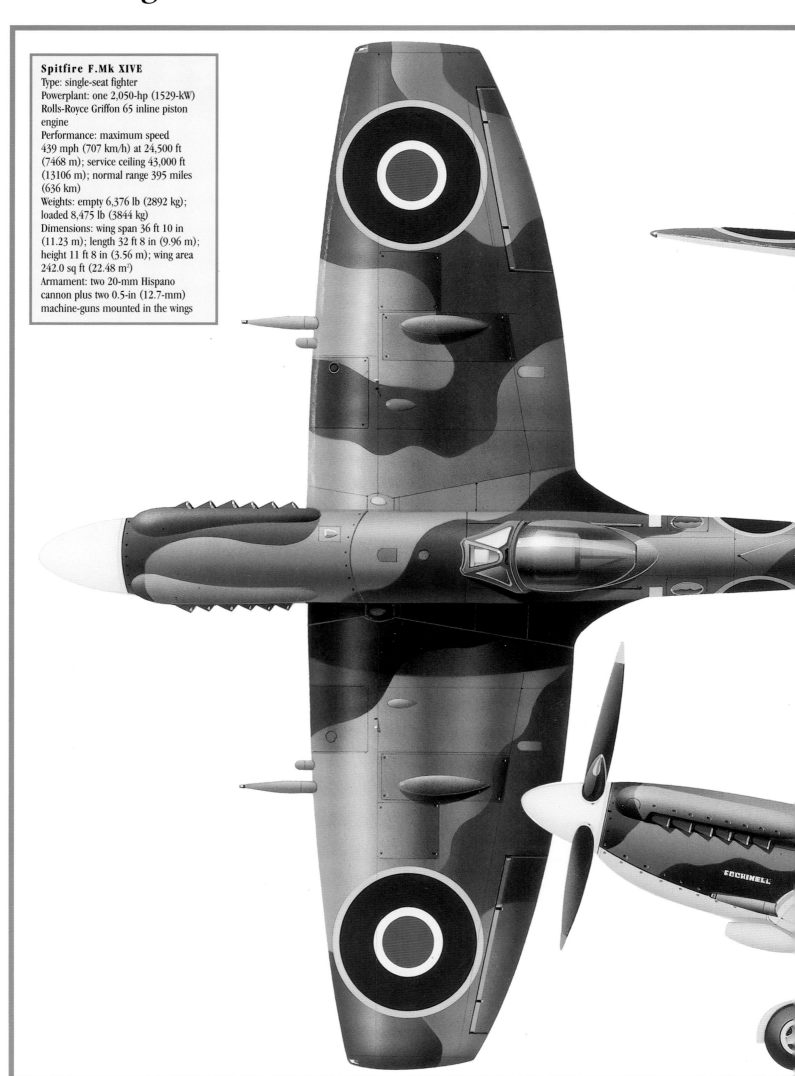

Spitfire F.Mk XIVE
Type: single-seat fighter
Powerplant: one 2,050-hp (1529-kW)
Rolls-Royce Griffon 65 inline piston
engine
Performance: maximum speed
439 mph (707 km/h) at 24,500 ft
(7468 m); service ceiling 43,000 ft
(13106 m); normal range 395 miles
(636 km)
Weights: empty 6,376 lb (2892 kg);
loaded 8,475 lb (3844 kg)
Dimensions: wing span 36 ft 10 in
(11.23 m); length 32 ft 8 in (9.96 m);
height 11 ft 8 in (3.56 m); wing area
242.0 sq ft (22.48 m²)
Armament: two 20-mm Hispano
cannon plus two 0.5-in (12.7-mm)
machine-guns mounted in the wings

Supermarine Spitfire FR.Mk XIVE

Named Fochinell, *this Spitfire FR.Mk XIVE was flown by No. II (AC) Squadron in Germany during September 1945, as part of the British Air Forces of Occupation. In its tactical reconnaissance role the FR.Mk XIVE could carry a single oblique camera, which was positioned to point to port or starboard through windows located below and to the rear of the cockpit canopy. All Mk XIVs had a new broad-chord tail to counteract the greater torque of the Griffon engine.*

Supermarine Spitfire Mk XIV

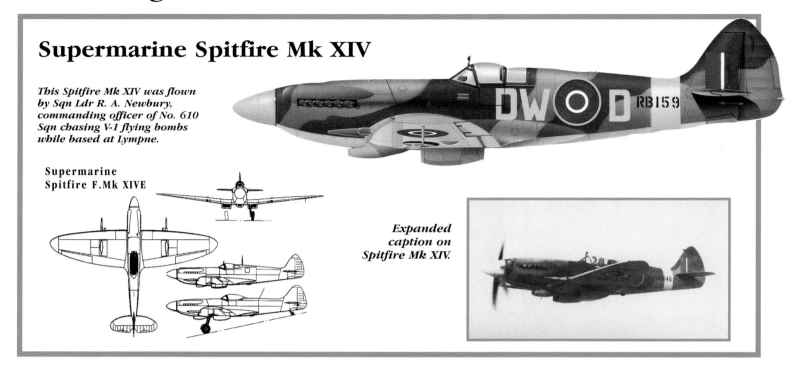

This Spitfire Mk XIV was flown by Sqn Ldr R. A. Newbury, commanding officer of No. 610 Sqn chasing V-1 flying bombs while based at Lympne.

**Supermarine
Spitfire F.Mk XIVE**

Expanded caption on Spitfire Mk XIV.

basically an LF.Mk V at high speed at low level. Only 100 were built, in 1942, the final 45 being based on the Mk VII and thus having the broad pointed rudder and retractable tailwheel. These were the first of the Griffon Spitfires, a totally different breed with a different set of flight characteristics. On take-off, for example, the Mk XII swung violently to the right (unless the rudder was trimmed hard-left) instead of more gently to the left.

Greater power at higher altitude

Rolls-Royce developed the Griffon as they had the Merlin, and with the 60-series introduced a two-stage supercharger and intercooler to give very much greater power at all levels, and almost double at high altitudes. The result was the most formidable of all Spitfires to see widespread war service, the Mk XIV. This was a Mk VIII, or late Mk XII, with the great Griffon 65, resulting in an even longer nose than that of the Mk XII and needing a five-bladed propeller to absorb the power of well over 2,000 hp (1492 kW).

To counter the destabilising effect of the long nose, the fin and rudder were further increased in chord, and to cool the engine symmetric radiator and oil cooler ducts, of much greater depth than those of the Mk IX, were fitted. The wing was a Universal (E) or C, the latter having the cannon in the outer instead of the inner positions and for the first time being wired for rocket projectiles. The 957

Above: MB293 was a Spitfire MK IIC converted to L.Mk IIC standard shortly after completion in November 1942. Here it is seen during trials in 1944 of the Mk III light universal carrier with small bombs and reconnaissance flares.

Left: The Royal Auxiliary Air Force used late-mark Spitfires after the war. No. 602 (City of Glasgow) squadron, which had used the old Mk V right up to March 1944, briefly used the Mks IX and XVI and then went on to Griffon-engined marks, this Mk 21 being one of nine used in 1947.

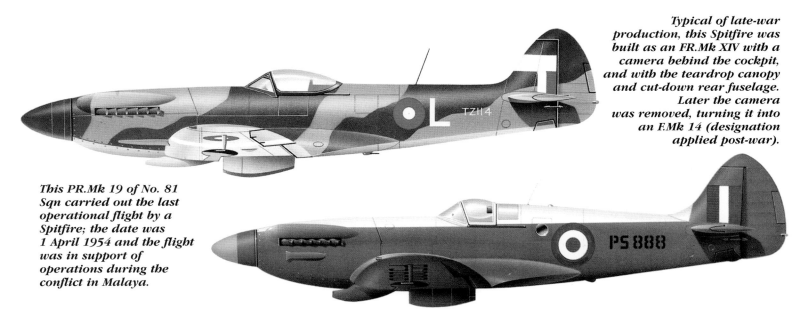

Typical of late-war production, this Spitfire was built as an FR.Mk XIV with a camera behind the cockpit, and with the teardrop canopy and cut-down rear fuselage. Later the camera was removed, turning it into an F.Mk 14 (designation applied post-war).

This PR.Mk 19 of No. 81 Sqn carried out the last operational flight by a Spitfire; the date was 1 April 1954 and the flight was in support of operations during the conflict in Malaya.

Mk XIVs built included many FR.Mk XIVEs with clipped wings, oblique cameras and a teardrop hood. The cut-down rear fuselage reduced directional stability close to zero.

Sptifire FR.MK XVIII

It the end of the war the standard fighter mark being delivered was the Mk XVIII, basically a refined Mk XIV with a strengthened airframe, increased internal tankage and standard teardrop hood/cutdown rear fuselage. The FR.Mk XVIII had cameras in place of the added rearfuselage tanks. Biggest fuel capacity of all was boasted by the similar PR.Mk XIX, which at the end of the war was replacing the Mk XI. Despite its higher fuel consumption, with a two-stage Griffon 66, the Mk XIX had even greater range than the Mk XI, as well as increased altitude and speed.

After the war the two-stage Griffon machines remained in service, restyled Mks 14, 18 and 19, and it was a Mk 19 that conducted the RAF's last Spitfire sortie, during operations in Malaya on 1 April 1954.

The Spitfire Mks 21, 22 and 24 were largely redesigned aircraft, with different wings and even further increased weight and four cannon armament. Prototypes flew from 1944 onwards, but they were essentially post-war versions. With Seafires, discussed in the next chapter, they brought total production up to 22,890 examples.

Though unmistakably Spitfires, these Mk 21s have hardly a single part in common with any of the Merlin-engined versions, and in particular introduced a completely redesigned wing. In turn this type served as the basis for even more advanced marks of Seafire.

Naval Fighters

Most British naval fighters were totally outclassed by the Bf 109 and Fw 190 and could barely defeat the early-war Italian fighters. Only in the final year of the war did good Seafires and two-seat Fireflies get into action.

From 1918 until July 1937 the Royal Navy's Fleet Air Arm (FAA) was a foolishly divided service, the RAF having control of design and provision of aircraft, even the embarked FAA Flights being RAF units, with the light-blue service also providing one-third of the pilots. Carrier-based aircraft are more difficult to design than land-based ones, but the FAA's fighters in 1937 were outdated into the bargain. At the start of the war there were just two types that might be called fighters.

One was the excellent Sea Gladiator, a normal Gladiator with catapult hooks, an arrester hook and a belly fairing covering a dinghy. The other was the Blackburn Skua, a trim but underpowered monoplane designed to combine the duties of dive bomber and fighter, and with an observer in the rear cockpit. Right up to the 1960s the Admirality stuck to the belief that sea-going fighters had to have a backseater to navigate, and in World War II this made purpose-designed naval fighters slow and unwieldy. The Skua did have four forward-firing machine-guns, and gained the UK's first fighter victory of the war (over a Dornier Do 18),

but it was quite outclassed as a fighter. A turret-armed development, the Roc, was even more useless; a floatplane version was unable to exceed 178 mph (286 km/h).

Fairey Fulmar

In the early war years there was only one British naval fighter worth having, and that had been designed as a land-based bomber! The Fairey Fulmar had a long rear cockpit canopy for the observer, and of necessity was larger than single-seaters; and its weight was increased by folding wings and the strength needed for catapult launches and arrested landings. It had eight machine-guns in the folding outer wings, and handled superbly; with a 2,000-hp (1492-kW) engine it would have been a pretty good fighter, but with an early Merlin of half this power it was pure flying skill that brought victories over the Bf 109, and nearly all its successes were gained in the Mediterranean theatre against Italian aircraft. Total production was 600.

Many Fulmars served aboard CAM (catapult-armed merchantman) ships, shot off to fend off Luftwafte Focke-Wulf

Left: With its wide-track undercarriage the Hurricane was more suitable for navalisation than Britain's other premier fighter of the early war years, the Spitfire. This Sea Hurricane is departing the escort carrier HMS Vindex *on an anti--submarine patrol over an inhospitable Atlantic.*

Below: When the Fairey Firefly entered squadron service in late 1943, the Fleet Air Arm at last had a robust, well-armed, two-seat fighter. In the hands of a capable pilot, the Firefly could more than hold its own against its single-seat counterparts. This is an early F.Mk I.

British Fighters of World War II

Presenting a puzzle to the spotter, this Canadian Car and Foundry-built Hurricane Mk X was painted in FAA colours and given an arrester hook as a Sea Hurricane IB, though differing in detail from most of that mark. It was then reassigned for day use with No. 440 Sqn of the RCAF. Note the green obliteration of the words ROYAL NAVY immediately above the serial.

Fw 200s and Junkers Ju 88s, afterwards ditching in the sea. The chief CAM fighter was the Hurricane, and from 1941 several marks of fully navalised Sea Hurricane served aboard carriers in a more normal mode in which the fighter was (hopefully) recovered after each mission. None had folding wings, and though useful they were strictly interim machines. Hawker never built the planned carrier-based Typhoon or Tempest, and the ultimate naval piston fighter, the Sea Fury, entered service after World War II.

Spitfire at sea

By far the most important British naval fighters of World War II were the Seafires. Mitchell had studied a naval Spitfire back in 1936, but no interest was shown until in 1941, the need was urgent (though the tough Grumman Wildcat, an American import at the time called the Martlet, gave the FAA some air-combat capability). For a start about 100 Spitfire Mk VBs were transferred to the FAA and served at RN air stations ashore. Many were fitted with hooks and used for deck training. Then AST (Air Service Training) at Hamble rebuilt about 100 Spitfire Mk Vs (nearly all of them Mk Vbs) as the first true Seafires, with mark number IB. They had catapult spools, hooks, naval radio and other equipment, and equipped No. 807 Sqn in June 1942. The first victories were gained against French fighters over Algeria in November 1942.

Supermarine Seafire Mk IIC

Next came the Seafire Mk IIC, with Universal wing, basic Spitfire Mk VC airframe with local strengthening, and various low-blown engines, the most powerful being of over 1,600 hp (1194 kW) and driving a four-bladed propeller. These led to the chief wartime variant, the Seafire Mk III, the first with folding wings. The wings were pushed upwards manually, the tips folding down to reduce height. The Merlin 32 or 55 drove a four-bladed propeller, and as in the case of the Mk IIC a proportion were completed as camera-equipped reconnaissance machines. Cunliffe-Owen Aircraft delivered 350 Seafire Mk IIIs and Westland another 870, and these saw action on many fronts, especially at the Salerno landings where they were the only Allied airpower during the first four crucial days.

Above: This rare, high-quality, wartime photograph shows a Sea Hurricane Mk IB, the first British wartime naval fighter that could actually go to sea and make some impression on the enemy. Most of these early machines were converted RAF Hurricanes, often with a long record of combat duty. This example has added plates ahead of the cockpit to shield the pilot's eyes from exhaust flames at night.

Right: As the Royal Navy's first operational monoplane the Blackburn Skua had to overcome much doubt and prejudice. Sadly, its poor performance made it almost useless as a fighter, though one did achieve the first British air combat victory of the war.

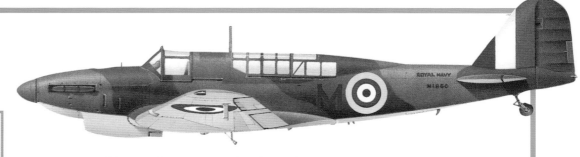

Fairey Fulmar

Fairey Fumar of the Royal Navy engaged in the Mediterranean theatre in 1942.

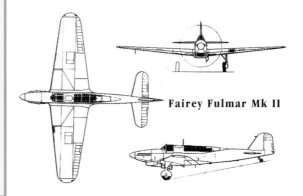

Fairey Fulmar Mk II

Fairey Fulmar Mk I.

Fulmar F.Mk I
Type: two-seat carrier-based fighter
Powerplant: one 1,080-hp
(805-kW) Rolls-Royce Merlin VIII inline
piston engine
Performance: maximum speed 247
mph (398 km/h) at 9,000 ft (2745 m);
service ceiling 21,500 ft (6555 m);
patrol endurance 4 hours with reserves
Weights: empty 8,720 lb (3955 kg);
maximum take-off 10,700 lb
(4853 kg)
Dimensions: span 46 ft 5 in
(14.15 m); length 40 ft 2 in (12.24 m);
height 14 ft 0 in (4.27 m); wing area
342 sq ft (31.77 m2)
Armament: eight 0.303-in (7.7-mm)
Browning machine-guns in wings

To avoid confusion Spitfire mark numbers were not repeated in Seafires, so the next was the Mk XV. This was a great advance, for it had a low-blown single-stage Griffon and was in many ways like a navalised Spitfire Mk XII. Deck landing was improved by switching from the A-frame hook to the US-style sting hook at the base of the rudder. Four FAA squadrons had formed and were working up when the European war ended, but Griffon Seafires just saw action in the Far East. Cunliffe-Owen built 134 Mk XVs and Westland a further 256, and the two companies followed with 189 Mk XVIIs with a cut-down rear fuselage, teardrop canopy and increased internal fuel. By 1945 far more powerful two-stage Griffon Seafires were flying, culminating with the great Mk 47 which was the ultimate member of the Spitfire/Seafire family and fought in Korea.

Urgency was missing from the Admiralty's search for a seagoing fighter able to hold its own in combat, and two specifications of 1938 were evaluated for two years and then amalgamated in 1940. By this time the talking had to lead somewhere, and it is to the credit of Fairey Aviation that the resulting Firefly Mk I was in the air before the end of 1941. This was essentially a tremendously improved Fulmar, with a Griffon engine, patented Youngman high-lift flaps, the fashionable elliptical wing and four cannon. Good features included excellent handling at low speeds and a pilot view better than for any other tailwheel type fighter, the pilot having a bulged canopy above the leading

The CAM (Catapult Armed Merchantman) ships were not exactly aircraft carriers, but they could fire Fulmar, Hurricane or Sea Hurricane fighters with the aid of cordite rockets. After engaging the enemy the luckless fighter pilot then had to take to his parachute – perhaps into the North Atlantic in winter, lethal in about a minute's exposure – and be picked up by a friendly vessel.

Above: The Seafire Mk III was basically a Spitfire Mk IIC with a Merlin 32 or 55 engine. This drove a four-bladed propeller and gave high power at low level. The wings folded upwards just inboard of the guns and were braced by telescopic jury struts fitted after landing. The tips folded to give adequate clearance in Royal Navy carrier hangars.

Above: Though burdened by a navigator (observer) and the additional weight of equipment required for carrier operations, the Fairey Firefly had just enough performance to be useful. The wartime marks were outclassed in combat by Japanese single-seat fighters. This F.Mk 1 served aboard HMS Indefatigable.

Above: Though only peripherally fighters, the Sea Mosquito TR.Mk 33s had four cannon and could give as good an account of themselves at low level as any other fighter Mosquito. These multi-role aircraft could carry a torpedo; their thimble-nose radar was used primarily for detecting surface targets.

Right: Seafire Mk IIC trainers on the deck of a Royal Navy fleet carrier. This mark did not have folding wings and retained the Rotol three-bladed propeller of many Spitfire Mk Vs. Note the folded Albacore at the stern.

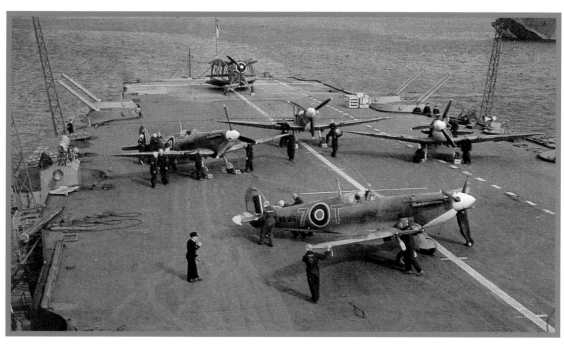

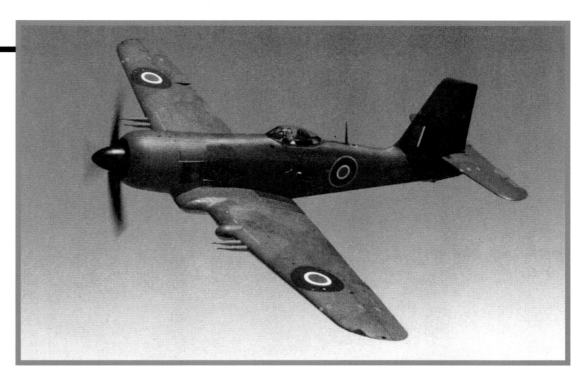

The worst thing about the Firebrand was the seven years it took to develop, so that only six Sabre-engined Mk IIs reached the Navy (non-operational, with No. 708 Sqn) during the war. This photograph shows the version that finally made the grade, the Centaurus-powered TF.IV, seen on test in July 1945.

edge. The Firefly F.Mk I could also carry up to 2,000 lb (907 kg) of bombs or eight 60-lb (27-kg) rockets, and towards the end of the war flew effective ground-attack missions. Drawbacks were that Fairey's chaotic administration delayed release in numbers until late 1943, and the basic fact that a large two-seater simply could not have the same performance as other fighters. Like the Fulmar the Firefly had no defence to the rear, and in combat had to rely on its good turn radius with the flaps in the high-lift mode, and the skill of the pilot. From the 471st Firefly a more powerful engine was fitted, and production included the FR.Mk I with ASH search radar, the Mk II night fighter with AI Mk X radar and, at the end of the war, the much more powerful FR.Mk IV with a two-stage Griffon and radiators moved to the wing leading edges.

Naval fighter prototypes

There were numerous naval fighters that never reached the wartime squadrons. One of Blackburn's designs, the B-44 to specification N2/42, was for a Sabre-engined sea-plane with a float retracting in the air to form the under-side of the fuselage (rather like a variable-height flying-boat). This was dropped, but the same company spent the entire war trying to develop a single-seat fighter able to carry a torpedo. Such a machine could never have been a

good fighter - except for shooting down aircraft other than fighters - but in aiming torpedoes against warships it would have been slightly less vulnerable than the 104-mph (167-km/h) Swordfish. Named Firebrand, the first of these versatile machines flew in February 1942. Most wartime Firebrands had the troublesome Sabre engine, but the version which at last went into production had the air-cooled Centaurus, and the TR.Mk IV (torpedo fighter) version at last entered service in September 1945, a month after the fighting stopped.

At the end of the war Hawker was well advanced with the Sea Fury Mk X, first flown in February 1945 as the carrier version of what had begun as the Tempest Light Fighter. This outstanding Centaurus-powered machine later became the FAA's last piston-engine fighter-bomber and saw action in Korea. Westland took on the difficult job of making a successor to the Firebrand and eventually, years after the war, the Wyvern entered service powered by the Python turboprop.

Possibly taken on the last day of the war, this photograph shows Lt Cdr Eric 'Winkle' Brown conducting deck trials with the first Hawker Sea Fury aboard the light carrier HMS Formidable. The Sea Fury arrived just too late to see operational service during the war and was a staggering contrast compared with the wartime British naval fighters.

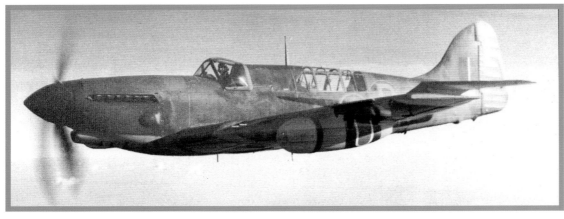

Once fitted with the two-stage Griffon the Fiarey Firefly went from being fairly good to being a masterpiece. This was one of a series of Mk IV prototypes, mostly converted Mk Is of 1944; this example has the larger vertical tail and clipped wings but has yet to acquire the final carb-air chin inlet.

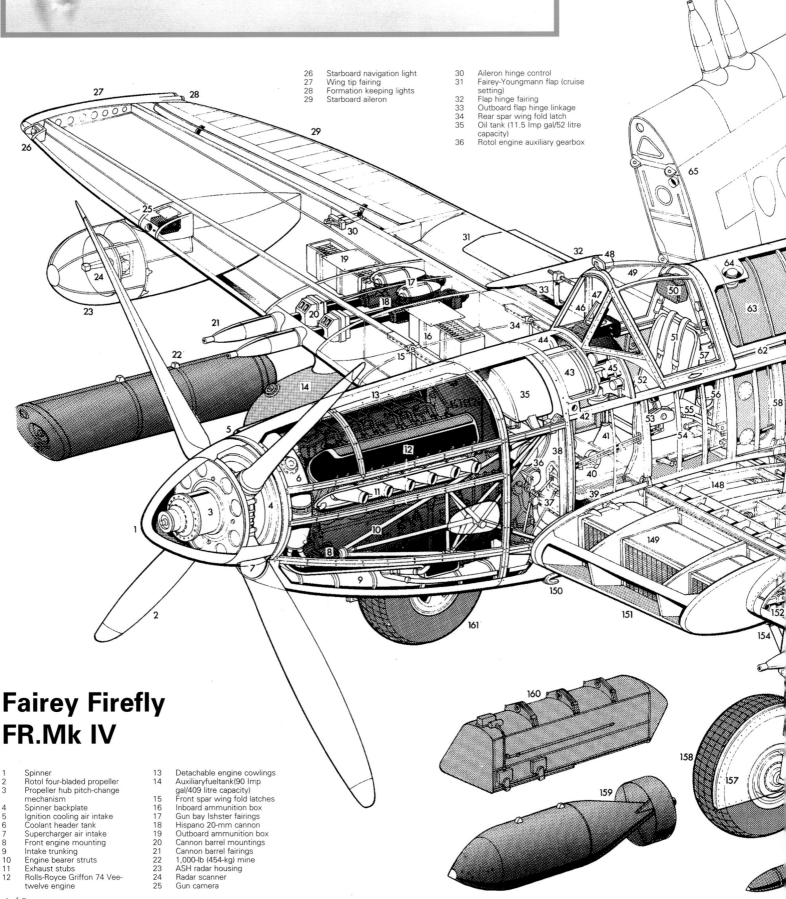

26	Starboard navigation light	30	Aileron hinge control
27	Wing tip fairing	31	Fairey-Youngmann flap (cruise setting)
28	Formation keeping lights	32	Flap hinge fairing
29	Starboard aileron	33	Outboard flap hinge linkage
		34	Rear spar wing fold latch
		35	Oil tank (11.5 Imp gal/52 litre capacity)
		36	Rotol engine auxiliary gearbox

Fairey Firefly
FR.Mk IV

1	Spinner	13	Detachable engine cowlings
2	Rotol four-bladed propeller	14	Auxiliaryfueltank(90 Imp gal/409 litre capacity)
3	Propeller hub pitch-change mechanism	15	Front spar wing fold latches
4	Spinner backplate	16	Inboard ammunition box
5	Ignition cooling air intake	17	Gun bay Ishster fairings
6	Coolant header tank	18	Hispano 20-mm cannon
7	Supercharger air intake	19	Outboard ammunition box
8	Front engine mounting	20	Cannon barrel mountings
9	Intake trunking	21	Cannon barrel fairings
10	Engine bearer struts	22	1,000-lb (454-kg) mine
11	Exhaust stubs	23	ASH radar housing
12	Rolls-Royce Griffon 74 Vee-twelve engine	24	Radar scanner
		25	Gun camera

37 Engine control rods
38 Fireproof bulkhead
39 Heater duct
40 Rudder pedals
41 Control column
42 Fuselage lifting bar attachment
43 Hydraulic fluid tank
44 Windscreen de-icing fluid tank
45 Instrument panel
46 Windscreen
47 Gyro gunsight
48 Pilot's rear view mirror
49 Sliding cockpit canopy cover
50 Headrest
51 Safety harness
52 Pilot's seat
53 Throttle and propeller controls
54 Catapult spool release
55 Flap lever
56 Fire extinguisher
57 Thermos flask
58 Fuselage double frame
59 Wing spar attachment joint
60 Tailplane control push-pull rods
61 Fuselage top longeron
62 Canopy sliding rail
63 Main fuel tank (146 Imp gal/ 664 litre capacity)
64 Fuel filler cap
65 Starboard wing, folded position
95 Port elevator construction
96 Elevator horn balance
97 Tailplane construction
98 Tailwheel retraction jack
99 Rear fuselage steel tube construction
100 Retractable tailwheel
101 Tailwheel doors (closed after extension of wheel)
102 Tailwheel well
103 Tailplane attachment joint
104 Rear fuselage bulkhead
105 Bottom longeron
106 Arrester hook housing
107 Rear fuselage frame construction
108 Detachable rear catapult spool attachment

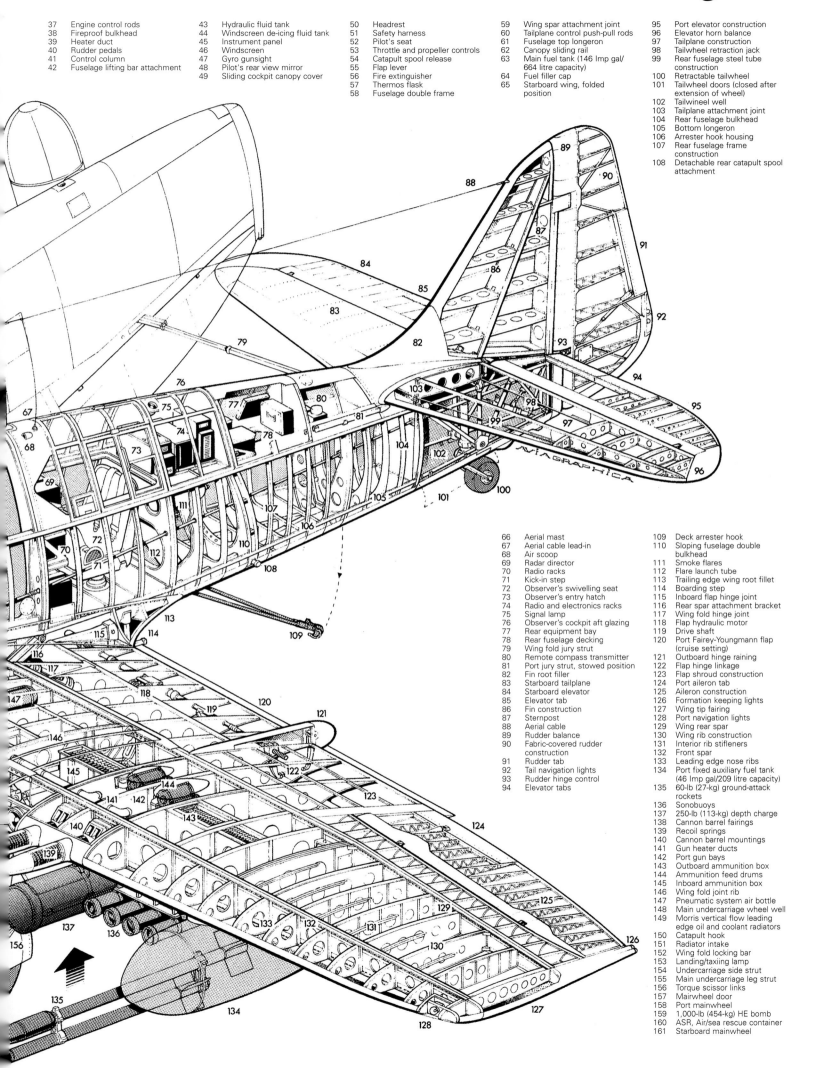

66 Aerial mast
67 Aerial cable lead-in
68 Air scoop
69 Radar director
70 Radio racks
71 Kick-in step
72 Observer's swivelling seat
73 Observer's entry hatch
74 Radio and electronics racks
75 Signal lamp
76 Observer's cockpit aft glazing
77 Rear equipment bay
78 Rear fuselage decking
79 Wing fold jury strut
80 Remote compass transmitter
81 Port jury strut, stowed position
82 Fin root filler
83 Starboard tailplane
84 Starboard elevator
85 Elevator tab
86 Fin construction
87 Sternpost
88 Aerial cable
89 Rudder balance
90 Fabric-covered rudder construction
91 Rudder tab
92 Tail navigation lights
93 Rudder hinge control
94 Elevator tabs
109 Deck arrester hook
110 Sloping fuselage double bulkhead
111 Smoke flares
112 Flare launch tube
113 Trailing edge wing root fillet
114 Boarding step
115 Inboard flap hinge joint
116 Rear spar attachment bracket
117 Wing fold hinge joint
118 Flap hydraulic motor
119 Drive shaft
120 Port Fairey-Youngmann flap (cruise setting)
121 Outboard hinge raining
122 Flap hinge linkage
123 Flap shroud construction
124 Port aileron tab
125 Aileron construction
126 Formation keeping lights
127 Wing tip fairing
128 Port navigation lights
129 Wing rear spar
130 Wing rib construction
131 Interior rib stifleners
132 Front spar
133 Leading edge nose ribs
134 Port fixed auxiliary fuel tank (46 Imp gal/209 litre capacity)
135 60-lb (27-kg) ground-attack rockets
136 Sonobuoys
137 250-lb (113-kg) depth charge
138 Cannon barrel fairings
139 Recoil springs
140 Cannon barrel mountings
141 Gun heater ducts
142 Port gun bays
143 Outboard ammunition box
144 Ammunition feed drums
145 Inboard ammunition box
146 Wing fold joint rib
147 Pneumatic system air bottle
148 Main undercarriage wheel well
149 Morris vertical flow leading edge oil and coolant radiators
150 Catapult hook
151 Radiator intake
152 Wing fold locking bar
153 Landing/taxiing lamp
154 Undercarriage side strut
155 Main undercarriage leg strut
156 Torque scissor links
157 Mainwheel door
158 Port mainwheel
159 1,000-lb (454-kg) HE bomb
160 ASR, Air/sea rescue container
161 Starboard mainwheel

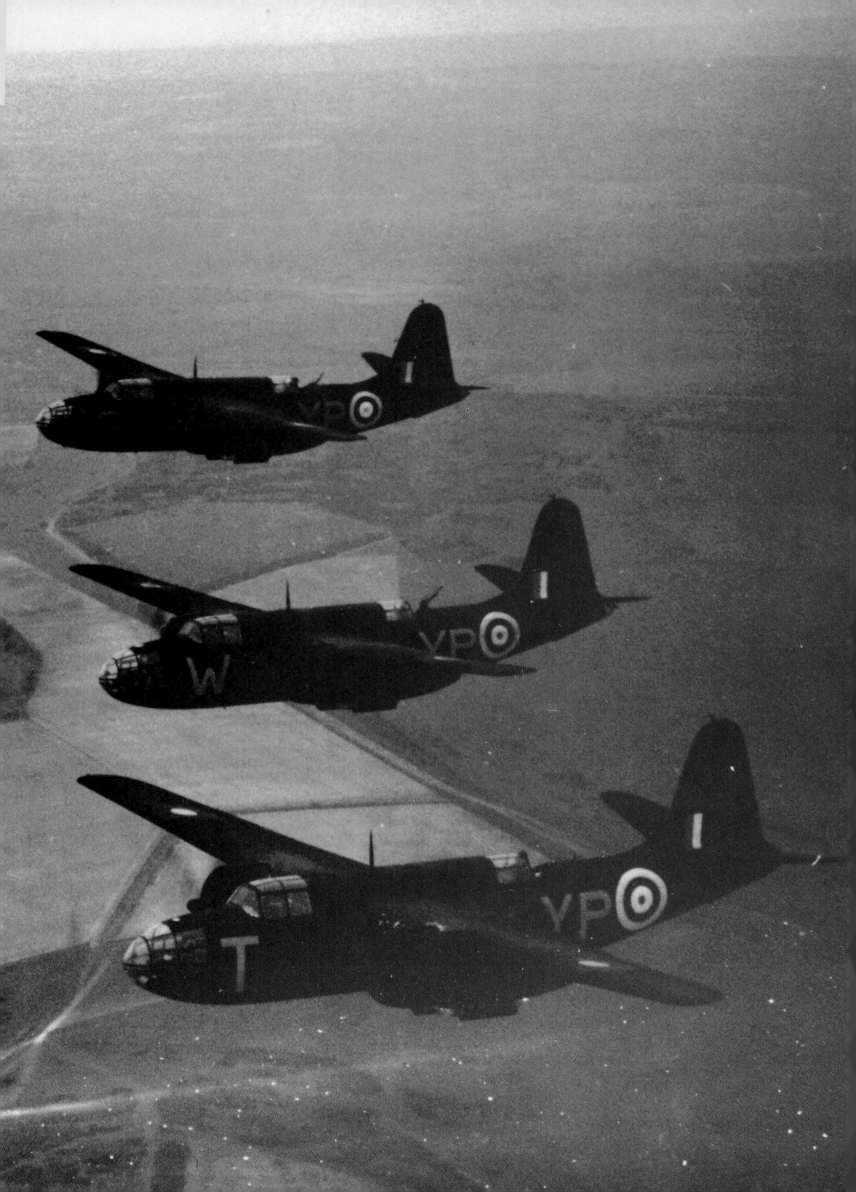

Night and Long-range Fighters

Until late in the Battle of Britain the only long-range or night-fighter in the RAF was a poorly armed converted bomber. The massive Beaufighter and superlative Mosquito then at last rectified the gaps left behind by the official procurement system.

In the simple days before World War II a night-fighter was just a day fighter with night equipment, such as a battery, navigation lights, cockpit lighting and flares which could be dropped to illuminate the landing field. The actual task of finding enemy aircraft at night was so difficult it was largely ignored; there were no set rules or techniques and, as far as the UK was concerned, not even an effective defence organisation such as had been created 'the hard way' in World War I.

Salvation lay in the invention of radar. Though the UK was not - as is often supposed - the only country to devel-op radar before World War II, British workers did achieve one tremendous advance that transformed the possibility of fitting radar into an aircraft. This was the magnetron valve, the creator of microwave radio waves with a wavelength of a few centimetres. Such short waves could be generated by radars small enough to go into vehicles, including aircraft, and so transformed the war, tilting the balance for a while (until magnetrons were captured by the enemy) in favour of the Allies. But a handful of brilliant engineers, led by Dr Ted Bowen, created airborne radar (at the time called RDF.2) even before the magnetron existed.

Left: The American Douglas Havoc shouldered part of the RAF's night-fighting duties during the early years of the war. Its contribution was largely negated by experiments that bore no tangible fruit.

Below: The most numerous mark of Mosquito was the FB.Mk VI fighter-bomber, which combined the guns of the Mk II with a substantial load of bombs or rockets. The Mosquito also proved to be a superlative night-fighter.

British Fighters of World War II

This Blenheim Mk IF was converted from bomber to fighter standard in 1938 and fitted with AI Mk II radar in 1939. It is shown after withdrawal from front-line duty, serving with No. 54 OTU (Operational Training Unit) at Church Fenton in 1941.

Potentially very important night fighters, some of the RAF's Douglas Havocs were squandered on trials with the LAM (aerial mine) and Turbinlite (aerial searchlight) systems. This example was an early Twin Wasp-powered Havoc Mk I three-seat intruder and served with No. 23 Sqn at Ford.

The Mosquito Mk II night-fighter brought a great increase in flight performance over previous RAF night-fighters, and with the original AI0 Mk IV radar it was possible to mount four machine-guns in the nose as well as four 20-mm cannon under the cockpit floor.

A transmitter capable of fitting an aircraft yet working on wavelengths of several metres (7 m was chosen in January 1937) could not have much power. The peak power of the pulses of the first set was 95 watts, about the same as an electric-light bulb, and the set first flew in an Anson on 16 August 1937. After intensive development this led to a fully engineered-set called AI (Airborne Interception) Mk I, flown in a Fairey Battle on 21 May 1939. Though it was temperamental, could lie convincingly and went wrong at the drop of a hat, it could occasionally indicate the presence, and rough direction and range, of a hostile aircraft from a distance about the same as the set's height above

the ground (up to about 20,000 ft/6095 m, or 3.8 miles/6.1 km). But the task of finding a target among the dim flickering glass on the cathode-ray tubes called for great skill by the operator. In early sets there was one display to give an up/down indication and a second to give left/right, both giving an idea of target range.

The first radar-equipped night fighters were 21 Blenheim Mk IFs, hastily fitted with AI Mk II in July/September 1939. In the first half of 1940 over 60 Blenheims received the somewhat better AI Mk III. Most aircrew disliked and resisted the new invention (it was even worse in the Luftwaffe where officer pilots refused to accept steering commands

A priceless colour photograph showing the Hurricane Mk IIC night intruder flown by the CO of No. 87 Sqn in 1941-42. Though not equal to the German single-seaters, the Hurricane proved valuable in a variety of other important combat roles including attack bomber, naval fighter, rocket carrier and big-gun tank buster.

The Defiant was seemingly well armed with four guns mounted in a power-operated turret. However, the type proved vulnerable to attack from below and after a series of losses was switched to nightime operations in 1941. The DZ codes on this weatherbeaten example indentified the famed No. 151 Sqn, based at RAF Wittering.

Boulton Paul Defiant

Boulton Paul Defiant Mk II
Type: two-seat night-fighter
Powerplant: one 1,280-hp (954-kW)
Rolls-Royce Merlin XX inline piston
engine
Performance: maximum speed
313 mph (504 km/h) at 19,000 ft
(5790 m); cruising speed 260 mph
(418 km/h); service ceiling 30,350 ft
(9250 m); range 465 miles (748 km)
Weights: empty 6,282 Ib (2849 kg);
maximum take-off 8,424 Ib
(3821 kg)
Dimensions: span 39 ft 4 in
(11.99 m); length 35 ft 4 in
(10.77 m); height 11 ft 4 in
(3.45 m); wing area 250 sq ft
(23.23m²)
Armament: four 0.303-in (7.7-mm)
machine-guns in power-operated
dorsal turret

Defiant NF.Mk II night-fighter with AI Mk VI radar of No. 151 Sqn based at RAF Wittering.

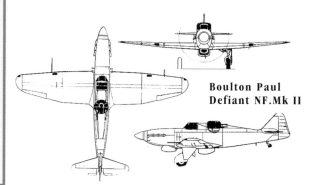

**Boulton Paul
Defiant NF.Mk II**

*Defiant NF.Mk II with AI Mk VI
radar, of No. 151 Sqn.*

*Right: Defiants of No. 264
Sqn, the original operator
of this turret-armed fighter
in daylight in early 1940.
The photograph was taken
during the Blitz period,
before these aircraft had
gained airborne radar
(and when B-Type roundels
were used with abnormally
wide yellow outer rings).*

*Below: Hurricane Mk I
night-fighters depart at
dusk, probably in late
1940. Though not equipped
with radar, the Hurricane
had one of the best success
rates of all RAF fighters at
night in the pre-1942 era.*

British Fighters of World War II

In the Mediterranean theatre most Beaufighters were used for long-range day escort and ground attack. This Fairey-built Mk IC of No. 252 Sqn wears a camouflage scheme applied for use in Egypt.

from sergeants sitting in the back), and many officials campaigned to have AI radar abandoned. The officials could not understand radar, but they could comprehend such crazy ideas as the Turbinlite and long Aerial Mine (and LAM).

Turbinlite and LAM

Turbinlite was a searchlight, carried in a large aircraft. In fact, to know where to aim the light the carrier had to have AI radar; and instead of projecting a beam of light it would have been better to have projected cannon shells. Instead the idea was that, once the hostile aircraft was nicely illuminated, and staying straight and level so that the searchlight stayed on target, Hurricanes could come in and shoot it down. Officials must have been puzzled that years of effort by large numbers of aircraft on this crazy scheme succeeded in shooting down only one aircraft, and that belonged to the RAF. The main Turbinlite carrier was the

excellent Douglas Havoc, a British conversion of an American light bomber with outstanding performance, but some Bristol Beaufighter and de Havilland Mosquito conversions were also made.

Limited successes of LAM

LAM stood for Long Aerial Mine, and it was a natural step from LAM (said as a word) to its codename of Mutton. Again the main night fighter involved was the Havoc, and the idea was to suspend a small bomb on a 2,000-ft (610-m) cable, either towed behind the fighter or allowed to fall on a parachute. An aircraft flying into the cable was expected to draw the bomb smartly up against itself, to explode on impact. This again appealed to technology illiterates, and the whole of 1941-42 was wasted on a technique that was quite dangerous – to its exponents.

But if these harebrained schemes brought little success, neither at first did AI radar. The technical difficulties, combined with the total disbelief of its operators, told against it in 1940-41, and the few night victories were gained by black-painted Hurricanes, Spitfires, Blenheims and Defiants, carrying little special equipment beyond metal plates to shield the exhaust from the pilots' eyes. In late August

Left: The world's first aircraft radomes were constructed in autumn 1941 to cover the scanner of the AI Mk VII, the first centimetric radar. This first flew in November 1941 in Beaufighter Mk IF X7579. Soon called a 'thimble' radome, it had no effect on flying qualities.

Below: Operations in the Mediterranean theatre quickly caused aircraft to deteriorate, and this Beaufighter Mk IC looks distinctly war-weary. This aircraft was probably operating in Tunisia in early 1943. It is still fitted with the horizontal tailplane which caused severe problems including longitudinal instability at low speeds and in the climb.

Bristol Beaufighter

Beaufighter TF.Mk X

Type: two-seat anti-shipping strike fighter/torpedo bomber

Powerplant: two 1,770-hp (1320-kW) Bristol Hercules XVIII radial piston engines

Performance: maximum speed 303 mph (488 km/h) at 1,300 ft (395 m); cruising speed 249 mph (401 km/h); service ceiling 15,000 ft (4570 m); range 1,470 miles (2366 km)

Weights: empty 15,600 Ib (7076 kg); maximum take-off 25,200 Ib (11431 kg)

Dimensions: wing span 57 ft 10 in (17.63 m); length 41 ft 8 in (12.70 m); height 15 ft 10 in (4.83 m); wing area 503 sq ft (46.73 m²)

This Bristol Beaufighter Mk IF night-fighter was employed by No. 25 Sqn at RAF North Weald in October 1940, scoring its first victory on 15 November. This squadron and No. 29. Sqn (at Wellingore) were the first units to receive Beaufighters.

Armament: four forward-firing 20-mm cannon, six forward-firing 0.303-in (7.7-mm) machine-guns and one 0.303-in (7.7-mm) Vickers 'K' gun in dorsal position, plus one torpedo and two 250-lb (113-kg) bombs or eight 90-lb (41-kg) rocket projectiles

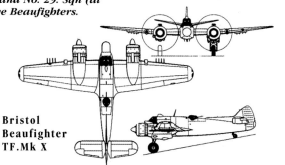

Bristol Beaufighter TF.Mk X

Left: Though in no way inferior to other variants as a day fighter, the Beaufighter IC was intended for Coastal Command or desert missions chiefly against surface targets. The nearer aircraft has a non-dihedral tailplane; the observer can be seen facing forward, while the DF loop fairing above the fuselage is prominent on both aircraft.

Below: An invasion-striped Beaufighter VI of No. 445 Sqn, RAAF, operating with a Coastal Command strike wing in 1944, salvoes rockets whilst in level flight against simulated targets.

Bristol Beaufighter

T4638

T4638 was the 16th Bristol Beaufighter Mk IF night-fighter built by the Fairey Aviation Company. It is equipped with AI Mk IV radar, characterised by the broad arrow nose aerial and outer wing arrays, and carries an armament of four 20-mm cannon and six 0.303-in (7.7-mm) machine-guns. T4638 joined No. 604 (County of Middlesex) Squadron at Middle Wallop in 1941. At this time the squadron, led by Wing Commander John Cunningham, was the top-scoring night-fighter unit in the RAF, and had been one of the first to receive the Beaufighter at the height of the Battle of Britain in September 1940. Although crews had been slow to master the use of AI radar, by the end of the German night blitz of 1940-41 the Beaufighter had become the world's most effective night-fighter.

The heroic defence of Malta from the summer of 1940 had been sharply reduced by a lack of night-fighters. When Beaufighters were received in 1941 they lacked radar, but still operated round the clock. This Mk IF taxiing at Luqa is probably from the initial detachment of No. 89 Sqn.

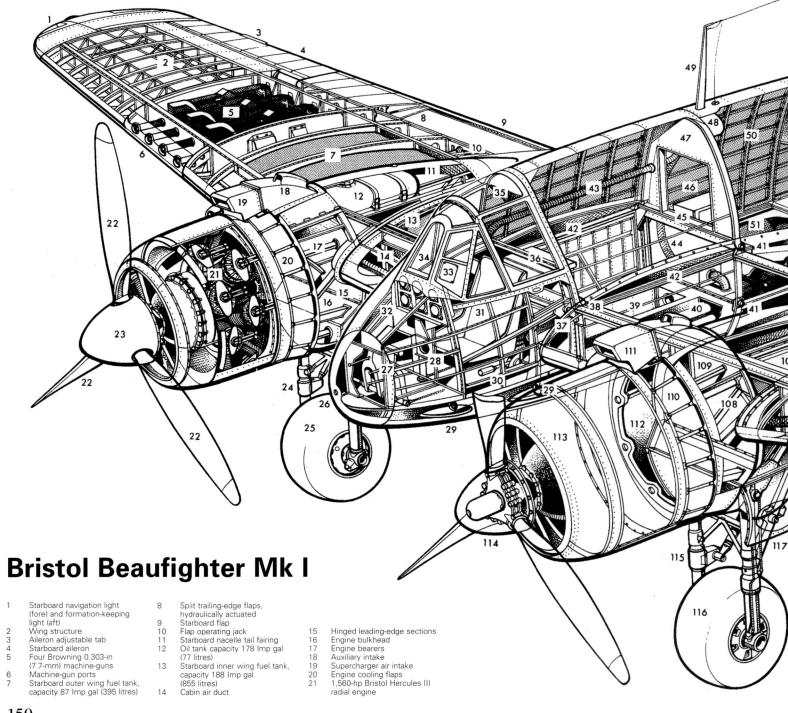

Bristol Beaufighter Mk I

1	Starboard navigation light (fore) and formation-keeping light (aft)	8	Split trailing-edge flaps, hydraulically actuated	
2	Wing structure	9	Starboard flap	
3	Aileron adjustable tab	10	Flap operating jack	15 Hinged leading-edge sections
4	Starboard aileron	11	Starboard nacelle tail fairing	16 Engine bulkhead
5	Four Browning 0.303-in (7.7-mm) machine-guns	12	Oil tank capacity 178 Imp gal (77 litres)	17 Engine bearers
6	Machine-gun ports	13	Starboard inner wing fuel tank, capacity 188 Imp gal (855 litres)	18 Auxiliary intake
7	Starboard outer wing fuel tank, capacity 87 Imp gal (395 litres)			19 Supercharger air intake
		14	Cabin air duct	20 Engine cooling flaps
				21 1,560-hp Bristol Hercules III radial engine

All the deficiencies of previous Beaufighters were rectified in the Mk X, the last wartime mark. Designated Mk 10 post war, it featured a different mark of Hercules engine, a Mark VIII radar that was used mainly in the surface attack mode, larger elevators and, in later examples, a dorsal fin. Full gun armament was retained, plus the ability to carry a torpedo, or eight rockets, as in this aircraft of No. 445 Sqn, RAAF. The observer had a Vickers 'K' gun for rear defence.

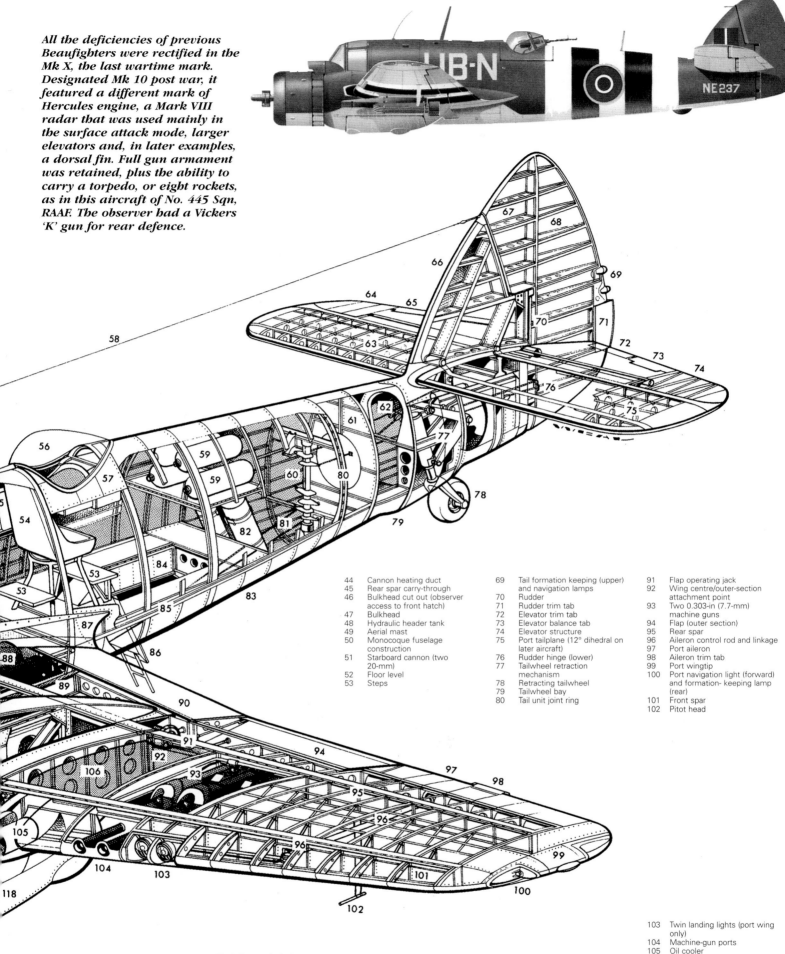

44 Cannon heating duct
45 Rear spar carry-through
46 Bulkhead cut out (observer access to front hatch)
47 Bulkhead
48 Hydraulic header tank
49 Aerial mast
50 Monocoque fuselage construction
51 Starboard cannon (two 20-mm)
52 Floor level
53 Steps

69 Tail formation keeping (upper) and navigation lamps
70 Rudder
71 Rudder trim tab
72 Elevator trim tab
73 Elevator balance tab
74 Elevator structure
75 Port tailplane (12° dihedral on later aircraft)
76 Rudder hinge (lower)
77 Tailwheel retraction mechanism
78 Retracting tailwheel
79 Tailwheel bay
80 Tail unit joint ring

91 Flap operating jack
92 Wing centre/outer-section attachment point
93 Two 0.303-in (7.7-mm) machine guns
94 Flap (outer section)
95 Rear spar
96 Aileron control rod and linkage
97 Port aileron
98 Aileron trim tab
99 Port wingtip
100 Port navigation light (forward) and formation- keeping lamp (rear)
101 Front spar
102 Pitot head

22 de Havilland Hydromatic propeller
23 Propeller spinner
24 Lockheed oleo-pneumatic shock absorber
25 Starboard mainwheel, with Dunlop brakes
26 Forward identification lamp in nose cap
27 Rudder pedals
28 Control column
29 Cannon ports
30 Seat adjusting lever
31 Pilot's seat
32 Instrument panel
33 Clear vision panel

34 Flat bullet-proof windscreen
35 Fixed canopy (sideways-hinged on later aircraft)
36 Spar carry-through step
37 Nose centre-section attachment point
38 Fuselage/centre-section attachment point
39 Pilot's entry/emergency escape hatch
40 Underfloor cannon blast tubes
41 Fuselage/centre-section attachment points
42 Centre-section attachment longeron reinforcement
43 Cabin air duct

54 Observer's swivel seat (normally forward facing)
55 Radio controls and intercom
56 Observer's cupola
57 Hinged panel
58 Aerial
59 Oxygen bottles
60 Vertical control cable shaft
61 Sheet metal bulkhead
62 Control cables
63 Tailplane structure
64 Elevator
65 Elevator balance tab
66 Fin structure
67 Rudder balance
68 Rudder framework

81 Control cables
82 Parachute flare chute
83 Fuselage skinning – flush riveted Alclad
84 Observer's entry/ emergency escape hatchway
85 Lower fuselage longeron
86 Entry ladder/emergency exit chute
87 Wing root fairing fillet
88 Port cannon breeches and magazine drum
89 Dinghy location – multi-seat 'H' or 'K' type in blow-out stowage
90 Flap (inner section)

103 Twin landing lights (port wing only)
104 Machine-gun ports
105 Oil cooler
106 Port outer wing fuel tank
107 Mainwheel well
108 Engine bearers
109 Front spar/undercarriage attachment
110 Engine cooling flaps
111 Supercharger air intake
112 Engine mounting ring
113 Cowling nose ring
114 Non-feathering (early) or feathering constant speed (late) propellers
115 Mainwheel leg
116 Port mainwheel
117 Retraction jack
118 Undercarriage door

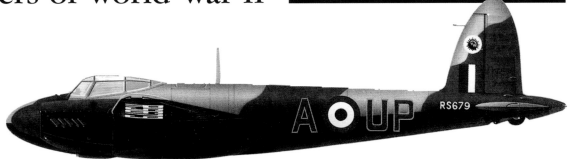

This Mosquito FB. Mk 6 (post-war designation) was built in 1945 by Airspeed and is shown in post-war markings while operating from Wahn (Cologne) and Celle with the British Air Force of Occupation. The badge of the unit, No. 4 Sqn, appears on the fin.

1940 the RAF received another of its great warplanes that resulted from initiative by the manufacturer. The Bristol Beaufighter was created quickly by fitting two powerful Hercules engines on the wing of a Beaufort torpedo bomber, and fitting a new fuselage with a pilot in the nose, an observer at the back and four cannon under the floor. For good measure six machine-guns were added in the wings, and the 'Beau' was also tailor-made to carry radar. It joined the RAF without it, but by November 1940 the first Beaufighter Mk IFs were in service with the new AI Mk IV radar. Like the Mk III this sent out its pulses of radio waves from a nose aerial looking like a harpoon, and received echoes on vertical or inclined dipoles on the outer wings, so connected up that they furnished the operator with the azimuth and elevation (direction in the horizontal and vertical planes) of the target.

In the Beaufighter the observer sat far removed from the pilot, under a transparent cupola, his swivelling seat usually facing aft so that he could attend to the radar displays and controls. Between passing steering commands to the pilot he had to change the drums of ammunition on the

Below: This Mosquito FB.Mk VI belonged to No. 143 Sqn and was based at Banff in 1945. The rockets being loaded have the slender 25-lb (11-kg) armour-piercing heads, though for soft-skinned ships the 60-lb (27-kg) high-explosive pattern was also used.

four cannon, until at the 401st aircraft this arrangement was changed for the belt feed that Bristol had recommended from the very start. In daylight the Beaufighter was at a disadvantage in close combat with a smaller fighter, but at night it was deadly, once the total night system of ground radar, ground controller, secure radio voice communications, reliable airborne radar and a good team of observer and pilot had been put together.

Mosquito – deadly at night

By 1941 an even better night-fighter was flying, again the result of company initiative triumphing over hordes of officials who tried to kill the idea. This was the de Havilland Mosquito, and after being delayed for a year before the war was at last allowed to go ahead in a batch of 50. Lord Beaverbrook, appointed Minister of Aircraft Production after Dunkirk, tried to cancel it, but once the prototype had flown in November 1940 this wooden twin-Merlin aircraft was uncancellable. It was simply too good, and could outfly a Hurricane with one engine feathered. Of the batch of 50, 30 were to be fighters, with four cannon under the nose, four machine-guns in the nose, a door on the right side to the staggered side-by-side cockpit, a wide flat bullet-proof windscreen and the AI Mk IV radar. Faster than a 1941 Spitfire, this fine aircraft was later developed in many other night-fighter versions.

de Havilland Mosquito

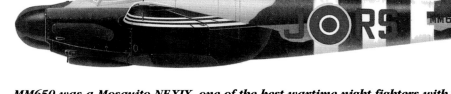

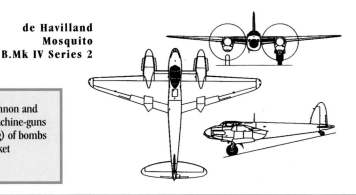

de Havilland Mosquito FB.Mk VI
Type: two-seat fighter-bomber
Powerplant: two 1,620-hp (1208-kW) Rolls-Royce Merlin 25 Vee-12 piston engines
Performance: maximum speed 362 mph (583 km/ h) at 5,500 ft (1676 m); maximum cruising speed 325 mph (523 km/h) at 15,000 ft (4570 m); service ceiling 33,000 ft (10060 m); range with internal bomb load 1,650 miles (2655 km)
Weights: empty 14,300 lb (6486 kg); maximum take-off 22,300 lb (10115 kg)
Dimensions: wing span 54 ft 2 in (16.51 m); length 40 ft 10¾ in (12.43 m); height 15 ft 3 in (4.65 m); wing area 454.0 sq ft (42.18 m²)

MM650 was a Mosquito NF.XIX, one of the best wartime night fighters with the so-called 'bull nose'. In this aircraft the nose housed the America SCR-720 radar (AI Mk X). Fitted with two-stage Merlins. The aircraft is shown with inasion stripes and was assigned to No. 157 Sqn at Swannington.

de Havilland Mosquito B.Mk IV Series 2

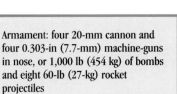

Armament: four 20-mm cannon and four 0.303-in (7.7-mm) machine-guns in nose, or 1,000 lb (454 kg) of bombs and eight 60-lb (27-kg) rocket projectiles

The magnetron valve led the way to radar working on centimetric wavelengths, and the resulting AI Mk VIII first flew in a Beaufighter in November 1941. Instead of spidery aerials it had a new antenna in a so-called thimble nose radome, and the new radar had important advantages in projecting a pencil-like beam ahead of the fighter. The beam could be scanned (pointed) in various repeating patterns, and give clearer pictures of the enemy's position, especially at low level where the previous sets were almost useless. By March 1943 the Mosquito had appeared in Mk XII form with a thimble nose radar, which necessitated removal of the four machine-guns. Marshall's at Cambridge quickly converted 97 Mosquito F.Mk IIs to NF.Mk XII standard with a bull nose radome over AI Mk VIII. These entered service at Hunsdon in late March 1943 with No.85 Sqn, commanded by the RAF's most famous night-fighter pilot, John Cunningham (like Beamont, after the war a test pilot). The NF.Mk XIIs were followed by 270 NF.Mk XIIIs with the improved airframe of the Mosquito FB.Mk VI and increased fuel capacity. Then Marshall's converted Mk II fighters into the FB.Mk XVII with a Universal Nose able to house AI Mk VIII or the outstanding American AI Mk 10 (SCR-720). Newly built aircraft to this standard were called NF.Mk XIX, with low-blown Merlin 25s and paddle-blade propellers. Last of the wartime 'Mossies' was the Mk 30, a Mk XIX with the high-blown two-stage Merlin 72, 76 or 113. The Mk 30 was by far the most efficient Allied night-fighter of the war, and like earlier versions carried the war, with cannon shells and special electronic-warfare devices, into the heart of Germany.

Mosquitoes first operated from bases outside Britain from December 1942 when No. 23 Sqn took its Mk II night-fighters to Luqa, Malta. They quickly scored by night and day against air and ground targets. The majority of the aircraft flew without radar in the intruder role, wearing the hybrid day-/night-fighter camouflage seen here.

New Technology

Though Britain pioneered the turbojet and actually got the Meteor I into squadron service ahead of any other jet in the world, few were ordered and the type made little impact on the war. And the Martin-Baker M.B.5, Supermarine Spiteful, Vickers Type 432, Westland Welkin and other new types never displaced such stalwarts as the Spitfire and Mosquito.

So ubiquitous was the Spitfire that the RAF hardly used any other British single-seat fighters in the later part of World War II, though there were plenty of new designs. The Spitfire itself was intended to be replaced by an extremely fast and agile machine, the Spiteful, which began life as a modified Spitfire fuselage riding on a totally new wing of only 210-sq ft (19.50-m) area and laminar-flow section. With a wide-track landing gear and very powerful two-stage Griffon engine the Spiteful seemed ideal, and one of the variants, the F.XVI, was the UK's fastest piston-fighter at 494 mph (795 km/h): it would have been simple to assemble the airframe, engine and propeller differently to exceed 500 mph (805 km/h) by a substantial margin, but this good-looking machine never entered service. Not least of the unexpected results was that at high Mach numbers the new laminar wing was inferior to the old Spitfire wing and almost certainly the post-war Attacker jet fighter would have been better had it had the old wing instead of the new one inherited from the Spiteful.

The only other wartime-developed fighters with a single piston engine were the Martin-Baker M.B.3 and M.B.5. The former was powered by a Sabre and carried the tremendous armament of six Hispano cannon, but was tragically destroyed in a fatal crash caused by engine failure on 12 September 1942. The M.B.5 was even better, and easily reached 460 mph (740 km/h) on its 2,340-hp (1746-kw) Griffon 83, driving a DH contra-rotating propeller, but despite outstanding engineering and good handling it was not put into production.

High-altitude requirement

Two technically interesting twin-engined fighters were built to specification F.7/41 calling for a high-altitude fighter with six cannon, a pressurised cockpit and two Merlin 61 engines. The Vickers Type 432 looked rather like a Mosquito but carried the fashionable Spitfire elliptical shapes to the limit, having elliptical wings, tailplane and fin/rudder unit. It flew in December 1942 and in many ways was an outstanding aircraft. Its rival, the Westland Welkin, flew a month earlier and was noted for its great span, adopted in order to reach the greatest possible altitude. In some respects the Welkin resembled a twin-Merlin development of the Whirlwind, but it was so much larger and heavier that performance was unimpressive, and the great span made rate of roll poor. There were many other shortcomings, and compressibility effects on the wing

Left: Along with the Hawker Sea Fury, the de Havilland Sea Hornet arguably represented the pinnacle of British wartime piston-engine fighter development. The Hornet arrived just too late to see operational wartime service.

The first Gloster G.40, built to specification E.28/39, is seen flying in 1943 with extra fins. The first aircraft was lost in an accident, but the second was retained by the Science Museum in London.

became evident at even shallow angles of dive, so that this sluggish machine could not catch other aircraft if they dived away. Despite this 67 production Welkins were delivered, and another was completed as a two-seater radar-equipped night-fighter.

de Havilland Hornet

A far better twin-engined fighter was the de Havilland Hornet. In many ways a smaller version of the Mosquito, this could have been flown in 1941 instead of 1944, and would have been a most valuable combat aircraft with

great range, performance and versatility. As it was, it just missed the war, though it later served as a single-seat day interceptor and fighter-bomber with the RAF and FAA, and with the latter as a two-seat radar-equipped carrier-based night and all-weather fighter. The reason it did not fly in 1941 was that it was never ordered (and DH was overloaded with other work); when it did appear it was, like its predecessor, solely the result of initiative by the company.

One machine that could not have been a private venture by the company was the Gloster E.28/39, because this was built to fly the Whittle turbojet which, to the surprise of

almost everyone except the tiny team at Power Jets, actually worked. The E.28/39 was a small and compact single-engined machine, sitting very low on tricycle landing gear and with the cockpit well forward. Provision was made for four machine-guns firing ahead, but these were never fitted. Instead Gloster was assigned the more difficult task of building a fully operational jet fighter to specification F.5/40. Two turbojets were to be used, and these were mounted well outboard on the sharply tapered wings, the cockpit being in the nose of the long slim fuselage with two (originally there were to be three) cannon on each side. The tricycle landing gear had levered suspension, and the tailplane was mounted very high on the fin.

F.9/40 first flight

The first F.9/40 flew on two DH H.1 engines (later named Goblin) on 5 March 1943. Other prototypes had the Power Jets W2/500, Rover W.2B and Rolls-Royce W.2B/23, all variants of the Whittle W.2 design, and another had slim underslung nacelles for the Metrovick F.2 (later named Beryl). Development was quite rapid, the problems lying not with the engines but with such pedestrian things as the ailerons, rudder and nosewheel. Eventually the F.9/40 became the Meteor F.I with the Rolls-Royce Welland, a derivative of the W.2B/23. It reached RAF No. 616 Sqn on 12 July 1944, making it the first operational jet fighter in

Above: This beautiful study captures a trio of production de Havilland Sea Hornet FR.Mk 20 fighter-reconnaissance aircraft serving with No. 801 Sqn from RNAS Ford in 1947. Later the Fleet Air Arm received the two-seat NF.Mk 21 night fighter which was appreciably slower.

Above: Most of the 67 production Westland Welkin F.Mk I high-altitude interceptors wore PRU Blue with Type B (red/blue) insignia. Unfortunately the Welkin was crippled by poor rate of roll (plus other shortcomings) and never entered operational service. A single aircraft in a later serial range (PF370) was completed as a two-seat radar-equipped night interceptor.

Left: Though outstanding in most respects, the Supermarine Spiteful had a completely new wing of so-called laminar-flow profile which at high subsonic Mach numbers proved markedly inferior to the old wing of the Spitfire. This particular Spiteful was the first of just 17 production F.Mk XIVs. The type's impressive performance was immediately eclipsed by the new jets.

British Fighters of World War II

Gloster Meteor

Gloster Meteor F.Mk III of No. 245 Sqn.

Gloster Meteor F.Mk 1
Type: single-seat day-fighter
Powerplant: two 1,700-lb (7.56-kN) thrust Rolls-Royce W.2B/23C Welland turbojets
Performance: maximum speed 415 mph (668 km/h) at 10,000 ft (3050 m); service ceiling 40,000 ft (12190 m)
Weights: empty 8,140 lb (3692 kg); maximum take-off 13,795 lb (6257 kg)
Dimensions: span 43 ft 0 in (13.11 m); length 41 ft 3 in (12.57 m); height 13 ft 0 in (3.96 m); wing area 374.0 sq ft (34.74 m²)
Armament: four 20-mm cannon

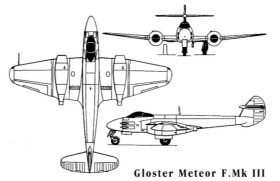

Gloster Meteor F.Mk III

Gloster Meteor F.Mk I.

Left: Before going to join 2nd TAF in Belgium in early 1945 No. 616 Sqn was re-equipped with the Meteor F.Mk III, with a much improved windscreen and sliding canopy. This photograph was taken in Germany in April 1945, by which time the Derwent-engined Mk III was already in service.

Below: Though not intended as a fighter, the Trent-Meteor is of historic importance as the world's first turboprop aircraft. It was built as a regular Meteor F.I fighter (EE227) and converted with Trent engines driving small five-bladed propellers in September 1945.

de Havilland Vampire

De Havilland Vampire F.Mk I of No. 247 Sqn, RAF.

de Havilland Vampire F.Mk 1
Type: single-seat day-fighter
Powerplant: one de Havilland Goblin
DGn.1 turbojet (first 41 aircraft) of
2,700-lb (12.00-kN) thrust
Performance: (full-rated engine)
maximum speed 540 mph (869 km/h)
at 20,000 ft (6095 m); service ceiling
44,000 ft (13410 m); range 730 miles
(1175 km)
Weights: empty 6,372 lb (2890 kg);
maximum take-off 8,578 lb (3891 kg)
Dimensions: wing span 40 ft 0 in
(12.19 m); length 30 ft 9 in (9.37 m);
height 8 ft 1 in (2.46 m); wing area
266. 0 sq ft (24.7 m²)
Armament: four 20-mm Hispano
cannon

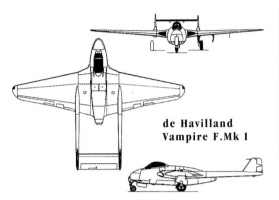

de Havilland Vampire F.Mk I

De Havilland Vampire F.Mk I.

the world. Almost at once the Meteors went into action against V-1 flying bombs, and as a temporary fault was found with the guns a few pilots downed bombs by tipping them over with a wing tip. From September 1944 Gloster delivered the improved Meteor F.Mk III with many refinements including a sliding instead of hinged canopy; from the 16th example the Mk III had the Derwent I engine with 'straight through' combustion chambers, and late in the war longer engine nacelles were fitted.

Vampire just makes the war

Only one other British jet fighter was flown during the war. The de Havilland D.H.100, at first called Spider Crab but later named Vampire, was a smaller machine than the Meteor and most attractive machine with a layout that had

been considered for the E.28/39. The engine was mounted in the rear of a short fuselage nacelle, fed by wing-root inlets, and the tail was carried on twin booms. Metal stressed-skin construction was used except for the nacelle, which was of wooden construction. Armament comprised four cannon under the cockpit in the nose. The first Vampire flew on 20 September 1943 and demonstrated outstanding handling, but DH was overloaded and eventually production had to be assigned to English Electric, the first Mk I flying on 20 April 1945.

Though the first prototype D.H.100 Vampire had graceful vertical tails of traditional de Havilland shape, the tops were cut off in the production F.Mk I model which went into production at English Electric in 1944. The Vampire has been viewed by some as the best of all British wartime fighters.

German
Warplanes
of
World War II

Warplanes for Blitzkrieg

Germany's air force went to war with highly professional and motivated airmen despite its relatively short existence. Its aircraft had been honed to effectiveness by participation in the Spanish Civil War and, available in large numbers, were among the best in Europe.

When Germany went to war in 1939 she had planned on defeating her European opponents within three years, and determined to do so by overcoming France and the UK before turning against the Soviet Union, thereby avoiding the nightmare situation of facing powerful enemies in the West and East simultaneously.

The Luftwaffe was a highly professional force, yet had only been in existence for some six years, and its aircraft, though to some extent tested in the combat conditions of the Spanish Civil War, were regarded as no more than adequate to maintain superiority over other European air forces for those three years.

Moreover, whether or not the Luftwaffe would be able to engage in any sort of strategic air offensive during the

three years was highly questionable. Plans to create a strategic bomber force had been scrapped in 1936 when Hitler vetoed production of small numbers of large aircraft in favour of much larger production of smaller aircraft.

Indeed, unlike the Royal Air Force (which was a wholly self-contained service, independent of the army and navy), the Luftwaffe was largely staffed by ex-army officers who regarded it as an army-support arm whose main purpose was to act as a highly mobile artillery and assault force. Long-range bombing, maritime air operations and air-to-air combat were regarded as being almost superfluous in Germany's Blitzkrieg (lightning warfare) concept.

Thus when Germany invaded Poland, in September 1939, the overwhelming force brought into action in the

Left: The Luftwaffe entered World War II with a world-class fighter in the shape of the Messerschmitt Bf 109. The type had already been blooded - and proven- in combat during Spanish Civil War. This line-up of early Bf 109Es was photographed early in the war, when, although the Luftwaffe was suffering losses, in general it seemed unstoppable.

Below: Widely and affectionately known as 'Tante Ju' ('auntie Junkers'), the Ju 52/3m originated as a dual-purpose airliner/bomber design in the early 1930s. It provided almost all the necessary transportation of airborne forces during the German invasions of Poland, Norway, the Low Countries, France and the Balkans.

Junkers Ju 87R (S2+MR) of 7./StG 77 during the Balkan campaign of April 1941. This version of the Ju 87, with long-range underwing fuel tanks, was first used operationally during the Norwegian campaign a year earlier.

The Ju 87B was the standard version of this notorious dive-bomber during the first two years of the war; this example, 6G+JR, carries the insignia of 7./StG 51 as worn during the Battle of France of May-June 1940.

air comprised large numbers of tactical bombers and ground-support aircraft which could be called down to strike battlefield targets by the army.

Principal among the aircraft flown by the Luftwaffe in 1939 were the Junkers Ju 87 (the famous Stuka) dive-bomber and the Dornier Do 17 medium bomber. With its grotesque, cranked-wing appearance and with sirens attached to its fixed landing gear, the Ju 87 was employed largely as a terror weapon although, provided it faced no fighter opposition, it was used to devastating effect and with great accuracy against small pinpoint targets. It was, however, extremely vulnerable during its steep dive and later came to be regarded as a sitting duck by fighter pilots.

The sleek Dornier Do 17 was an efficient medium bomber by the standards of the time, could carry a useful bomb load of over 2,205 lb (1000 kg) and had a top speed of more than 250 mph (400 km/h). It did display one of the

flaws inherent in many German bombers, concentrating all crew members in the nose of the aircraft so that the gunners had many blind spots in their fields of fire.

Excellent He 111 bomber

The Heinkel He 111 was less vulnerable in this respect. This excellent heavy bomber had also received its baptism of fire in Spain in its early forms, but the much improved He 111P was only reaching the Luftwaffe in significant numbers when German troops marched into Poland. Capable of carrying a bomb load of about 4,409 lb (2000 kg) and possessing a top speed of nearly 250 mph (400 km/h),

Ju 87Bs of StG 77, each carrying a 1,102-lb (500-kg) bomb under the fuselage, on a raid probably during the first two years of the war. In contrast to the RAF's practice of flying close formations, the Luftwaffe preferred the close formation seen here.

Warplanes for Blitzkrieg

Focke-Wulf Fw 200 Condor

This Fw 200 (F8+DH) of 1.Staffel was based at Bordeaux-Mérignac late in 1940 for maritime operations over

Focke-Wulf Fw 200C-8/U10

Focke-Wulf Fw 200C-3/U4 Condor
Type: seven-crew long-range maritime reconnaissance bomber
Powerplant: four 1,000-hp (746-kW) BMW-Bramo 323R-2 radial piston engines
Performance: maximum speed 224 mph (360 km/h) at 15,420 ft (4700 m); service ceiling 19,685 ft (6000 m); range 2,211 miles (3560 km)
Weights: empty 37,478 lb (17000 kg); maximum take-off 50,044 lb (22700 kg)
Dimensions: wing span 107 ft 9½ in (32.84 m); length 76 ft 11½ in (23.85 m); height 20 ft 8 in (6.30 m); wing area 1,290.0 sq ft (118.0 m²)
Armament: one 7.92-mm (0.31-in) gun in forward dorsal turret, one 13-mm (0.51-in) machine-gun in rear dorsal position, two 13-mm (0.51-in) machine-guns in beam positions, one 20-mm cannon in forward position of ventral gondola and one 7.92-mm (0.31-in) machine-gun in aft ventral position, plus a maximum bomb load of 4,630 lb (2100 kg)

The Fw 200C-3/U2 entered Luftwaffe service in late 1941; it had a Lotfe 7D bombsight but featured reduced gun armament.

the He 111 was certainly one of the best heavy bombers in Europe in 1939-40. It had a defensive armament of six machine-guns and was accordingly able to put up a respectable defence against most contemporary fighters. It was the He 111 that carried out the devastating and wide-

ly criticised raids on Warsaw and Rotterdam during the first year of the war, attacks that brought to a shocked world the concept of total war.

Another bomber that was just beginning to join the Luftwaffe in September 1939 was the superb Junkers Ju 88,

Refuelling an Fw 200C-3 of 2.Staffel, KG 40. Normally based at Bordeaux-Mérignac, France, these aircraft were detached to the Stalingrad Front during the winter of 1942-43 for use as bomber-transports.

Below: A line-up of Ju 87Bs of Stukageschwader 2 'Immelmann', probably in the Mediterranean theatre during 1941. The nearest two aircraft bear the 'scottie dog' insignia of the Geschwader's II.Gruppe.

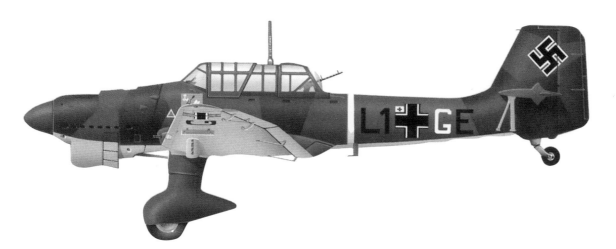

The codes L1+GE identify this Ju 87B as an aircraft of Stab IV (Stuka) Gruppe Lehrgeschwader 1. This general-purpose geschwader was unusual in possessing five Gruppen with medium bombers, dive bombers and heavy fighters (Zerstöreren).

often mistakenly regarded as a dive-bomber on account of the dive-brakes fitted under the wings, but in fact a fast medium bomber whose attacks were frequently carried out in a shallow dive from medium or low level. Able to carry a 2,205-lb (1000-kg) bombload, the early Ju 88 had a top speed of nearly 300 mph (480 km/h), as fast as or faster than half the fighters in service with European air forces.

The Luftwaffe's fighter arm (the *Jagdverband*) had standardised on a single aircraft, the brilliant Messerschmitt Bf 109, a small, fast and highly manoeuvrable single-seater that was more than a match for any opponent that Germany expected to meet early in the war. If it earned any criticism it was for its poor armament, which certainly fell short of RAF Fighter Command's eight-gun batteries in

the Hawker Hurricane and Supermarine Spitfire. No one could foresee that the war would drag on for six years, or that the Bf 109 would fight right up to the last day nor would destroy more enemy aircraft than any other fighter. The type would eventually be built in greater numbers than any other aircraft in the world.

Zerstörer concept

Despite the lack of a strategic bombing force, already mentioned, Germany went to war with a well-balanced range of combat aircraft and, in some respects, its operational concepts were less constricted by traditional ideas than among her opponents. The Luftwaffe had, for example, evolved a radical type of heavy fighter, or *Zerstörer* (destroyer), of

Left: The Do 17E-1 was the first production model of the Dornier bomber. A small number of this variant was delivered to the Legion Condor serving in Spain with the Nationalist Forces in 1937; it had been relegated to second-line duties with the Luftwaffe by September 1939.

Below: The standard Do 17 version at the outbreak of war was the Do 17Z. These examples are seen over Poland in 1939.

which the new Messerschmitt Bf 110 was the first and had entered service shortly before the war.

Possessing a top speed of over 350 mph (560 km/h) and heavy armament, this fighter was regarded as a devastating weapon; while regarded as the brainchild of Hermann Goering himself, the *Zerstörergeschwader* (destroyer groups) were hailed as the elite arm of the Luftwaffe, on a par with the army generals' favourite, the *Stukageschwader* (dive-bomber groups); perhaps it was no accident that many of their crews were drawn from Goering's fellow Prussian gentry.

Luftwaffe support types

Among the supporting aircraft were the rugged three-engine Junkers Ju 52/3m troop transports, developed directly from a civil airliner; the four-engine Focke-Wulf Fw 200 Condor, also a former airliner which came to be adapted for military purposes, this time for maritime reconnaissance; the Henschel Hs 126, a short-range recon-naissance aircraft with short take-off performance and used for battlefield surveillance, and a vital element of the *Blitzkrieg* tactic; the Dornier Do 18 flying-boat and Heinkel He 59 coastal reconnaissance floatplane; and the Heinkel He 115 minelaying floatplane.

This then was Germany's air arsenal, a powerful and well-balanced range of excellent aircraft, flown by well-trained, professional and dedicated crews, and supplied by

an efficient manufacturing industry fairly well dispersed throughout the German hinterland.

All went well for the Luftwaffe during the first eight months of the war. Poland was crushed despite a gallant but forlorn resistance by her outmoded air force. In truth the Luftwaffe was scarcely extended, and the campaign served only to feed the myth of *Blitzkrieg* invincibility. The dive-bombers attacked without serious intervention by opposing fighters, and the Heinkels achieved suitably impressive devastation in the sprawling capital of Warsaw. Poland had been crushed in less than a month.

The Norwegian campaign, though always a lost cause for the UK, posed its own problems for the Luftwaffe, not least of which were the distances involved and the relative absence of airfields. Ju 52/3ms were used to land airborne forces at key points in the south while the Bf 110s were the only available fighters with adequate range to provide cover. Only in the final stages of the campaign was the Luftwaffe given a foretaste of things to come when, in the far north, unescorted bombers and transports faced the RAF's mod-ern Hurricane fighters, and suffered accordingly.

A schwarm of Bf 109 'Emils' flies low along the Channel coast in 1940. Combat experience gained during the early stages of Blitzkrieg allowed German pilots to crush all aerial opposition over France within just six weeks. The situation proved markedly different when attention was turned to the attack on Britain.

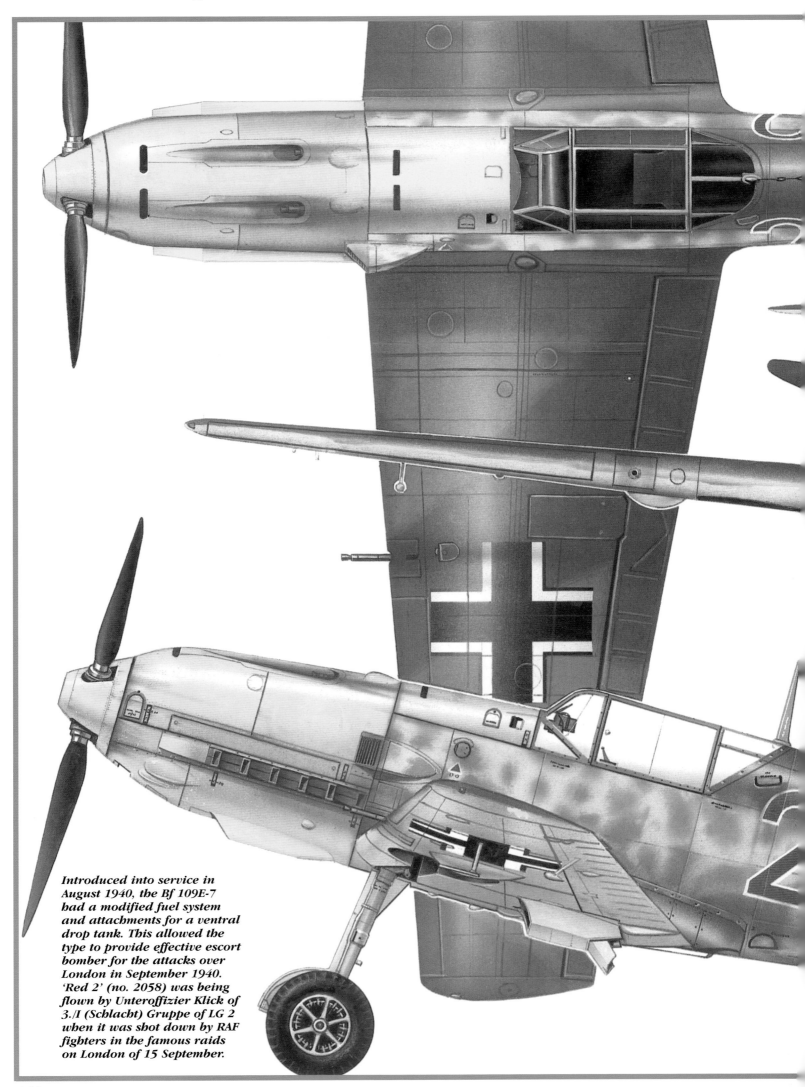

Introduced into service in August 1940, the Bf 109E-7 had a modified fuel system and attachments for a ventral drop tank. This allowed the type to provide effective escort bomber for the attacks over London in September 1940. 'Red 2' (no. 2058) was being flown by Unteroffizier Klick of 3./I (Schlacht) Gruppe of LG 2 when it was shot down by RAF fighters in the famous raids on London of 15 September.

Messerschmitt Bf 109

Messerschmitt Bf 109E-7
Powerplant: one 1,200-hp (895-kW) Daimler-Benz DB 601N inverted V-12 liquid-cooled inline piston engine
Performance: maximum speed 359 mph (578 km/h) at 12,300 ft (3749 m); initial climb rate 3,300 ft (1006 m) per minute; ceiling 36,500 ft (11125 m); range 680 miles (1094 km)
Weights: empty 4,440 lb (2014 kg); maximum take-off 6,100 lb (2767 kg)
Dimensions: wing span 32 ft 4 in (9.86 m); length 28 ft 8 in (8.74 m); height 11 ft 2 in (3.40 m); wing area 174.00 sq ft (16.16 m²)
Armament: one hub-firing 20-mm MG FF/M cannon and four 7.92-mm (0.31-in) MG 17 machine-guns in nose and wings

Keith Fretwell

German Warplanes of World War II

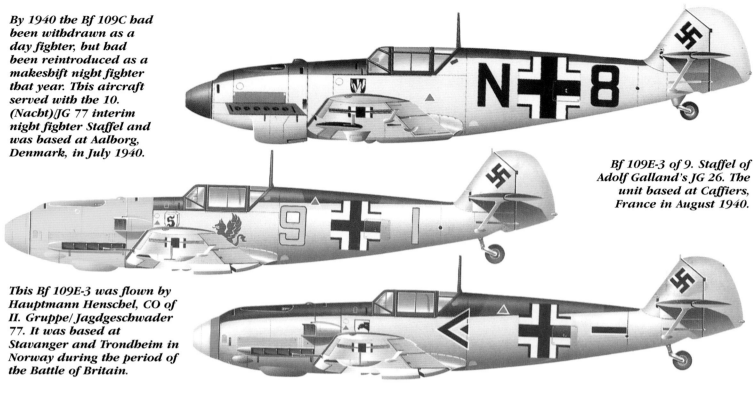

By 1940 the Bf 109C had been withdrawn as a day fighter, but had been reintroduced as a makeshift night fighter that year. This aircraft served with the 10. (Nacht)/JG 77 interim night fighter Staffel and was based at Aalborg, Denmark, in July 1940.

Bf 109E-3 of 9. Staffel of Adolf Galland's JG 26. The unit based at Caffiers, France in August 1940.

This Bf 109E-3 was flown by Hauptmann Henschel, CO of II. Gruppe/ Jagdgeschwader 77. It was based at Stavanger and Trondheim in Norway during the period of the Battle of Britain.

Messerschmitt Bf 109E-4

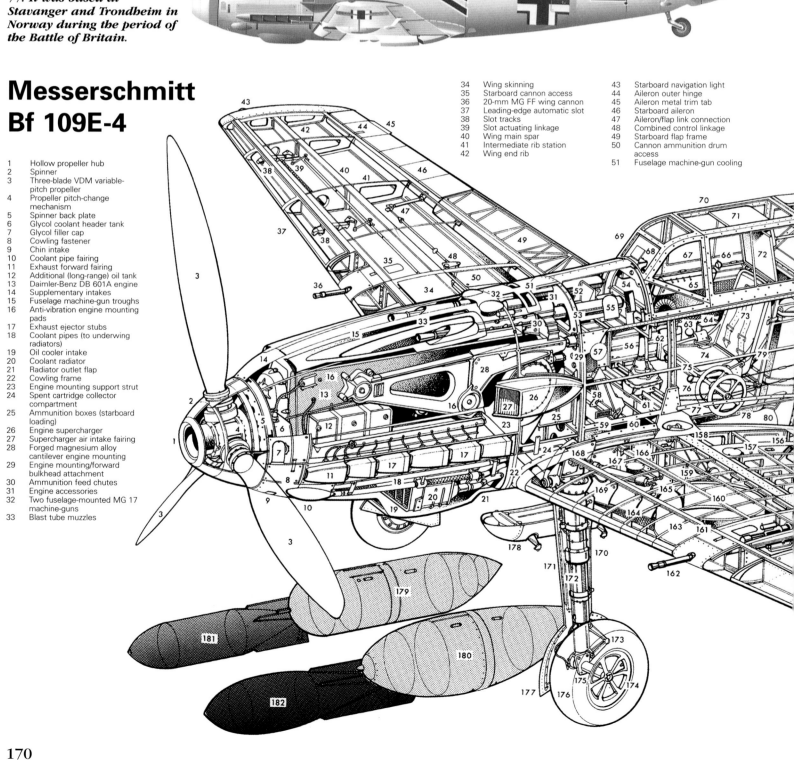

1. Hollow propeller hub
2. Spinner
3. Three-blade VDM variable-pitch propeller
4. Propeller pitch-change mechanism
5. Spinner back plate
6. Glycol coolant header tank
7. Glycol filler cap
8. Cowling fastener
9. Chin intake
10. Coolant pipe fairing
11. Exhaust forward fairing
12. Additional (long-range) oil tank
13. Daimler-Benz DB 601A engine
14. Supplementary intakes
15. Fuselage machine-gun troughs
16. Anti-vibration engine mounting pads
17. Exhaust ejector stubs
18. Coolant pipes (to underwing radiators)
19. Oil cooler intake
20. Coolant radiator
21. Radiator outlet flap
22. Cowling frame
23. Engine mounting support strut
24. Spent cartridge collector compartment
25. Ammunition boxes (starboard loading)
26. Engine supercharger
27. Supercharger air intake fairing
28. Forged magnesium alloy cantilever engine mounting
29. Engine mounting/forward bulkhead attachment
30. Ammunition feed chutes
31. Engine accessories
32. Two fuselage-mounted MG 17 machine-guns
33. Blast tube muzzles

34. Wing skinning
35. Starboard cannon access
36. 20-mm MG FF wing cannon
37. Leading-edge automatic slot
38. Slot tracks
39. Slot actuating linkage
40. Wing main spar
41. Intermediate rib station
42. Wing end rib

43. Starboard navigation light
44. Aileron outer hinge
45. Aileron metal trim tab
46. Starboard aileron
47. Aileron/flap link connection
48. Combined control linkage
49. Starboard flap frame
50. Cannon ammunition drum access
51. Fuselage machine-gun cooling

The red 'worm' insignia on the nose of this Bf 109E denotes 2. Staffel, Jagdgeschwader 3 'Udet'; aircraft of 1. Staffel carried the insignia in white, and those of 3. Staffel in yellow.

A Bf 109E-4 (note absence of hub-firing cannon) bearing the markings of Geschwaderstab, Jagdgeschwader 1. This unit that was not involved in the Battle of Britain.

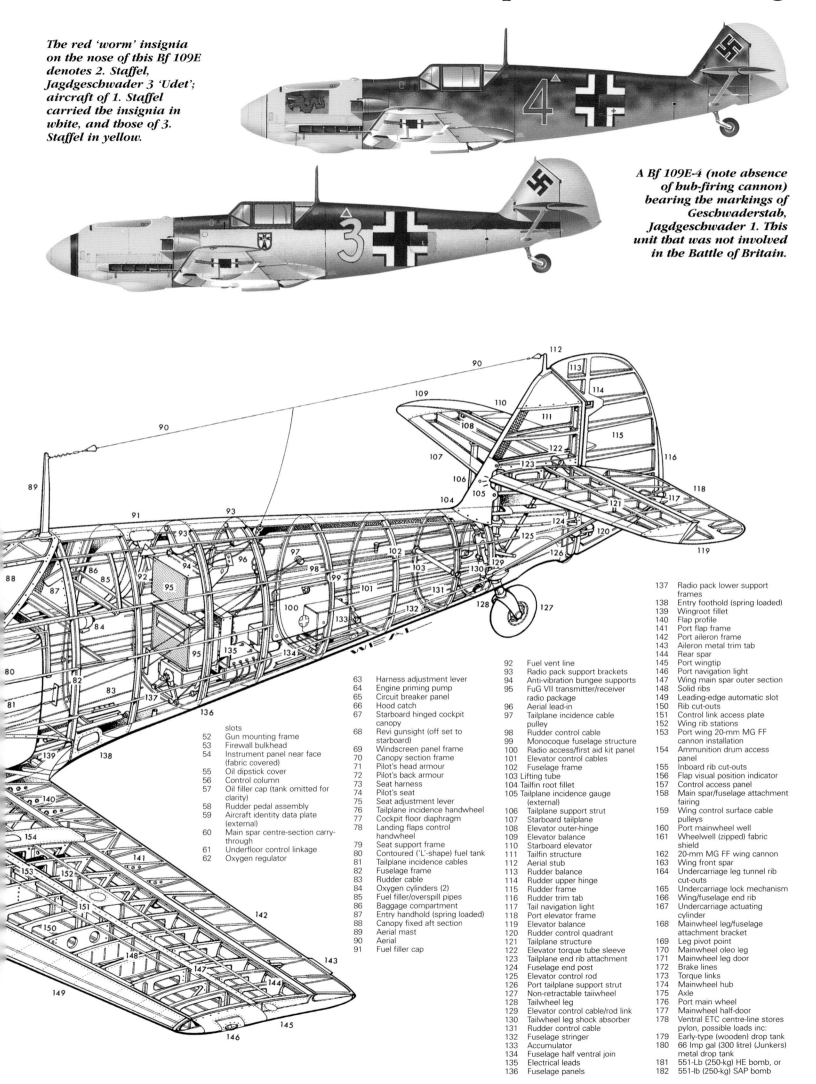

slots
52 Gun mounting frame
53 Firewall bulkhead
54 Instrument panel near face (fabric covered)
55 Oil dipstick cover
56 Control column
57 Oil filler cap (tank omitted for clarity)
58 Rudder pedal assembly
59 Aircraft identity data plate (external)
60 Main spar centre-section carry-through
61 Underfloor control linkage
62 Oxygen regulator
63 Harness adjustment lever
64 Engine priming pump
65 Circuit breaker panel
66 Hood catch
67 Starboard hinged cockpit canopy
68 Revi gunsight (off set to starboard)
69 Windscreen panel frame
70 Canopy section frame
71 Pilot's head armour
72 Pilot's back armour
73 Seat harness
74 Pilot's seat
75 Seat adjustment lever
76 Tailplane incidence handwheel
77 Cockpit floor diaphragm
78 Landing flaps control handwheel
79 Seat support frame
80 Contoured ('L'-shape) fuel tank
81 Tailplane incidence cables
82 Fuselage frame
83 Rudder cable
84 Oxygen cylinders (2)
85 Fuel filler/overspill pipes
86 Baggage compartment
87 Entry handhold (spring loaded)
88 Canopy fixed aft section
89 Aerial mast
90 Aerial
91 Fuel filler cap

92 Fuel vent line
93 Radio pack support brackets
94 Anti-vibration bungee supports
95 FuG VII transmitter/receiver radio package
96 Aerial lead-in
97 Tailplane incidence cable pulley
98 Rudder control cable
99 Monocoque fuselage structure
100 Radio access/first aid kit panel
101 Elevator control cables
102 Fuselage frame
103 Lifting tube
104 Tailfin root fillet
105 Tailplane incidence gauge (external)
106 Tailplane support strut
107 Starboard tailplane
108 Elevator outer-hinge
109 Elevator balance
110 Starboard elevator
111 Tailfin structure
112 Aerial stub
113 Rudder balance
114 Rudder upper hinge
115 Rudder frame
116 Rudder trim tab
117 Tail navigation light
118 Port elevator frame
119 Elevator balance
120 Rudder control quadrant
121 Tailplane structure
122 Elevator torque tube sleeve
123 Tailplane end rib attachment
124 Fuselage end post
125 Elevator control rod
126 Port tailplane support strut
127 Non-retractable tailwheel
128 Tailwheel leg
129 Elevator control cable/rod link
130 Tailwheel leg shock absorber
131 Rudder control cable
132 Fuselage stringer
133 Accumulator
134 Fuselage half ventral join
135 Electrical leads
136 Fuselage panels

137 Radio pack lower support frames
138 Entry foothold (spring loaded)
139 Wingroot fillet
140 Flap profile
141 Port flap frame
142 Port aileron frame
143 Aileron metal trim tab
144 Rear spar
145 Port wingtip
146 Port navigation light
147 Wing main spar outer section
148 Solid ribs
149 Leading-edge automatic slot
150 Rib cut-outs
151 Control link access plate
152 Wing rib stations
153 Port wing 20-mm MG FF cannon installation
154 Ammunition drum access panel
155 Inboard rib cut-outs
156 Flap visual position indicator
157 Control access panel
158 Main spar/fuselage attachment fairing
159 Wing control surface cable pulleys
160 Port mainwheel well
161 Wheelwell (zipped) fabric shield
162 20-mm MG FF wing cannon
163 Wing front spar
164 Undercarriage leg tunnel rib cut-outs
165 Undercarriage lock mechanism
166 Wing/fuselage end rib
167 Undercarriage actuating cylinder
168 Mainwheel leg/fuselage attachment bracket
169 Leg pivot point
170 Mainwheel oleo leg
171 Mainwheel leg door
172 Brake lines
173 Torque links
174 Mainwheel hub
175 Axle
176 Port main wheel
177 Mainwheel half-door
178 Ventral ETC centre-line stores pylon, possible loads inc:
179 Early-type (wooden) drop tank
180 66 Imp gal (300 litre) (Junkers) metal drop tank
181 551-Lb (250-kg) HE bomb, or
182 551-lb (250-kg) SAP bomb

Above: A Heinkel He 111H flying over London's docklands during the early evening raid of 7 September 1940 – the raid marked the end of the Luftwaffe's assault on RAF fighter bases, and incidentally represented Goering's fatal error which cost him likely victory in the Battle of Britain.

Above: After the Battle of Britain and the 'Blitz' of 1940-41 the Heinkel He 111 was moved away to other war theatres and scarcely ever again appeared over Britain. It continued to give sterling service in other roles right up to the end of the war.

Below: Groundcrew prepare an He 111H for flight; the nose insignia denotes KG 26 'Löwen-Geschwader (lion wing), a unit that was based at Stavanger, Norway, early in the Battle of Britain. KG 26 flew only one major daylight raid, on 15 August 1940, but suffered prohibitive losses.

Junkers Ju 52/3m

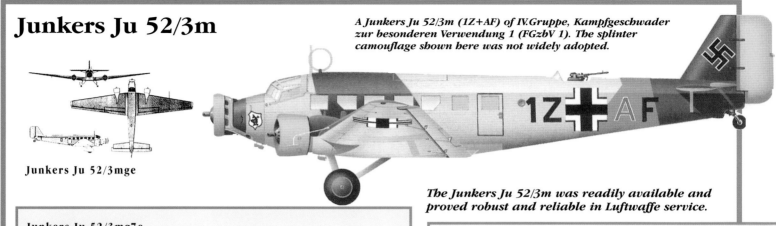

Junkers Ju 52/3mge

A Junkers Ju 52/3m (1Z+AF) of IV.Gruppe, Kampfgeschwader zur besonderen Verwendung 1 (FGzbV 1). The splinter camouflage shown here was not widely adopted.

The Junkers Ju 52/3m was readily available and proved robust and reliable in Luftwaffe service.

Junkers Ju 52/3mg7e
Type: 18-seat military transport
Powerplant: three 830-hp (619-kW) BMW 132T-2 nine-cylinder air-cooled radial piston engines
Performance: maximum speed 183 mph (295 km/h) at sea level; initial climb rate 680 ft (208 m) per minute; service ceiling 18,045 ft (5500 m); range 802 miles (1290 km)
Weights: empty 14,462 lb (6560 kg); maximum take-off 23,180 lb (10515 kg)
Dimensions: wing span 95 ft 11½ in (29.25 m); length 62 ft 0 in (18.80 m); height 14 ft 9 in (4.50 m); wing area 1,189.45 sq ft (110.5 m²)
Armament: (typical) one 7.92-mm (0.31-in) MG 15 machine-gun in dorsal position and two 7.92-mm (0.31-in) machine-guns firing abeam through side windows

Before the Norwegian campaign drew to its inevitable end, the great German attack in the West had been launched on 10 May, the full panoply of *Blitzkrieg* armoury and tactics being unleashed on France and the Low Countries. For a period of about one week the Luftwaffe was fighting the combined air forces of the UK, France, the Netherlands and Belgium.

Every type of German military aircraft was given a specific role. He 111s attacked Rotterdam as Do 17s roamed the skies over France; Ju 87s struck at targets in the path of the advancing German army as Bf 110s flew top cover; Bf 109s decimated the Dutch and Belgian air forces as Ju 52/3ms landed airborne forces on key objectives in the Low Countries, and Ju 88s struck at targets on the Belgian coast.

In a number of 'setpiece' attacks novel tactics were used: He 59 biplanes alighted on the Maas river, bringing 120 troops to capture the key bridge at Rotterdam; DFS 230 gliders landed with assault troops on the key Belgian fort of Eben Emael. And all the while Hs 126 reconnaissance aircraft buzzed to and fro over the rumbling *Panzer* forces.

Within a week the Netherlands had been overrun, and Belgium followed ten days later. France eventually collapsed in mid-June, her air force unable to blunt the thrusts of *Blitzkrieg* and being constantly forced to abandon its poorly prepared airfields. In the north of the country, as the UK tried desperately to recover her battered army from Dunkirk, the Luftwaffe was forced into its first major and prolonged air battle against a modern fighter force. While

The Heinkel He 111H was a rugged heavy bomber by early wartime standards. Its performance and load-carrying abilities were roughly comparable with those of the RAF's Wellington, but like the British aircraft, the He 111 was transferred to the night bombing role after suffering heavy losses sustained by day.

the German air fighting tactics proved superior to those of the RAF, the bombers were suddenly found to be surprisingly vulnerable to the onslaughts of determined fighter pilots in modern aircraft. The much-vaunted Ju 87 was seen to be particularly brittle in the rough-house melee with enemy fighters; even the Bf 110 was seen to be a ponderous weapon in the presence of British fighters.

British appreciation of German types

The British, on the other hand, found German aircraft to be rugged in combat, demanding much more than fleeting hits to ensure their destruction. The Bf 109E was seen to be a match for the Spitfire, the former's relative lack of armament being largely offset by the British pilots' lack of combat experience.

The great Battle of Britain brought the greater part of the Luftwaffe into full-scale conflict with the British air defence system although, through lack of range in the Bf 109, the battle was largely confined to the south of England. The lessons of Dunkirk were that in daylight the formations of Do 17s, He 111s and Ju 87s required close escort and, in the light of the Bf 110's vulnerability (particularly in the presence of Hurricanes), this resulted in the Bf 109 being tied to the bomber formations as close escort; in so doing, the Luftwaffe was restricted twofold: the single-seat fight-

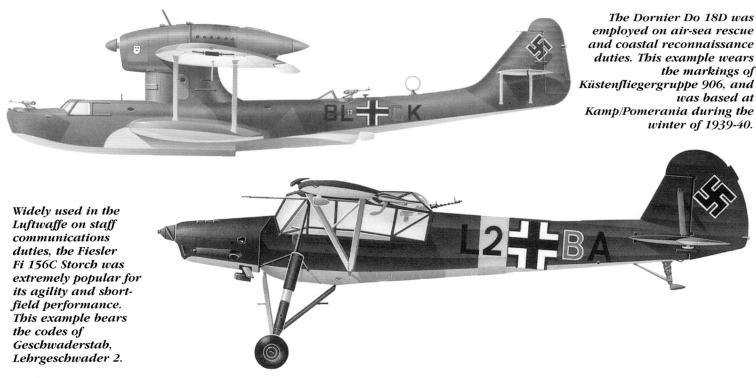

The Dornier Do 18D was employed on air-sea rescue and coastal reconnaissance duties. This example wears the markings of Küstenfliegergruppe 906, and was based at Kamp/Pomerania during the winter of 1939-40.

Widely used in the Luftwaffe on staff communications duties, the Fiesler Fi 156C Storch was extremely popular for its agility and short-field performance. This example bears the codes of Geschwaderstab, Lehrgeschwader 2.

ers could not meet the defending fighters on equal terms, and the bombers could not at least in safety and in daylight venture further than some 100 miles (160 km) beyond the English south and east coasts.

The Battle of Britain represented the first major setback for the Luftwaffe, both in materiel and morale. None of its aircraft, with the likely exception of the Bf 109, was seen to be invincible, least of all the vaunted Ju 87 and the Bf 110, the former having been withdrawn as being wholly unsuitable in the continuing presence of enemy fighters.

It was at this point, the first turning point of the war, that the *Oberkommando der Luftwaffe* (OKL - Luftwaffe High

A pair of Bf 110C-2s of 1./ZG 52 based at Charleville in June 1940 during the Battle of France. Though fast and well-armed, the Bf 110 proved extremely vulnerable in the presence of more agile single-seat fighters.

Command) realised that considerable improvement of its aircraft was now needed, and quickly, if German initiative in the war was to be maintained. Beginning in the autumn of 1940 the German aircraft industry, which had hitherto been operating at no more than walking pace, was ordered to gear itself for massive efforts to support the great assault on Russia which Hitler was already planning for 1941.

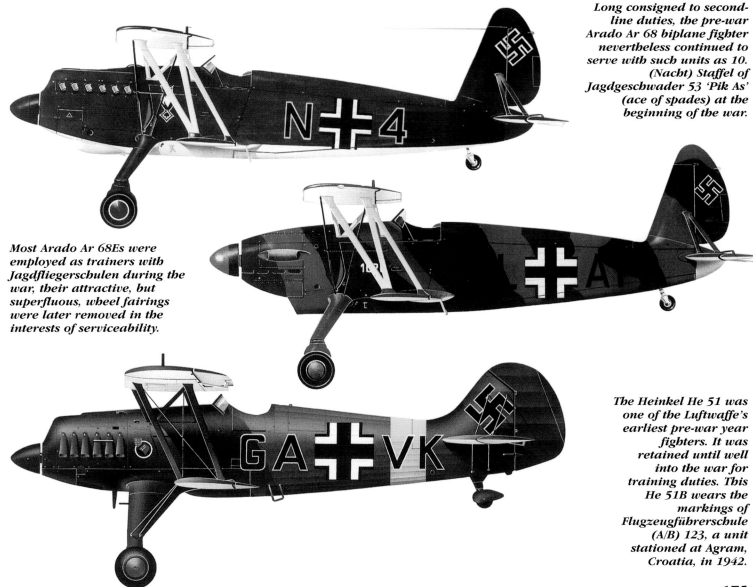

Long consigned to second-line duties, the pre-war Arado Ar 68 biplane fighter nevertheless continued to serve with such units as 10. (Nacht) Staffel of Jagdgeschwader 53 'Pik As' (ace of spades) at the beginning of the war.

Most Arado Ar 68Es were employed as trainers with Jagdfliegerschulen during the war, their attractive, but superfluous, wheel fairings were later removed in the interests of serviceability.

The Heinkel He 51 was one of the Luftwaffe's earliest pre-war year fighters. It was retained until well into the war for training duties. This He 51B wears the markings of Flugzeugführerschule (A/B) 123, a unit stationed at Agram, Croatia, in 1942.

Heinkel He 111

Heinkel He 111H-6
Type: five-seat medium night-bomber/pathfinder and glider tug
Powerplant: two 1,350-hp (1006-kW) Junkers Jumo 211F-2 inline piston engines
Performance: maximum speed 270 mph (435 km/h) at 19,685 ft (6000 m); service ceiling 27,890 ft (8500 m); normal range 1,212 miles (1950 km)
Weights: empty 19,136 lb (8680 kg); maximum take-off 30,864 lb (14000 kg)
Dimensions: wing span 74 ft 1 in (22.60 m); length 53 ft 9 in (16.40 m); height 13 ft 1 in (4.00 m); wing area 931.10 sq ft (86.50 m²)
Armament: one 20-mm MG FF cannon, one 13-mm (0.51-in) MG 131 machine-gun and up to seven 7.92-mm (0.31-in) MG 15 and MG 81 machine-guns, plus one 4,409-lb (2000-kg) bomb carried externally and one 1,102-lb (500-kg) bomb internally, or eight 551-lb (250-kg) bombs all internally

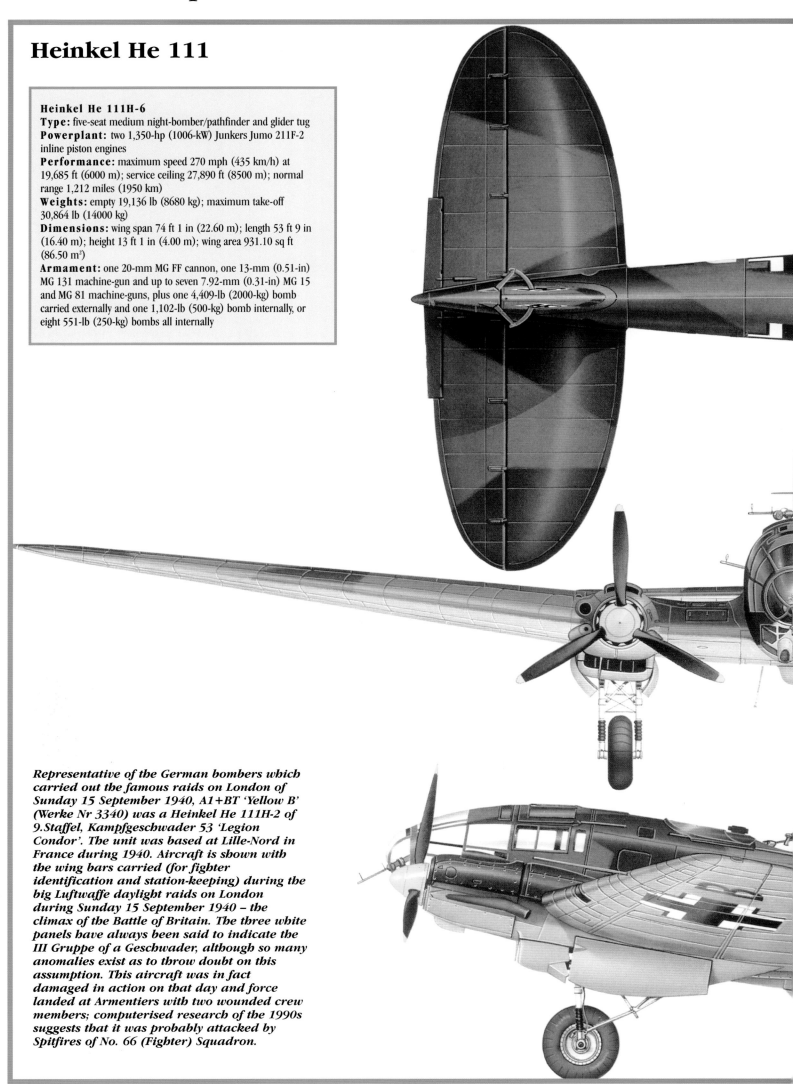

Representative of the German bombers which carried out the famous raids on London of Sunday 15 September 1940, A1+BT 'Yellow B' (Werke Nr 3340) was a Heinkel He 111H-2 of 9.Staffel, Kampfgeschwader 53 'Legion Condor'. The unit was based at Lille-Nord in France during 1940. Aircraft is shown with the wing bars carried (for fighter identification and station-keeping) during the big Luftwaffe daylight raids on London during Sunday 15 September 1940 – the climax of the Battle of Britain. The three white panels have always been said to indicate the III Gruppe of a Geschwader, although so many anomalies exist as to throw doubt on this assumption. This aircraft was in fact damaged in action on that day and force landed at Armentiers with two wounded crew members; computerised research of the 1990s suggests that it was probably attacked by Spitfires of No. 66 (Fighter) Squadron.

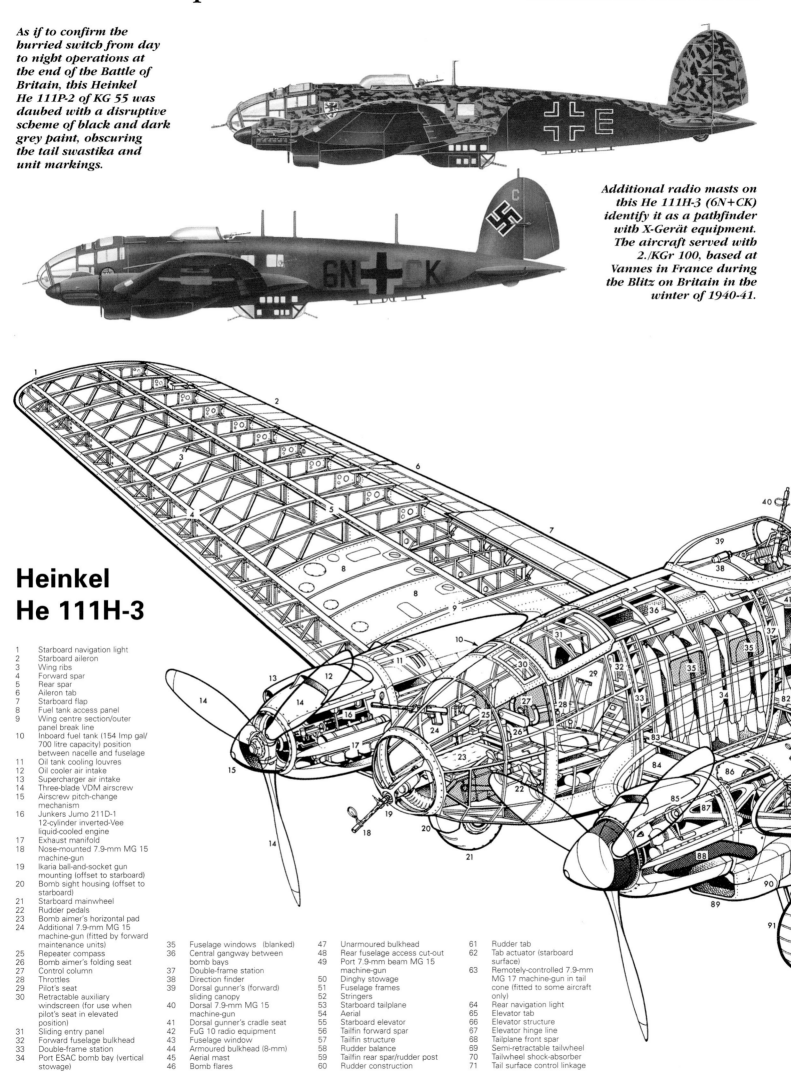

As if to confirm the hurried switch from day to night operations at the end of the Battle of Britain, this Heinkel He 111P-2 of KG 55 was daubed with a disruptive scheme of black and dark grey paint, obscuring the tail swastika and unit markings.

Additional radio masts on this He 111H-3 (6N+CK) identify it as a pathfinder with X-Gerät equipment. The aircraft served with 2./KGr 100, based at Vannes in France during the Blitz on Britain in the winter of 1940-41.

Heinkel He 111H-3

1 Starboard navigation light
2 Starboard aileron
3 Wing ribs
4 Forward spar
5 Rear spar
6 Aileron tab
7 Starboard flap
8 Fuel tank access panel
9 Wing centre section/outer panel break line
10 Inboard fuel tank (154 Imp gal/700 litre capacity) position between nacelle and fuselage
11 Oil tank cooling louvres
12 Oil cooler air intake
13 Supercharger air intake
14 Three-blade VDM airscrew
15 Airscrew pitch-change mechanism
16 Junkers Jumo 211D-1 12-cylinder inverted-Vee liquid-cooled engine
17 Exhaust manifold
18 Nose-mounted 7.9-mm MG 15 machine-gun
19 Ikaria ball-and-socket gun mounting (offset to starboard)
20 Bomb sight housing (offset to starboard)
21 Starboard mainwheel
22 Rudder pedals
23 Bomb aimer's horizontal pad
24 Additional 7.9-mm MG 15 machine-gun (fitted by forward maintenance units)
25 Repeater compass
26 Bomb aimer's folding seat
27 Control column
28 Throttles
29 Pilot's seat
30 Retractable auxiliary windscreen (for use when pilot's seat in elevated position)
31 Sliding entry panel
32 Forward fuselage bulkhead
33 Double-frame station
34 Port ESAC bomb bay (vertical stowage)

35 Fuselage windows (blanked)
36 Central gangway between bomb bays
37 Double-frame station
38 Direction finder
39 Dorsal gunner's (forward) sliding canopy
40 Dorsal 7.9-mm MG 15 machine-gun
41 Dorsal gunner's cradle seat
42 FuG 10 radio equipment
43 Fuselage window
44 Armoured bulkhead (8-mm)
45 Aerial mast
46 Bomb flares

47 Unarmoured bulkhead
48 Rear fuselage access cut-out
49 Port 7.9-mm beam MG 15 machine-gun
50 Dinghy stowage
51 Fuselage frames
52 Stringers
53 Starboard tailplane
54 Aerial
55 Starboard elevator
56 Tailfin forward spar
57 Tailfin structure
58 Rudder balance
59 Tailfin rear spar/rudder post
60 Rudder construction

61 Rudder tab
62 Tab actuator (starboard surface)
63 Remotely-controlled 7.9-mm MG 17 machine-gun in tail cone (fitted to some aircraft only)
64 Rear navigation light
65 Elevator tab
66 Elevator structure
67 Elevator hinge line
68 Tailplane front spar
69 Semi-retractable tailwheel
70 Tailwheel shock-absorber
71 Tail surface control linkage

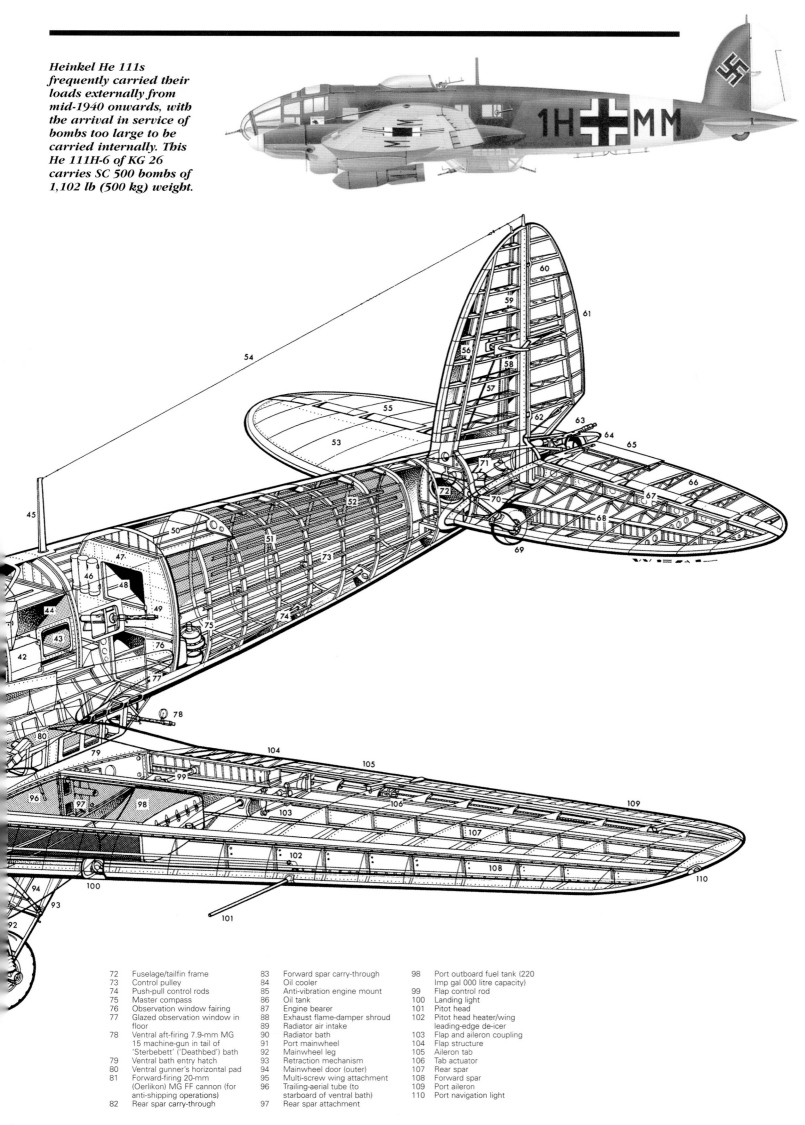

Heinkel He 111s frequently carried their loads externally from mid-1940 onwards, with the arrival in service of bombs too large to be carried internally. This He 111H-6 of KG 26 carries SC 500 bombs of 1,102 lb (500 kg) weight.

72 Fuselage/tailfin frame
73 Control pulley
74 Push-pull control rods
75 Master compass
76 Observation window fairing
77 Glazed observation window in floor
78 Ventral aft-firing 7.9-mm MG 15 machine-gun in tail of 'Sterbebett' ('Deathbed') bath
79 Ventral bath entry hatch
80 Ventral gunner's horizontal pad
81 Forward-firing 20-mm (Oerlikon) MG FF cannon (for anti-shipping operations)
82 Rear spar carry-through

83 Forward spar carry-through
84 Oil cooler
85 Anti-vibration engine mount
86 Oil tank
87 Engine bearer
88 Exhaust flame-damper shroud
89 Radiator air intake
90 Radiator bath
91 Port mainwheel
92 Mainwheel leg
93 Retraction mechanism
94 Mainwheel door (outer)
95 Multi-screw wing attachment
96 Trailing-aerial tube (to starboard of ventral bath)
97 Rear spar attachment

98 Port outboard fuel tank (220 Imp gal 000 litre capacity)
99 Flap control rod
100 Landing light
101 Pitot head
102 Pitot head heater/wing leading-edge de-icer
103 Flap and aileron coupling
104 Flap structure
105 Aileron tab
106 Tab actuator
107 Rear spar
108 Forward spar
109 Port aileron
110 Port navigation light

Multi-Front Nightmare

Complicated by Britain's dogged survival of the air assaults of 1940-41, Hitler's critical timetable for the conquest of Europe demanded a speedy victory over the Soviet Union, but simultaneous war on the Western, Eastern and Southern Fronts created an impossible strain on the Luftwaffe's resources.

As if reluctant to concede defeat in the daylight skies over Britain in September 1940, Goering ordered the Luftwaffe to commence a prolonged night assault against British towns and cities. The offensive was to last for almost nine months and was targeted principally against London, the vulnerable hub of British commerce and government that lay within easy reach of all German bombers with full bomb bays. Night after night the Heinkel He 111s, Dornier Do 17s and Junkers Ju 88s droned their way through darkened skies, scarcely troubled by the paltry British night-fighter defences.

Though the British civil population was the Luftwaffe's target, attempts were made to strike specific strategic objectives, often involving long flights over hostile territory. For such purposes specialist pathfinding bombers were used. It was the task of Kampfgruppe 100, using special He 111s, to employ special radio aids (*X-Gerät*, receiving HF signals transmitted by a *Knickebein*, or 'crooked leg', transmitter) to find and illuminate the target for the benefit of the main raiding force. In due course the British evolved means to distort the enemy signals and thereby prevent the concentration of an enemy raid.

Left: This Ju 87D was operating with III./StG. 1 on the Eastern Front. Aircraft like the Ju 52/3m in the background played a vital role later in the war, supplying Germany's beleaguered armies with ammunition and food.

Below: Typifying the style of Luftwaffe air support operations during the great German land advances of the first two years of the war, this scene depicts Ju52/3m transports delivering fuel stocks for a Bf 110 unit.

Dornier Do 17

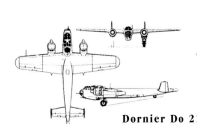

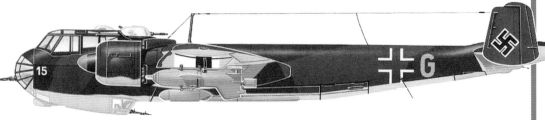

Dornier Do 217E-2

The Dornier Do 217 represented an ingenious upgrade of the ageing Do 17; this Do 217E-5 was adapted to carry two Henschel Hs 293A stand-off guided weapons under the wings.

Dornier Do 17Z-2
Type: four-seat medium bomber
Powerplant: two BMW-Bramo 323P Fafnir nine-cylinder radial piston engines, each rated at 1,000 hp (746 kW) for take-off and 940 hp (701 kW) at 13,120 ft (4000 m)
Performance: maximum speed 255 mph (410 km/h); service ceiling 22,965 ft (7000 m); range 720 miles (1160 km); standard tactical radius 205 miles (330 km)
Weights: empty 11,484 lb (5209 kg); empty equipped 13,145 lb (5962 kg); maximum overload 19,481 lb (8837 kg)
Dimensions: wing span 59 ft 0⅓ in (18.00 m); length 51 ft 9⅔ in (15.79 m); height 14 ft 11½ in (4.56 m); wing area 592 sq ft (55.0 m²)
Armament: two forward-firing 7.92-mm (0.31-in) MG 15 machine-guns, either fixed or free-mounted, two MG 15s firing from side windows, one MG 15 firing aft from dorsal and ventral positions in forward compartment; maximum internal bomb load of 2,205 lb (1000 kg)

Below: Bombs stacked under a Dornier Do 17Z-2 of 10./KG 2 'Holzhammer' (wooden hammer wing).

By May 1941 Hitler's attack on Russia lay only a month away, and most of the *Kampfgeschwader* (bomber groups) were moved from France and Belgium to the East in readiness, It was at this time that the first examples of a new bomber, the Dornier Do 217, were being delivered to units in France, at first to join the Focke-Wulf Fw 200 in anti-shipping duties over the Atlantic. The Do 217 was a much-improved and modernised development of the plainly obsolescent Do 17, being able to carry twice the bombload and capable of a speed of 320 mph (515 km/h). In time the Do 217 became one of the mainstays of the Luftwaffe's bomber force in the West.

Other developments had occurred during the winter of 1940-41. Italy entered the war in June 1940 and in due course embarked on adventures in Egypt and East Africa, supplementing the dire course of events already taking place in the Balkans. These rapidly became bogged down as a result of inadequate planning and unexpectedly stubborn Allied resistance. Italian calls for assistance had brought a growing force of Luftwaffe aircraft to the Mediterranean, and in due course to the Balkans.

As the first *Gruppe* of specially tropicalised Messerschmitt Bf 109Es (I. Gruppe of JG 27) arrived in Sicily early in 1941 to support what was later to become famous as General Rommel's *Deutsches Afrika Korps*, Hitler determined to eliminate Yugoslavia and Greece as a potential threat to the southern flank of his future Russian front (and thereby extricate Italy from an embarrassing stalemate).

Triumph in Crete

British and Greek Hawker Hurricanes and Gloster Gladiators, which had successfully matched the Italian aircraft, now faced the modern German air force. Within six weeks the German army and the Luftwaffe were once more triumphant, and the British were forced to evacuate their forces, first to Crete and finally to Egypt. The Junkers Ju 88s in particular left their mark on the Greek campaign, carrying out a number of brilliant low-level raids on ports and airfields. In the subsequent invasion of Crete the Luftwaffe once more employed airborne forces, dropping large numbers of paratroops from, and landing others in, Junkers Ju 52/3ms, and flying in small groups of troops in

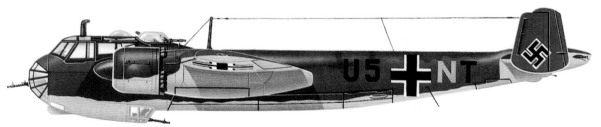

KG 2 started receiving the improved Do 217E in 1941. Wearing the codes of the Geschwader's 9. Staffel, this E-2 version had an electrically-operated dorsal turret with a single 13-mm (0.51-in) machine-gun.

A Junkers Ju 88A-1 (9K+GL) of I/KG 51 'Edelweiss' based at Melun-Villaroche, France, in October 1940. The black undersides and toned-down markings were adopted during the night Blitz on Britain.

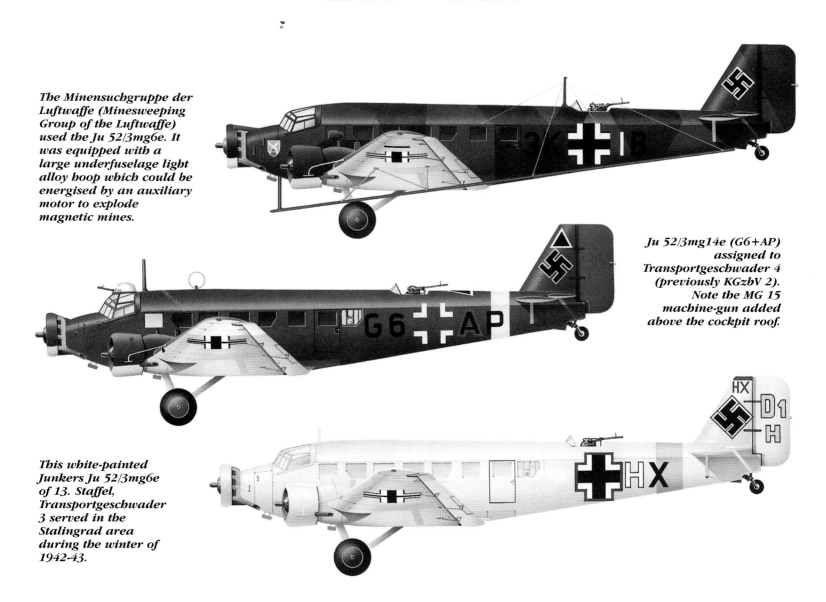

The Minensuchgruppe der Luftwaffe (Minesweeping Group of the Luftwaffe) used the Ju 52/3mg6e. It was equipped with a large underfuselage light alloy hoop which could be energised by an auxiliary motor to explode magnetic mines.

Ju 52/3mg14e (G6+AP) assigned to Transportgeschwader 4 (previously KGzbV 2). Note the MG 15 machine-gun added above the cockpit roof.

This white-painted Junkers Ju 52/3mg6e of 13. Staffel, Transportgeschwader 3 served in the Stalingrad area during the winter of 1942-43.

DFS 230 gliders, though sustaining very heavy losses in the process. German plans were already well underway to produce a true assault glider, the Gotha Go 242, but having only been initiated less than a year before these were not ready in time for the Crete operation.

Thus by mid-1941 the nature of the war had been decided for Germany as one involving that traditional nightmare, enemies to the east and west (and now to the south), and

in the air. Only Turkey, Switzerland, Sweden, Spain and Portugal remained neutral; Italy, Austria, Hungary, Rumania, Bulgaria and Finland had or were about to join the Axis, while Poland, Czechoslovakia, Denmark, Norway,

A Junkers Ju 88A-4 of III. Gruppe, Lehrgeschwader 1 on the Eastern Front in 1942. It carries a 551-lb (250-kg) SC 250 and 1,102-lb (500-kg) SC 500 bomb.

Messerschmitt Bf 110

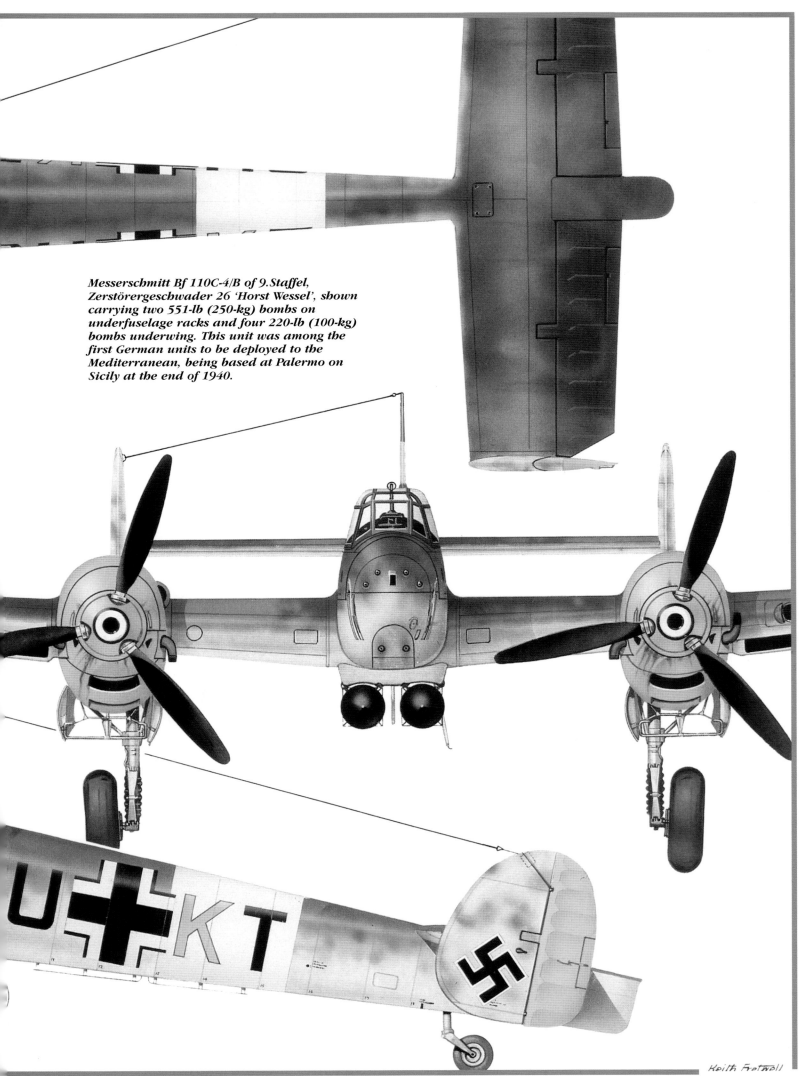

Messerschmitt Bf 110C-4/B of 9.Staffel, Zerstörergeschwader 26 'Horst Wessel', shown carrying two 551-lb (250-kg) bombs on underfuselage racks and four 220-lb (100-kg) bombs underwing. This unit was among the first German units to be deployed to the Mediterranean, being based at Palermo on Sicily at the end of 1940.

Keith Fretwell

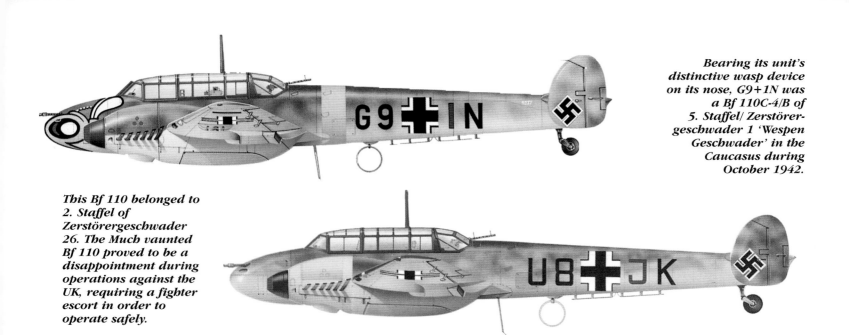

Bearing its unit's distinctive wasp device on its nose, G9+1N was a Bf 110C-4/B of 5. Staffel/ Zerstörergeschwader 1 'Wespen Geschwader' in the Caucasus during October 1942.

This Bf 110 belonged to 2. Staffel of Zerstörergeschwader 26. The Much vaunted Bf 110 proved to be a disappointment during operations against the UK, requiring a fighter escort in order to operate safely.

1	Hirschgeweih (Stag's Antlers) array for FuG 2201b Lichtenstein SN-2 radar	9	Twin 30-mm Rheinmetall Borsig M K 108 (Rüstsatz/Field conversion Set 3) with 135rpg	17	Pitot tube	
2	Single-pole type antenna for FuG 212 Lichtenstein C-1 radar	10	Armoured bulkhead	18	FuG 227/1 Flensburg homing aerial fitted to some aircraft by forward maintenance units (to home on Monica tail-warning radar emissions)	
3	Camera gun	11	Supercharger intake			
4	Cannon muzzles	12	Position of nacelle-mounted instruments on day fighter model	19	Stressed wing skinning	
5	Cannon ports	13	Exhaust flame damper	20	Starboard aileron	
6	Blast tubes	14	Auxiliary tank	21	Trim tab	
7	Starboard mainwheel	15	Three-blade VDM airscrew	22	Slotted flap	
8	Armour plate (10 mm)	16	Leading-edge automatic slat	23	Hinged canopy roof	
				24	Armoured glass windscreen	

	(60 mm)	33	Radar operator's swivel seat
25	Instrument panel	34	D/F loop
26	Cockpit floor armour (4 mm)	35	Aerial mast
27	Twin 20-mm Mauser MG 151 cannon with 300 rounds (port) and 350 rounds (starboard)	36	Upward-firing cannon muzzles
28	Pilot's seat	37	Two 30-mm MK 108 cannon in Schräge Musik installation firing obliquely upward (optional installation supplied as Factory Conversion Set)
29	Control column		
30	Pilot's back and head armour (8 mm)		
31	Cannon magazine	38	Ammunition drums
32	Centre section carry-through	39	Aft cockpit bulkhead
		40	FuG 10 HF R/T set

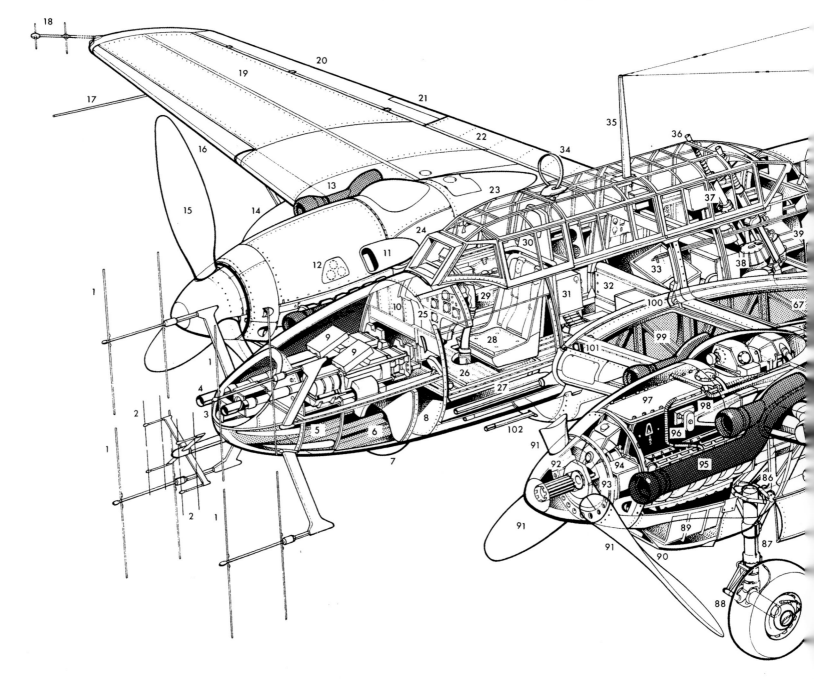

Multi-Front Nightmare

Messerschmitt Bf 110C-4
Type: two-seat heavy fighter
Powerplant: two 1,100-hp (821-kW) Daimler-Benz DB 601A inline piston engines
Performance: maximum speed 349 mph (560 km/h) at 22,965 ft (7000 m); initial climb rate 2,165 ft (660 m) per minute; service ceiling 32,810 ft (10000 m); normal range 482 miles (775 km)
Weights: empty 11,464 lb (5200 kg); maximum take-off 14,881 lb (6750 kg)
Dimensions: wing span 53 ft 4¾ in (16.27 m); length 41 ft 6¾ in (12.65 m); height 11 ft 6 in (3.50 m); wing area 413.3 sq ft (38.4 m²)
Armament: two 20-mm MG 151 cannon and four 7.92-mm (0.31-in) MG 17 machine-guns in the nose, firing forward, and one 7.92-mm (0.31-in) MG 812 twin machine-gun on flexible mounting in the rear fuselage firing aft

A Bf 110C-4/B of Schnellkampfgeschwader 210 over the Eastern Front. This unit had originated as Erprobungsgruppe 210 in 1940 but became ZG 1 'Wespen Geschwader' later, before becoming SKG 210; the aircraft shown retains ZG 1's wasp markings on the nose.

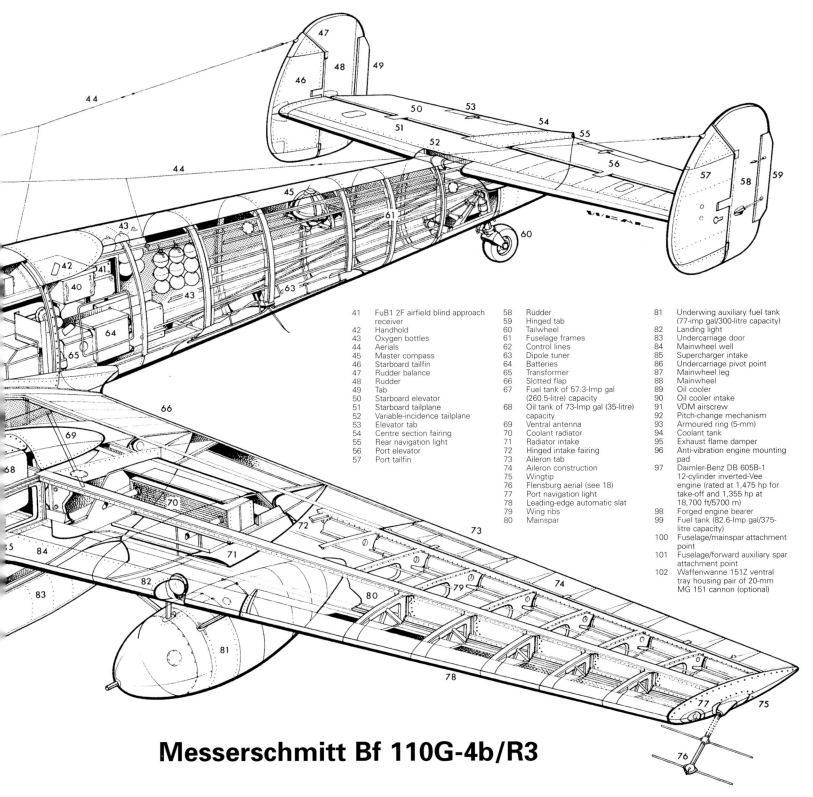

41	FuB1 2F airfield blind approach receiver	58	Rudder	81	Underwing auxiliary fuel tank (77-imp gal/300-litre capacity)
42	Handhold	59	Hinged tab	82	Landing light
43	Oxygen bottles	60	Tailwheel	83	Undercarriage door
44	Aerials	61	Fuselage frames	84	Mainwheel well
45	Master compass	62	Control lines	85	Supercharger intake
46	Starboard tailfin	63	Dipole tuner	86	Undercarriage pivot point
47	Rudder balance	64	Batteries	87	Mainwheel leg
48	Rudder	65	Transformer	88	Mainwheel
49	Tab	66	Slotted flap	89	Oil cooler
50	Starboard elevator	67	Fuel tank of 57.3-Imp gal (260.5-litre) capacity	90	Oil cooler intake
51	Starboard tailplane	68	Oil tank of 73-Imp gal (35-litre) capacity	91	VDM airscrew
52	Variable-incidence tailplane	69	Ventral antenna	92	Pitch-change mechanism
53	Elevator tab	70	Coolant radiator	93	Armoured ring (5-mm)
54	Centre section fairing	71	Radiator intake	94	Coolant tank
55	Rear navigation light	72	Hinged intake fairing	95	Exhaust flame damper
56	Port elevator	73	Aileron tab	96	Anti-vibration engine mounting pad
57	Port tailfin	74	Aileron construction	97	Daimler-Benz DB 605B-1 12-cylinder inverted-Vee engine (rated at 1,475 hp for take-off and 1,355 hp at 18,700 ft/5700 m)
		75	Wingtip	98	Forged engine bearer
		76	Flensburg aerial (see 18)	99	Fuel tank (82.6-Imp gal/375-litre capacity)
		77	Port navigation light	100	Fuselage/mainspar attachment point
		78	Leading-edge automatic slat	101	Fuselage/forward auxiliary spar attachment point
		79	Wing ribs	102	Waffenwanne 151Z ventral tray housing pair of 20-mm MG 151 cannon (optional)
		80	Mainspar		

Messerschmitt Bf 110G-4b/R3

187

German Warplanes of World War II

Above: By 1941 the Dornier Do 17 was regarded as obsolescent and was slowly being replaced by Heinkel He 111s and Junkers Ju 88s. This Dornier Do 17Z, probably serving with KG 2, was deployed in the Balkans in 1941.

Left: This photograph is often reproduced but nevertheless highlights the excellent effectiveness of the Luftwaffe's desert camouflage. It is applied to a Messerschmitt Bf 109E-4/Trop assigned to I/JG 27 under Hauptmann Eduard Neumann during 1941 in North Africa.

the Netherlands, Belgium, France, Yugoslavia, Albania and Greece had all been subjugated by Germany or Italy. In due course German aircraft were built in many of these countries to supplement production in the Fatherland.

Preparations for Barbarossa

It is worthwhile at this point, on the eve of Hitler's assault on the Soviet Union, to take stock of the Luftwaffe and its equipment. Most important arrival in service at this time was the new Messerschmitt Bf 109F, a considerably cleaned-up development of the now-ageing Bf 109E and powered by the beefy Daimler-Benz DB 601N or E. Its top speed of 391 mph (630 km/h) gave it a substantial edge over the early Supermarine Spitfires and Hurricanes of the RAF and over anything yet being flown by the Russians.

The bomber force in the East was composed almost entirely of He 111s and Ju 88s. The Heinkel type equipped

three *Geschwader* (with about 320 aircraft), soon to be joined by four further *Gruppen* (another 120 aircraft). The Junkers bomber was in service with two *Geschwader* (with some 200 aircraft). Junkers Ju 87s, once more brought into action in support of the Blitzkrieg, equipped seven *Stukagruppen* with around 270 aircraft, including a number of Ju 87Rs with long-range tanks.

Elsewhere the German air force was pared to the bone to allow the assembly of the greatest possible concentration of air power in the East. In France fighter defences were reduced to two *Geschwader* (JG 2 and JG 26) of Bf 109Fs but, reflecting the growing importance of operations over the Atlantic, the maritime reconnaissance unit (KG 40 with Focke-Wulf Fw 200 Condors) was strengthened by the arrival of the first more heavily-armed Fw 200Cs. In Norway, and also deployed for anti-shipping attacks, there remained two *Gruppen* of He 111s (I. and III. /KG 26), and

Above: The Ju 88 was one of the most adaptable of all German aircraft of the war. It served on almost every front from the north of Norway to the Mediterranean, and from the night Blitz on Britain to the assault on the Soviet Union.

Left: The big Heinkel He 177 was originally intended to provide the Luftwaffe with a strategic bombing force but encountered so many problems during its development that production examples only entered service in any numbers during the last 18 months of the war. This is the pre-production He 177A-0.

a *Geschwader* of Ju 88s. In the Mediterranean theatre an autonomous *Fliegerkorps* (air corps) deployed two *Gruppen* of tropicalised Bf 109Es (soon replaced by Bf 109Fs) and one of Ju 87s. In the Balkans air defence rested upon one *Gruppe* of Bf 109s, though theoretically this was available to cover the south Russian front.

Barbarossa - the first strikes

From the outset of Operation Barbarossa (the attack on Russia) the Luftwaffe seized and retained total air supremacy over the front. On the first day the Russians conceded the loss of over 1,200 aircraft, the majority destroyed on the ground by surprise attack. The *Jagdverband* chopped up all air opposition and very soon many Bf 109 pilots were amassing personal air victory tallies far in excess of any score ever before achieved. After an initial phase of devastating attacks on Soviet airfields, a

series of heavy raids on Moscow was carried out by an average of over 100 Ju 88s and He 111s. In the north, Ju 87s attacked the Soviet fleet at Kronshtadt, sinking the battleship *Marat*. (The pilot involved in this success was Hans-Ulrich Rudel, by far, the most successful dive-bomber pilot of the war.)

By mid-1941 the war situation was fairly satisfactory for Germany, with the initiative on almost all fronts still firmly in her grasp. However, the steady build-up of British strength was giving concern, especially in the slow but steady increase of RAF bomber strength in the West. Daylight attacks on France and the Low Countries were as yet pinpricks, but the growing weight of night raids on Germany had forced Goering to sanction the rapid build-up of night-fighter forces. This could be achieved largely by adaptation of existing fighters, in particular the Bf 110 and the Ju 88C (itself a *Zerstörer* adaptation of the bomber version).

German Warplanes of World War II

A disruptive white streaking was applied over the standard two-tone Mediterranean camouflage of this Ju 88A-4. The aircraft served with I./KG 54 'Totenkopf Geschwader' (death's head wing). It was based at Bergamo on Sicily in September 1943, during operations against the Allies at Salerno.

This 'sand' painted Ju 88A-10 (L1+EN) of 5. Staffel, Lehrgeschwader 1, based at Heraklion, Crete, in October 1942 for anti-shipping operations in the Aegean and Eastern Mediterranean. Led by Hauptmann Kollewe, this unit had sunk two British destroyers in a convoy on 11 May that year.

A Junkers Ju 88A-4 (4D+DT) of 9./KG 30 'Adler Geschwader' (eagle wing). This Geschwader's III. Gruppe was particularly successful in its attacks on Allied shipping in the Mediterranean during 1941, as illustrated by the tally painted on this Ju 88's fin.

As in the RAF, little serious attention had been given to the night-fighter by the Luftwaffe before the war. When, in 1940, British (and French) bombers carried out a number of desultory night raids, darkness itself seemed to be the best defence – as many bombers simply failed to find their targets. It was, however, the early raids on Berlin, the Ruhr and Italy (the last involving long trips over German-held territory) that spurred the formation of the first *Nachtjagdgeschwader* (night-fighter wings). These were equipped with about 90 Bf 110Cs without any specialised equipment.

More night fighter units form

By June 1941, when three *Geschwader* (NJG 1, 2 and 3) had been formed, the Bf 110D, Bf 110F-4 and Bf 110G-4 variants had been or were being specially developed for night-fighting, as well as small numbers of Do 17s, Do 217s and Ju 88Cs. The fighters could only carry rudimentary radar as yet and relied mainly upon Generalmajor Josef

Kammhuber's *Himmelbett* system of ground radar which guided the night-fighter right up to its target; not surprisingly, early night victories were scarce.

Hs 129 close-support aircraft

Throughout 1941 the German aircraft industry was undergoing an intense period of activity as the earlier requirements bore fruit in the shape of numerous prototypes. In the ground-support role there was the radical twin-engine Henschel Hs 129. This had in fact first flown in 1939 but had been found to be severely underpowered. Upon re-engining with French Gnome-Rhône radials in 1941 the type was ordered into production as the Hs 129B and entered service with the Luftwaffe in 1942.

The big four-engine Heinkel He 177 heavy bomber, whose engines were 'coupled' in two nacelles, had first flown in November 1939 but immediately ran into problems with engine overheating and tail flutter, and it was not

Two Messerschmitt Bf 109Fs of III./JG 54 'Grünherz' (green hearts) serving on the Leningrad front during the autumn of 1941. Commanded by Major Hannes Trautloft, this Geschwader had already achieved its 1,000th air combat victory in August that year.

until August 1941 that the first aircraft were delivered to KG 40 for service trials. Even then Luftwaffe crews complained bitterly about their aircraft, so that further development was required before the He 177A finally carried out its first raids in mid-1942.

Battlefield reconnaissance types

The extraordinary Blohm und Voss Bv 141 was a single-engine short-range reconnaissance aircraft with a conventional fuselage but with the two-seat crew nacelle offset to starboard and with no starboard tailplane. The purpose of this highly unusual configuration was to afford the crew an increased field of vision. The Bv 141 suffered endless problems during its development and, although trials continued during the first three years of the war with more than a dozen prototypes, the type was finally abandoned owing to the fact that the Focke-Wulf Fw 189 was performing the task of quite efficiently.

Of more conventional layout than the Bv 141, the Fw 189

The Messerschmitt Me 210 Zerstörer suffered teething problems during its development and was not considered a success. The variant shown here is the Me 210A-1, armed with two 20-mm cannon and two 7.92-mm (0.31-in) machine-guns. The Me 210 was superseded by the excellent Me 410.

Uhu (Owl) was a twin-boom twin-engine monoplane with a central three/four-seat nacelle. It had flown as long ago as July 1938 (with its designer, Kurt Tank, at the controls), but it was not until 1942 that significant numbers of Fw 189A-1s and Fw 189A-2s started joining Aufklärungsgruppe 10 'Tannenberg' and AufklGr 11 on the Eastern Front.

Another aircraft that was doomed to eclipse at this time was the Messerschmitt Me 210, a Zerstörer that had been conceived in 1937, just as the Bf 110 was joining the Luftwaffe. Great hopes were attached to the Me 210 two-seat twin-engine fighter and a special unit, Erprobungsgruppe 210, was formed early in the summer of 1940 to introduce the aircraft into Luftwaffe service.

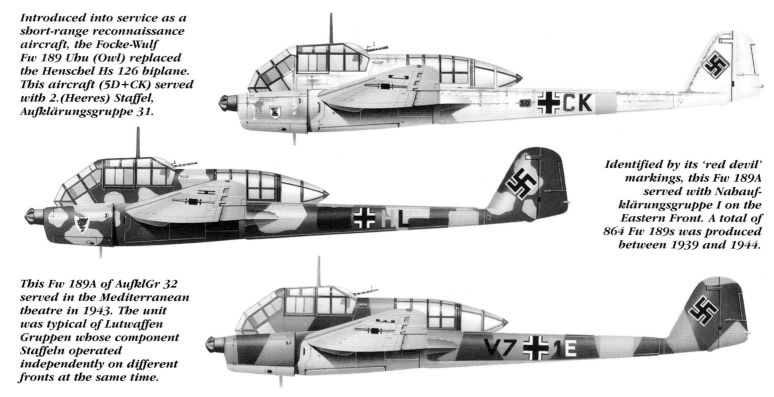

Introduced into service as a short-range reconnaissance aircraft, the Focke-Wulf Fw 189 Uhu (Owl) replaced the Henschel Hs 126 biplane. This aircraft (5D+CK) served with 2.(Heeres) Staffel, Aufklärungsgruppe 31.

Identified by its 'red devil' markings, this Fw 189A served with Nahaufklärungsgruppe I on the Eastern Front. A total of 864 Fw 189s was produced between 1939 and 1944.

This Fw 189A of AufklGr 32 served in the Mediterranean theatre in 1943. The unit was typical of Lutwaffen Gruppen whose component Staffeln operated independently on different fronts at the same time.

Henschel Hs 129

A Henschel Hs 129B-2/R2 of IV.(Pz)/SG 9 based at Czernowotiz, March 1944. Commanded by the brilliant Major Bruno Meyer, this new unit operated on a roving commission over the Eastern Front in 1944.

Henschel Hs 129B-1/R4

Henschel Hs 129B-1/R2
Type: single-seat anti-tank ground-support aircraft
Powerplant: two 700-hp (522-kW) Gnome-Rhône 14M radial piston engines
Performance: maximum speed 253 mph (407 km/h) at 12,750 ft (3830 m); time to 9,845 ft (3000 m) in 7 minutes; service ceiling 29,530 ft (9000 m); range 348 miles (560 km)
Weights: empty 8,783 lb (3984 kg); maximum take-off 11,263 lb (5109 kg)
Dimensions: wing span 46 ft 7 in (14.20 m); length 31 ft 11¾ in (9.75 m); height 10 ft 8 in (3.25 m); wing area 312.16 sq ft (29.0 m²)
Armament: two 20-mm MG 151/20 cannon and two 7.92-mm (0.31-in) MG 17 guns in nose, and one 30-mm MK 101 cannon with 30 rounds in fairing under the nose, plus a bombload of up to 772 lb (350 kg)

Although somewhat underpowered, the Hs 129B was eventually a fairly effective ground attack type.

In the event the Me 210 prototypes ran into so much trouble (as a result of marked directional instability and a tendency to spin at the slightest provocation) that ErprGr 210 never got its intended aircraft. Instead, production aircraft eventually served with II./ZG 1 on the Eastern Front late in 1941, but the toll of accidents was so great that the aircraft was withdrawn. Modifications were attempted in efforts to cure its shortcomings, and a new unit, Versuchs-staffel 210, was given the task of re-introducing the Me 210 into service in 1942, and a number later saw service in Sicily and the Balkans, but attention had meanwhile switched to the Me 410.

The truly outstanding aircraft that entered service in 1941 was Focke-Wulf Fw 190 single-seat, single-engine fighter. Designed by Kurt Tank, this was the only wholly-new combat type introduced into service with the Luftwaffe

This Ju 87B-2 (6G+AC) of Stab II./StG 1 on the Eastern Front late in 1941, wears a temporary camouflage of all-over soluble white paint. The red eagle insignia on the nose was retained after III./StG 51 was re-designated II./StG 1.

This Hs 129B-1 of 4./SG 2 was based at Tripoli, Libya, in December 1942. The Hs 129 proved unsuitable for operations in North Africa owing to difficulties in producing an efficient sand filter for its engines.

With Geschwaderstab markings superimposed over radio codes (NN+KF), this Hs 129B-3 carried a 75-mm BK7.5 tank gun in a jettisonable gondola under the fuselage. The aircraft served with 14.(Panzer) Staffel, SG 9, on the Eastern Front.

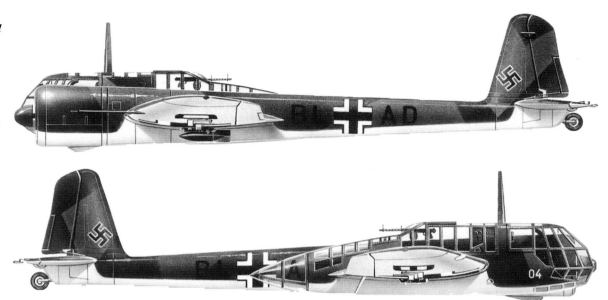

Characterised by a tall angular fin and rudder, the Blohm und Voss Bv 141A-0 (A-04 shown here) underwent trials at Rechlin in 1940 but was dropped in favour of the Focke-Wulf Fw 189 Uhu. Two years later plans were abandoned to form a special unit, Sonderstaffel 141, on the Eastern Front.

after the outbreak of war that was to be built in really significant quantities.

Having made its first flight on 1 June 1939, the aircraft underwent some alteration before entering production at a number of factories at the end of 1940. Against the widely adopted trend by designers, who favoured the sleek contours made possible by inline liquid-cooled engines, Tank designed the Fw 190 around the bulky but very powerful 14-cylinder BMW 801 air-cooled radial, but produced a superbly compact, low-drag installation that from the outset gave the new fighter a significantly greater top speed than that of the Messerschmitt Bf 109.

Me 210 troubles

The Focke-Wulf Fw 190A first joined the Luftwaffe based in France in August 1941. Its appearance came as an unpleasant surprise to the RAF. Eclipsing the Spitfire Mk V which formed the backbone of RAF Fighter Command, the Fw 190 swung the balance of air superiority in the Luftwaffe's favour. Within six months the new fighter came to provide the principal equipment of JG 2 and JG 26 '5chlageter" and successfully protected the German warships *Scharnhorst*, *Gneisenau* and *Prinz Eugen* during their spectacular dash up the English Channel in February 1942. The Fw 190 did not join the Luftwaffe, for operations on the Eastern Front until March 1942 when, in a reconnaissance version, it joined 9.(H)/LG 2.

Contender for the title of the war's most grotesque aircraft, the Blohm und Voss Bv 141 reconnaissance aircraft suffered endless difficulties and was abandoned in 1942 before entering production; the aircraft shown here (NC+RF) was the twelfth prototype, the Bv 141B-04.

The Focke-Wulf Fw 190A came as an unpleasant surprise to the RAF in Western Europe towards the end of 1941. An outstanding and versatile design, it proved more than a match for the Spitfire Mk V. The centreline bomb racks identify these aircraft as fighter-bombers.

The End of Supremacy

As Allied resources were harnessed to halt the German advances at Stalingrad and Alamein, America entered the war and fortunes changed inexorably against the European Axis powers. Henceforth German air power would be almost entirely geared to defence.

In December 1941 the United States of America entered the war against Germany, an event that must have convinced the less fanatically-blinded German leaders that, even if total defeat could be avoided, total victory would be impossible. Already the objective of a quick victory in the East had been compromised by the arrival of the Russian winter. And in North Africa the British were showing themselves generally capable of withstanding the joint armies of Germany and Italy. The Royal Air Force, now equipped with a sizeable force of four-engine Avro Lancasters, Handley Page Halifaxes and Short Stirlings, was beginning to mount devastating attacks on German cities, raids which the Luftwaffe's Nachtjagdverband seemed powerless to prevent. Certainly the objective of a victory in Europe within three years seemed to be receding.

Yet it would be some months before the effects of the USA's entry into the war would be felt. In the meantime the Luftwaffe redoubled its efforts to bring into service new, improved aircraft. The total number of *Jagdgruppen*, equipping with new versions of the Bf 109 and Fw 190, rose in six months by 14 with almost 500 extra aircraft; *Stukageschwader* increased by two with more than 200 aircraft, and *Kampfgruppen* by 11 with more than 300 aircraft.

Airborne gun improvements

Fighter armament was undergoing rapid change. The old MG FF 20-mm cannon had given place to the faster-firing MG 151/20; the rifle-calibre MG 17 was being overtaken by the 13-mm (0.51-in) MG 131, and the 15-mm machine-gun had entered service. More significant was the appearance of the excellent 30-mm MK 108 cannon which was superior to anything the RAF possessed for knocking down heavy bombers.

Defensive armament for bombers had also been improved with the introduction of twin MG 81 guns in place of the previous single MG 17s, and with 20-mm guns

Left: A line-up of Fw 190G-3 fighter-bombers of II. Gruppe Schlactgeschwader 2 'Immelmann', based at Deblin-Irena, Poland, probably in mid-1943. Shown here are 5. Staffel aircraft, some of which are displaying on their cowlings the 'gun-toting Mickey Mouse' emblem of the II. Gruppe.

Below: A Junkers Ju 87G armed with two underwing 37-mm cannon; this version was used to deadly effect against Soviet tanks at the great Battle of Kursk in July 1943. The special ammunition of the cannon was able to penetrate the armour of Soviet T-34 tanks.

German Warplanes of World War II

The 'winged U' badge identifies this Bf 109G-10 as belonging to Jagdgeschwader 3 'Udet'; commanded by Major Wolf-Dietrich Willke, JG 3 was one of the earliest units to receive the Gustav on the Southern Sector of the Russian Front late in 1942.

Bf 109G-2 of 4. Staffel, Jagdgeschwader 54 'Grünherz', based at Siverskaya, North Russian Front, mid-1942. The quartered spinner marking (not frequently used) indicated the first Staffel of II. Gruppe (i.e. 4. Staffel), the Gruppe also being shown by the horizontal red bar.

in movable, mountings. Bombloads were being substantially improved by the introduction of more powerful engines, notably the 1,750-hp (1306-kW) DB 603A and the BMW 801D of similar power. Great progress had also been made with water-methanol and nitrous-oxide power boosting. Engines fitted with these systems were capable of delivering over 2,000 hp (1492 kW) for short bursts.

Night-fighting improvements
In the field of night-fighting, the immediate need was neither for more speed nor for heavier armament, but for improvement in airborne radar, and in 1942 the Messerschmitt Bf 110 night-fighters beginning to join the Luftwaffe were equipped with *Lichtenstein BC* or *Lichtenstein C-1* radars which had a range of about two and a half miles (4 km). By the end of the year the German night-fighter force amounted to 389 aircraft of which at least 300 were Bf 110s. The *Nachtjagdverband* had, during 1942, destroyed more than 800 RAF bombers.

On the Russian front, 1942 witnessed the German army battle its way to the farthest extent of its eastward advance before being hammered to a halt at Stalingrad. The ferocity of the campaign resulted in enormous losses by both sides, although the Bf 109 and, latterly, the Fw 190 retained their superiority over all Soviet aircraft. British and US aircraft were beginning to arrive in fast-increasing numbers, however, being supplied by convoy round the North Cape and from the Middle East.

Enter the 'Gustav'
The most important fighter to join the Luftwaffe during 1942 was the Messerschmitt Bf 109G (affectionately named 'Gustav' by German pilots). Powered by a DB 605A engine rated at 1,475 hp (1,100 kW) with nitrous-oxide boost, the Bf 109G dispensed with the 7.92-mm (0.31-in) guns. mounting twin 13-mm (0.51-in) guns in addition to a variety of alternative wing guns; the most important variant was the Bf 109G-6 with a hub-firing 30-mm cannon. During 1942 the 'Gustav' joined JG2 in France, JG 1 in Germany, JG 3 and JG 52 in southern Russia, JG 5 in Scandinavia, and JG 27, JG 53 and JG 54 in the Mediterranean. Furthermore, III./JG 54 with Bf 109Gs had been brought home to Germany from the East for defence against the growing daylight attacks by American bombers.

A Bf 109G6 of 7./JG 27 flying escort to a Heinkel He 111 during the Aegean campaign of November 1943; at that time III/JG 27 was based at Athens. The characteristic bulges over the nose gun bodies can clearly be seen.

196

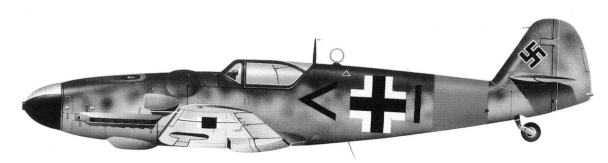

The Bf 109G-14/R2 fighter-bomber suffered from a shortfall in lateral stability while carrying underfuselage bombs; this was rectified by the installation of an enlarged wooden fin and rudder.

The Fw 190A-5/U8 was an early fighter-bomber version of the Fw 190. The aircraft shown here with drop tanks and centreline bomb rack served with I. Gruppe, Schnellkampfgeschwader 10 (fast bomber wing, SKG 10). It was based at Poix, France, for the sneak 'intruder' raids on Britain of the summer of 1943.

The Focke-Wulf Fw 190A continued to increase in numbers in the West, and by August the excellent Fw 190A-4 fighter-bomber had arrived. In that month the Allies launched their seaborne landing at Dieppe, one of whose aims was to attract the Luftwaffe into the air and to engage it with superior forces of Supermarine Spitfire Mk Vs and Mk IXs (hurriedly introduced to counter the Fw 190) and Hawker Typhoons.

Dieppe debacle

In the event neither the Spitfire Mk IX nor the Typhoon were available in adequate numbers. Both types were ineffectually committed to battle, with pilots of Spitfire Mk Vs finding themselves trounced by the new Fw 190s. The German fighter also surprised the Allies with its bombing attacks. All in all, the Dieppe operation proved to be a savage defeat for the RAF.

Also much in evidence at Dieppe was the Dornier Do 217E, which carried out a series of attacks during the Allied incursion. The Do 217E subsequently made heavy raids on Exeter, Norwich, York, Hull, Poole and Grimsby during 1942. Ten days after the start of the Dieppe raid Heinkel He 177A-1s joined in an attack on Bristol, which suffered its worst single incident of the war when a 551-lb (250-kg) bomb dropped from one of these aircraft killed and injured more than 100 people.

It was during 1942 that the Junkers Ju 88 underwent substantial development, much of which was intended to improve its combat potential in the Mediterranean theatre. Junkers Ju 88A-4s of five *Kampfgruppen* were moved to Sicily for operations to eliminate Malta as a British air and naval base, together with a *Gruppe* of Ju 88C intruders for night operations over the island. For some of the raids the bombers carried 2,205-lb (1000-kg) rocket-propelled bombs for attacks on concrete structures. And it was in the numerous heavy attacks on British convoys being sailed to the beleaguered island that the Ju 88 was particularly successful, proving to be too fast for the shipboard Hawker Sea Hurricanes to catch.

Improved Ju 87D

An improved version of the Junkers Ju 87 dive-bomber joined the Luftwaffe at the end of 1941 and thereafter gradually replaced the earlier Ju 87Bs. This was the Ju 87D, powered by the 1,400-hp (1044-kW) Junkers Jumo 211J engine. Obviously little could be done to transform the performance of such a fundamentally 'untidy' aircraft, although local improvements, including refining the nose shape, improving the rear cockpit and giving the aircraft better armour protection, certainly enhanced it as a weapon. The speed was increased by about 10 mph (16 km/h), but it was in the bombload that the Ju 87D benefited; the type

This Fw 190A-8 was flown by Unteroffizier Ernst Schröder of 5. Staffel, Jagdgeschwader 300 in November 1944 as part of the Defence of the Reich force. It was armed with four 20-mm cannon in the wings and two 13-mm (0.51-in) guns in the nose.

German Warplanes of World War II

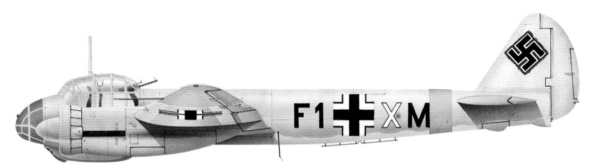

Operating in the Kursk area during during July 1943, this Fw 190A-4/U3 of Gefechtsverband Druschel (Battle Unit, Druschel) carries both staff markings and individual aircraft letter. Oberst Alfred Druschel was awarded the Oak Leaves and Swords to the Knight's Cross. Having served with the Luftwaffe since 1936, he was killed in the Operation Bodenplatte attacks of New Year's Day 1945.

The Ju 88C was a Zerstörer (heavy fighter) version of the Junkers Ju 88. This Ju 88C-6 (F1+XM) served with 4. (Zerstörer) Staffel, Kampfgeschwader 76, and was based at Taganrog in the Ukraine. In an attempt to deceive enemy pilots, the 'solid' nose has been painted to simulate the glazed panels of a standard Ju 88 bomber.

was able to carry a single 3,968-lb (1800-kg) bomb. From May 1942 the first units began to receive the new Stuka variant; these were 1./StG 2 on the Leningrad front and StG 3 in the Western Desert.

Formation of Schlachtgeschwader units

Heavy losses (from ground fire and enemy fighters) among the *Stukaverband* resulted in a net decrease in the Luftwaffe's dive-bomber strength during 1942, despite the new deliveries, and it was only by introduction of such aircraft as the ground-attack Henschel Hs 129 (already mentioned) and of the Fw 190 fighter-bomber that adequate close support for the German armies could be afforded. Indeed the entire *Stukaverband* underwent reappraisal,

Although the Do 217 was a distinct improvement on the much older Do 17, it suffered problems in its development as a dive bomber, and finished up in the level bombing role. Like so many German bombers it suffered from poor defensive armament. This example is a Do 217E-4.

and in May 1942 the new *Schlachtgeschwader* (assault groups) came into being with bomb-carrying Bf 109Fs and Bf 109Gs and the Hs 129; later still the Ju 87 was given an anti-armour attack role, while the Fw 190 replaced it on the *Stukageschwader*, which were in turn renamed *Schlacht-fliegergeschwader* (air attack groups) to embrace all ground support and assault forces.

Improvements and adaptations only

As the Axis advance was battered to a standstill at Stalingrad and Alamein, it became clear to the OKL that no longer could German industry be afforded the luxury of time to evolve and introduce wholly new aircraft, and that henceforth the keynote would be improvement and adaptation, and that only improvements which would not seriously jeopardise volume production of existing types could be countenanced.

There were of course to be significant exceptions to this policy, as will be seen; but, unlike the British and

Above: The Do 217K-1 was normally a night medium bomber. This example bears the insignia of Luftflotte 2 and was allocated directly to Luftflotte headquarters. As such, it was probably employed for reconnaissance duties.

Americans who were able to introduce such wholly new aircraft as the de Havilland Mosquito, North American P-51 Mustang, Hawker Tempest, Republic P-47 Thunderbolt and Lockheed P-38 Lightning, the backbone of the Luftwaffe up to the end of the war would remain the Fw 190, Bf 109, Do 217, Ju 87 and Ju 88, plus one or two others, such as the Me 410, on the point of entering operational service. By the same token, aircraft which had only recently entered service but which were seen to demand wasteful effort to bring them to anything like worthwhile efficiency would be ruthlessly dropped from production or swiftly relegated to second-line duties.

Above: Armed with two 37-mm cannon, the Ju 87G was introduced too late to participate in large numbers in the massive tank battles on the Eastern Front of mid-1943 but later became the scourge of Russian armour.

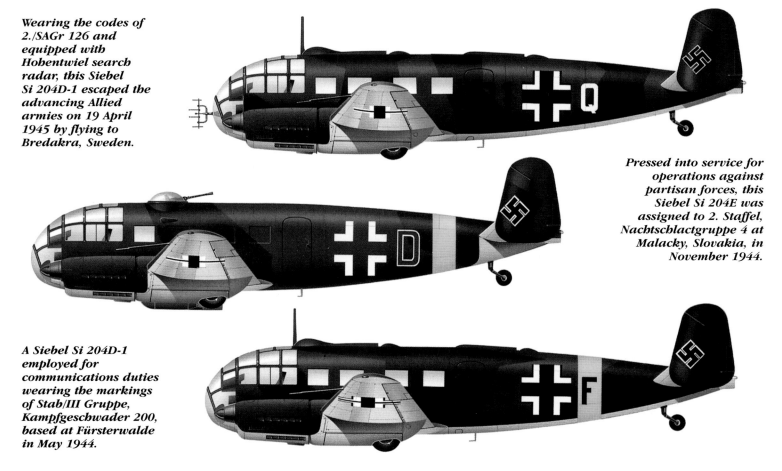

Wearing the codes of 2./SAGr 126 and equipped with Hohentwiel search radar, this Siebel Si 204D-1 escaped the advancing Allied armies on 19 April 1945 by flying to Bredakra, Sweden.

Pressed into service for operations against partisan forces, this Siebel Si 204E was assigned to 2. Staffel, Nachtschlactgruppe 4 at Malacky, Slovakia, in November 1944.

A Siebel Si 204D-1 employed for communications duties wearing the markings of Stab/III Gruppe, Kampfgeschwader 200, based at Fürsterwalde in May 1944.

Junkers Ju 87

> **Junkers Ju 87G-1**
> **Type:** anti-tank aircraft
> **Powerplant:** one 1,400-hp (1044-kW) Junkers Jumo 211J-1 inline piston engine
> **Performance:** maximum speed about 195 mph (314 km/h); cruising speed normally about 118 mph (190 km/h); rate of climb and service ceiling not known, but extremely poor; combat radius about 199 miles (320 km)
> **Weights:** empty about 9,700 lb (4400 kg); maximum take-off about 14,550 lb (6600 kg)
> **Dimensions:** wing span 49 ft 2 in (15.00 m); length 37 ft 8 in (11.50 m); height 12 ft 9 in (3.90 m); wing area 362.60 sq ft (33.69 m²)
> **Armament:** two 37-mm BK 3,7 cannon and one flexible 7.92-mm (0.33-in) MG 81 machine-gun, plus a useful bomb load when the underwing cannon were not being carried

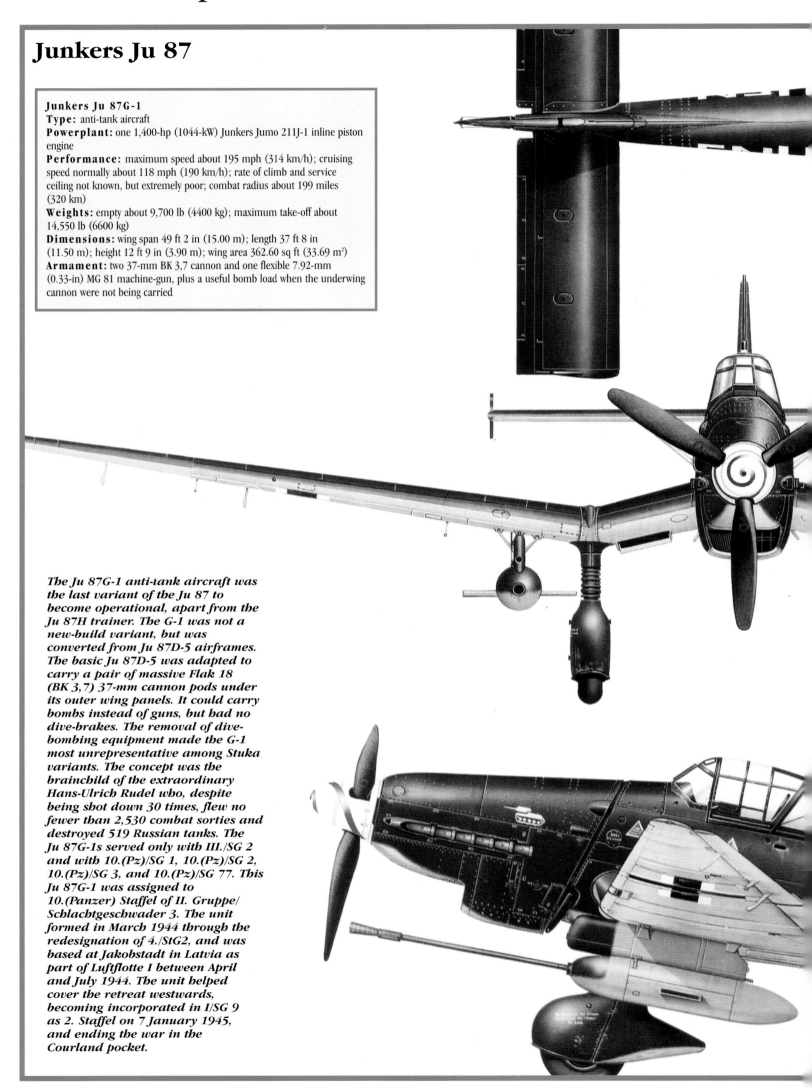

The Ju 87G-1 anti-tank aircraft was the last variant of the Ju 87 to become operational, apart from the Ju 87H trainer. The G-1 was not a new-build variant, but was converted from Ju 87D-5 airframes. The basic Ju 87D-5 was adapted to carry a pair of massive Flak 18 (BK 3,7) 37-mm cannon pods under its outer wing panels. It could carry bombs instead of guns, but had no dive-brakes. The removal of dive-bombing equipment made the G-1 most unrepresentative among Stuka variants. The concept was the brainchild of the extraordinary Hans-Ulrich Rudel who, despite being shot down 30 times, flew no fewer than 2,530 combat sorties and destroyed 519 Russian tanks. The Ju 87G-1s served only with III./SG 2 and with 10.(Pz)/SG 1, 10.(Pz)/SG 2, 10.(Pz)/SG 3, and 10.(Pz)/SG 77. This Ju 87G-1 was assigned to 10.(Panzer) Staffel of II. Gruppe/ Schlachtgeschwader 3. The unit formed in March 1944 through the redesignation of 4./StG2, and was based at Jakobstadt in Latvia as part of Luftflotte I between April and July 1944. The unit helped cover the retreat westwards, becoming incorporated in I/SG 9 as 2. Staffel on 7 January 1945, and ending the war in the Courland pocket.

German Warplanes of World War II

A Junkers Ju 87G-1 of Versuchskommando für Panzerbekampfung (Experimental Detachment for Tank Combat), Tarnewitz, April 1943. Hauptmann Rudel participated in trials with this unit and the following month took a Ju 87G-1 to the Crimea, using it in action for the first time at Temryuk.

1   Spinner
2   Pitch-change mechanism housing
3   Blade hub
4   Junkers VS 11 constant speed airscrew
5   Anti-vibration engine mounting attachments
6   Oil filler point and marker
7   Auxiliary oil tank (5.9-Imp gal/26.8-litre capacity)
8   Junkers Jumo 211J-1 12-cylinder inverted-Vee liquid-cooled engine
9   Magnesium alloy forged engine mount

10 Coolant (Glysantin-water) header tank
11 Ejector exhaust stubs
12 Fuel injection unit housing
13 Induction air cooler
14 Armoured radiator
15 Inertia starter cranking point
16 Ball joint bulkhead fixing (lower)

17 Tubular steel mount support strut
18 Ventral armour (0.315 in/8 mm)
19 Main oil tank (9.9-Imp gal/45-litre capacity)
20 Oil filling point
21 Transverse support frame
22 Rudder pedals

23 Control column
24 Heating point
25 Auxiliary air intake
26 Ball joint bulkhead fixing (upper)
27 Bulkhead
28 Oil tank (6.8-Imp gal/31-litre capacity)
29 Oil filler point and marker (Intava 100)
30 Fuel filler cap
31 Self-sealing starboard outer fuel tank (33-Imp gal/150-litre capacity)

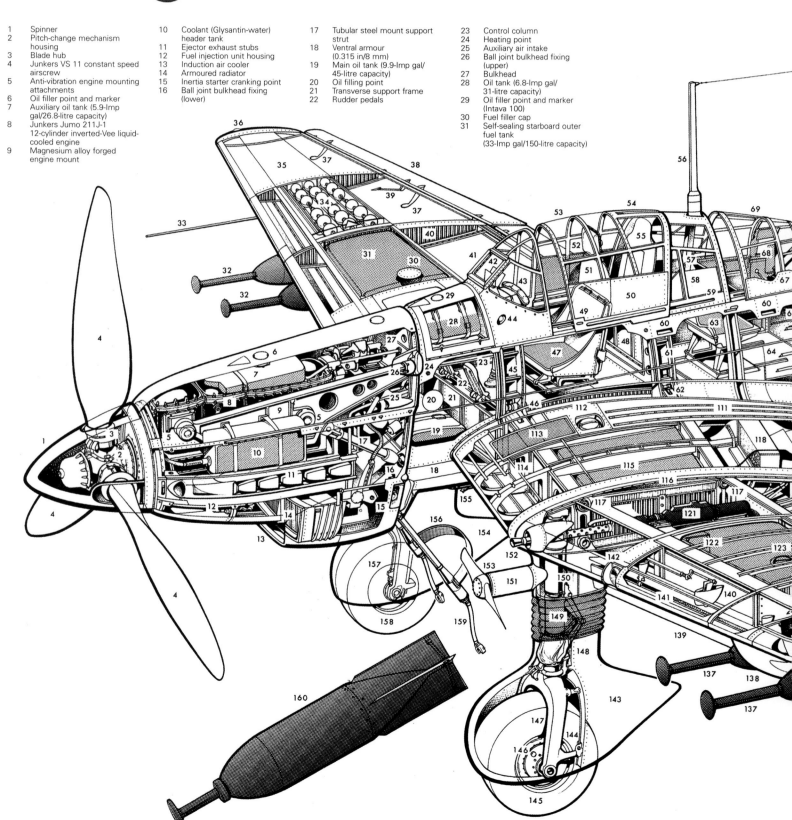

Junkers Ju 87D-3

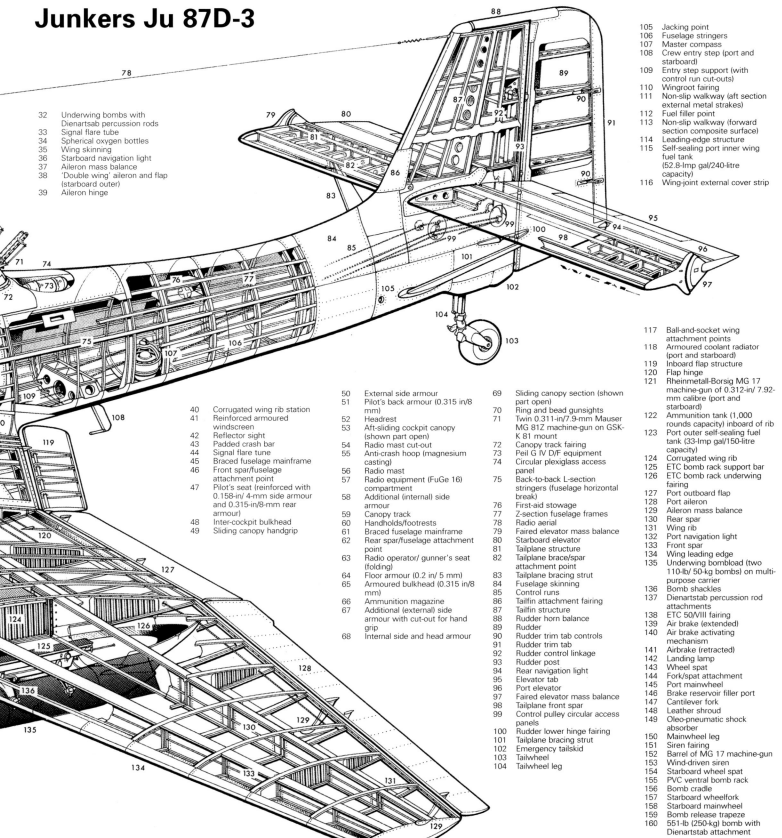

32 Underwing bombs with Dienartsab percussion rods
33 Signal flare tube
34 Spherical oxygen bottles
35 Wing skinning
36 Starboard navigation light
37 Aileron mass balance
38 'Double wing' aileron and flap (starboard outer)
39 Aileron hinge

105 Jacking point
106 Fuselage stringers
107 Master compass
108 Crew entry step (port and starboard)
109 Entry step support (with control run cut-outs)
110 Wingroot fairing
111 Non-slip walkway (aft section external metal strakes)
112 Fuel filler point
113 Non-slip walkway (forward section composite surface)
114 Leading-edge structure
115 Self-sealing port inner wing fuel tank (52.8-Imp gal/240-litre capacity)
116 Wing-joint external cover strip

117 Ball-and-socket wing attachment points
118 Armoured coolant radiator (port and starboard)
119 Inboard flap structure
120 Flap hinge
121 Rheinmetall-Borsig MG 17 machine-gun of 0.312-in/ 7.92-mm calibre (port and starboard)
122 Ammunition tank (1,000 rounds capacity) inboard of rib
123 Port outer self-sealing fuel tank (33-Imp gal/150-litre capacity)
124 Corrugated wing rib
125 ETC bomb rack support bar
126 ETC bomb rack underwing fairing
127 Port outboard flap
128 Port aileron
129 Aileron mass balance
130 Rear spar
131 Wing rib
132 Port navigation light
133 Front spar
134 Wing leading edge
135 Underwing bombload (two 110-lb/ 50-kg bombs) on multi-purpose carrier
136 Bomb shackles
137 Dienartstab percussion rod attachments
138 ETC 50/VIII fairing
139 Air brake (extended)
140 Air brake activating mechanism
141 Airbrake (retracted)
142 Landing lamp
143 Wheel spat
144 Fork/spat attachment
145 Port mainwheel
146 Brake reservoir filler port
147 Cantilever fork
148 Leather shroud
149 Oleo-pneumatic shock absorber
150 Mainwheel leg
151 Siren fairing
152 Barrel of MG 17 machine-gun
153 Wind-driven siren
154 Starboard wheel spat
155 PVC ventral bomb rack
156 Bomb cradle
157 Starboard wheelfork
158 Starboard mainwheel
159 Bomb release trapeze
160 551-lb (250-kg) bomb with Dienartstab attachment

40 Corrugated wing rib station
41 Reinforced armoured windscreen
42 Reflector sight
43 Padded crash bar
44 Signal flare tune
45 Braced fuselage mainframe
46 Front spar/fuselage attachment point
47 Pilot's seat (reinforced with 0.158-in/ 4-mm side armour and 0.315-in/8-mm rear armour)
48 Inter-cockpit bulkhead
49 Sliding canopy handgrip
50 External side armour
51 Pilot's back armour (0.315 in/8 mm)
52 Headrest
53 Aft-sliding cockpit canopy (shown part open)
54 Radio mast cut-out
55 Anti-crash hoop (magnesium casting)
56 Radio mast
57 Radio equipment (FuGe 16) compartment
58 Additional (internal) side armour
59 Canopy track
60 Handholds/footrests
61 Braced fuselage mainframe
62 Rear spar/fuselage attachment point
63 Radio operator/ gunner's seat (folding)
64 Floor armour (0.2 in/ 5 mm)
65 Armoured bulkhead (0.315-in/8 mm)
66 Ammunition magazine
67 Additional (external) side armour with cut-out for hand grip
68 Internal side and head armour

69 Sliding canopy section (shown part open)
70 Ring and bead gunsights
71 Twin 0.311-in/7.9-mm Mauser MG 81Z machine-gun on GSK-K 81 mount
72 Canopy track fairing
73 Peil G IV D/F equipment
74 Circular plexiglass access panel
75 Back-to-back L-section stringers (fuselage horizontal break)
76 First-aid stowage
77 Z-section fuselage frames
78 Radio aerial
79 Faired elevator mass balance
80 Starboard elevator
81 Tailplane structure
82 Tailplane brace/spar attachment point
83 Tailplane bracing strut
84 Fuselage skinning
85 Control runs
86 Tailfin attachment fairing
87 Tailfin structure
88 Rudder horn balance
89 Rudder
90 Rudder trim tab controls
91 Rudder trim tab
92 Rudder control linkage
93 Rudder post
94 Rear navigation light
95 Elevator tab
96 Port elevator
97 Faired elevator mass balance
98 Tailplane front spar
99 Control pulley circular access panels
100 Rudder lower hinge fairing
101 Tailplane bracing strut
102 Emergency tailskid
103 Tailwheel
104 Tailwheel leg

Enemy Pressure Grows

Ringed on almost every side by growing enemy forces, and deprived of Italy's doubtful war effort, Germany faced the spectre of defeat as the Allied air offensive was mounted against her armies in the field and with ever-increasing intensity against her cities.

Throughout the last 30 months of the war, Germany was almost entirely on the defensive. The European mainland was by 1943 under constant air attack by the Americans in daylight and by RAF Bomber Command at night. At last the British had evolved (by means of pathfinding techniques and the bomber stream) methods by which huge fleets of heavy bombers could reach and strike German towns and cities, while heavily armed formations of American Boeing B-17s and Consolidated B-24s were beginning to strike with great accuracy relatively small key targets deep inside Europe.

To counter the night raids the Luftwaffe continued to strengthen its night-fighter defences and in August 1943 introduced a simple but devastatingly effective new weapon, the *schräge Musik* (shrill music, or jazz) installa-

tion of a pair of upward-firing cannon (usually 20-mm) mounted amidships in Messerschmitt Bf 110G-4/R8s and, later, Junkers Ju 88G-6bs.

Night-fighter tactics

The tactics involved overtaking the night bomber from the rear and attacking from beneath (where there were no defensive guns), firing upwards into the engines and fuel tanks. For many months, while the very existence of the new weapon was scarcely suspected by the British, casualties increased rapidly and a number of German *experten* (aces) were frequently adding four, five or more four-engine bombers to their victory tallies on single nights.

A new and deadly night fighter started appearing in the *Nachtjagdgeschwader* in 1943. This was the Heinkel

Left: As Allied bombers began to exact a terrible toll on German cities, the Luftwaffe's fighter leaders struggled to convince their superiors that air defence was now of the utmost priority. Few experienced pilots were left, and the survivors seldom had fuel for their fighters.

Below: The excellent Messerschmitt Me 410 was produced to perform a number of duties. This Me 410A-3 (F6+WK) of 2.Staffel, Aufklärungsgruppe 122, was based at Trapani in May 1943. It was captured by the Allies and shipped over to the USA for evaluation.

He 219 with DB 603A engines and a top speed of 416 mph (670 km/h), and armed with two 30-mm and two 20-mm cannon. The He 219 had narrowly escaped being axed during the reappraisal of new German projects, but survived when it was pointed out that it was the only night-fighter capable of catching the de Havilland Mosquito, which was by 1943 appearing in increasing numbers in the night skies over Germany.

German airborne radar improvements

More significant were the improvements being made in German airborne radar, and by 1943 most Bf 110s, Ju 88s and He 219s were equipped with the FuG 212 *Lichtenstein C-1* with prominent 'toasting fork' aerial array on the nose. The first major setback for the Luftwaffe night defences occurred on the night of 24/25 July 1943 when the RAF started dropping Window, the codename for huge quantities of small metallised foil strips cut to half the wavelength of German radar. Within moments the entire screen provided by ground *Würzburg* and airborne *Lichtenstein*

Ever more frequently, the best of German fighters appeared on Allied gun-camera film during the last two years of the war. Here a Focke-Wulf Fw 190 is struck by cannon fire moments before the pilot baled out.

radars had been blinded by spurious signals. This was but another weapon in the growing armoury of radio countermeasures warfare, and led the Germans to adopt a number of expedients, including the use of day fighters on freelance night patrols for visual interception (not being dependent on radar), and the 'insertion' of Bf 110s into the bomber stream for visual attacks; the former (*Wilde Sau*, wild boar) tactics proved to be very effective on moonlit nights, and the latter (*Zahme Sau*, tame boar) worthwhile in the area of the target where ground fires silhouetted the British bombers.

By day the *Jagdverband* was using every available fighter to attack the big American bomber formations. It had been discovered early on that the B-17 and B-24 were relatively poorly armed in the nose, with the result that the favourite

During the latter half of the war the Bf 110 returned to its originally-intended role, that of 'heavy fighter' (or destroyer). This Bf 110G-2 of 5./ZG 76 was based at Grosenhain late in 1943. It carried four WfrGr 21 (21-cm/8.27-in) rocket launchers under the wings to combat American heavy bomber streams.

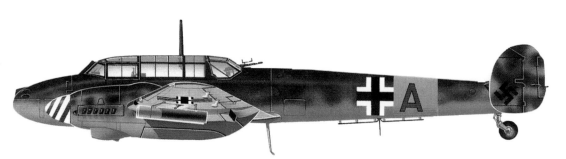

This He 111H-6 (7A+FA) of Gefechtsverband Kuhlmey was based at Imola, Finland in July 1944. The composite combat unit was led by Oberst Kurt Kuhlmey, a brilliant and popular commander who had won distinction flying Ju 87s and Fw 190s on almost every war front. Kuhlmey was awarded the Knight's Cross.

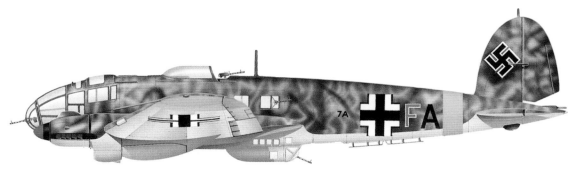

This Ju 88A-14 (Q1+JC), said to be of II./ZG 1, was based in Rumania during April 1944 for anti-shipping operations over the Black Sea; its armament was increased by the addition of a 20-mm MG FF cannon in the nose gondola.

Left: The Heinkel He 219 was one of the most outstanding night-fighters of the war. The He 219A-053 was used as a prototype for the He 219A-5/R1 (the first production version); it carried an armament of two 20-mm and two 30-mm cannon and proved easily capable of knocking down RAF night heavy bombers in large numbers.

Heinkel He 219

Heinkel He 219A-5R1

A Heinkel He 219A (G9+FH) of I./NGJ 1, the first unit to fly the He 219 on operations. The CO, Major Werner Streib, shot down five Lancasters in 30 minutes on the night of 11/12 June 1944.

Heinkel He 219A-7/R1
Type: two-seat high-altitude night-fighter
Powerplant: two 1,800-hp (1343-kW) Daimler Benz DB 603E inline piston engines
Performance: maximum speed 416 mph (670 km/h) at 22,965 ft (7000 m); initial climb rate 1,805 ft (550 m) per minute; absolute ceiling 41,665 ft (1270 m); range 1,243 miles (2000 km)
Weights: empty 24,691 lb (11200 kg); loaded 33,730 lb (15300 kg)
Dimensions: wing span 60 ft 8½ in (18.50 m); length 50 ft 11¾ in (15.54 m); height 13 ft 5½ in (4.10 m); wing area 479.00 sq ft (44.5 m²)
Armament: two 30-mm MK 108 cannon in wing roots, two 30-mm MK 103 and two 20-mm MG 151/20 cannon in ventral gun tray, and two upward-firing 30-mm Mk 108 cannon in rear cockpit

Although by no means an attractive aircraft, the He 219 had a purposeful air. This is an early prototype, possibly the He 219 V11.

*Right: A ground view of a
Gotha Go 244B-3 transport
showing the non-jettisonable
landing gear and the upward-
hinged rear loading door. The
Go 244 was capable of
carrying a Kübelwagen and
six to eight troops.*

method of attack, though demanding nerves of steel, was the head-on pass, and the fast-firing 15-mm and 20-mm cannon of the Messerschmitt Bf 109Gs and Focke-Wulf Fw 190A-5s were extremely effective.

More anti-bomber weapons

A new version of the latter was the Fw 190A-6 which could mount a battery of six 20-mm cannon, while the Fw 190A-6/R6 could carry a single 21-cm (8.3-in) rocket under each wing. Bf 110s, Junkers Ju 88s and Dornier Do 217s were also introduced as bomber-destroyers with large calibre weapons, and there were even plans to introduce such improbable aircraft as the Heinkel He 177 (as the He 177A-5) in the *Zerstörer* role, each with 33 upward-firing rockets. Among the novel, though not particularly successful, tactics was the aerial bombing of American bomber formations by Bf 109Gs and Fw 190s carrying 551-1b (250-kg) bombs, the first American bomber being destroyed in this manner on 22 March 1943.

An early milestone in the daylight defence against American bombers was reached on 17 August 1943 when more than 300 Bf 109s, Bf 110s, Fw 190s, Me 210s and Ju 88s intercepted a similar number of American bombers and destroyed 60 of them, damaging 100 others. On 14 October 228 bombers attacked the ball-bearing factories at Schweinfurt, losing 79 of their number shot down and 121 damaged by the German defences. It was at this point, with losses far outstripping the replacement rate, that the decision was taken to introduce American long-range fighter escorts, but it was some time before the superlative North American P-51 Mustang (which could accompany the bombers all the way to Berlin and back) could be brought into service.

Meanwhile the Fw 190A was being employed in a new role over the British Isles, that of daylight hit-and-run raider. A new unit, SKG10 (*Schnellkampfgeschwader* or

The six-engine Me 323 was a powered version of the Me 321. This example is taking off with the aid of six auxiliary rocket units in addition to its six Gnome-Rhône radials.

Enemy Pressure Grows

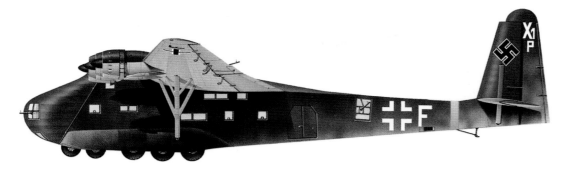

Nothing comparable with the Messerschmitt Me 323 transport was used by the Allies during the war. Owing to its obvious vulnerability it was not employed as an assault aircraft but for heavy-lift duties behind the front line; the Me 323E shown here was flown by 1./TG 5 behind the Southern Sector of the Russian Front late in 1943.

This Ju 88G-7a (2Z+AW) of IV./NJG 6, winter 1944-45, has had its squared-off vertical tail painted to represent the curved version of the earlier Ju 88C night fighter. The Ju 88G wears the muted blotching of Luftwaffe night fighters during the late war period.

fast bomber group), was flying Fw 190A-4/U8s with a 1,102-1b (500-kg) bomb under the fuselage and underwing drop tanks. Heavy damage was done in such raids on London, Eastbourne, Canterbury, Hastings and Ashford, and caused RAF Fighter Command to deploy quite disproportionate fighter strength to counter raids by seldom more than about a dozen Focke-Wulfs.

Defeat in North Africa

In North Africa and the Mediterranean, 1943 was a disastrous year for the Axis. After a period in which the Bf 109F and Bf 109G gained the upper hand, before the Second Battle of Alamein, the build-up of overwhelming Allied air strength crushed the Luftwaffe and Regia Aeronautica. It was during the Second Battle of Alamein that a young German pilot, Hauptmann Hans-Joachim Marseille, became the highest-scoring fighter pilot against the Western Allies. He racked up 158 air victories before being killed in an accident in a Bf 109G on 30 September 1942. By the time

the Axis armies had been crowded into the northern tip of Tunisia early in 1943, the Luftwaffe was almost powerless. Even when in June two *Gruppen* (II. and IV./SKG 10) of Fw 190A-4/U8s were transferred from France to Sicily, they proved unable to affect the course of battle. Desperate measures were adopted to supply fuel and ammunition to the Axis forces in Tunisia, unescorted formations of Junkers Ju 52/3ms and the huge six-engine Messerschmitt Me 323 transports being flown across the Sicilian narrows in daylight. On more than one occasion these formations were spotted by Allied fighter pilots who knocked them into the sea with consummate ease.

Me 323 Gigant - the giant transport

The Me 323 Gigant transport was capable of carrying 130 troops (or more in an emergency) and had been developed from the Me 321 Gigant (giant) glider principally as a supply aircraft for moving men and materiel on the Eastern Front, and was typical of the expedients being

Six Junkers Jumo engines identified the Me 323E-2/U1 which also introduced a power-operated nose turret housing a 13-mm (0.51-in) machine-gun; similar guns were also located in the cabin windows.

209

adopted by Germany at this stage of the war. Significantly it was never intended as an assault glider in the same concept as the British Airspeed Horsa and General Aircraft Hamilcar gliders. It is worth mentioning in passing here that for towing the huge Me 321 glider the Luftwaffe began by using trios of Bf 110s but later produced the extraordinary Heinkel He 111Z Zwilling (twin); this was, in effect, a pair of He 111 bombers joined together with a new centre wing on which a fifth engine was added.

Missile pioneering

Before leaving the war in the Mediterranean, one other aspect of Luftwaffe operations should be mentioned, namely the successful introduction of the radio-controlled rocket-assisted glide bombs, of which the Henschel Hs 293 was the best known. This missile consisted of a winged bomb, powered by a Walter 109 liquid-fuel rocket. The missile had a launch weight of 2,304 lb (1045 kg), of which 1,102 lb (500 kg) was explosive. The initial carrier aircraft

was the Do 217E-5, the bomber carrying a single Hs 293 under the wing. The weapon entered service with II./KG 40 and II./KG 100 on the west coast of France in August 1943. These units were transferred to the south of France in the following month and were used to no mean effect against Allied shipping in the Mediterranean, particularly during the Anzio landings. Other launch aircraft for Hs 293As included Heinkel He 111H-12s, He 177A-3s and He 177A-5s, Focke-Wulf Fw 200Cs, and Dornier Do 217Ks, Do 217Ms and Do 217Rs.

Another missile used with success was the controlled-trajectory armour-piercing X-1 *Fritz X* bomb. With a launch weight of 3,461 lb (1570 kg), these bombs were first carried by aircraft of III./KG 100, this unit being responsible

After the four-engine prototype Messerschmitt Me 323 was found to be underpowered, six Gnome-Rhône radials were fitted in the Me 323 V2 (second prototype) shown here. The structure of this huge aircraft was of welded steel tubing and wood, with fabric and wood covering.

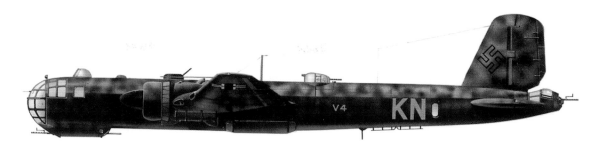

A Heinkel He 177A-5 (V4+KN) of II. Gruppe, Kampfgeschwader 1 'Hindenburg' based at Prowehren, East Prussia in mid-1944. Led by Oberstleutnant Horst von Riesen, KG 1 assembled about 90 of these bombers for attacks on Russian communications and military concentrations.

In May 1943 III. Gruppe of Zerstörergeschwader 1 became one of the first units to receive the Messerschmitt Me 410 Hornisse. This Me 410A-1 was flown by 9.Staffel from Gerbini.

for the sinking of the battleship *Roma* after Italy's capitulation in September 1943.

In northern Europe a new medium bomber joined in operations against the UK. This was the Junkers Ju 188, an extensively redesigned development of the excellent Ju 88 which, in the interests of maximum production, had itself been changed very little in four years. The Ju 188, powered initially by two 1,600-hp (1194-kW) BMW 801L and later by 1,700-hp (1268-KW) BMW 801D or G engines, had a top speed of 311 mph (500 km/h), which was not much more than the Ju 88, but could carry a bombload of up to 6,614 lb (3000 kg) or two torpedoes. With sharply pointed wings the German aircraft also appeared in reconnaissance form on the Russian front in 1943, and underwent continuous development right up to the end of the war, culminating in such versions as the Ju 188S-1/U close-support aircraft with 50-mm anti-tank cannon, and the Ju 188T, a 435-mph (700-km/h) reconnaissance version.

The final 'Zerstörer'

As already stated, the Messerschmitt Me 210 had proved a failure in service, and this aircraft was one of the casualties of the swingeing cuts imposed on Luftwaffe projects in 1942; a radical development, the Me 310, was also abandoned in favour of the Me 410, which gave much better

promise. Powered by DB 603A engines in lengthened nacelles, the Me 410 Hornisse (hornet) entered service in Germany and Italy in May 1943 with bomber, reconnaissance. and *Zerstörer Gruppen* simultaneously. With a top speed of 388 mph (625 km/h) the new aircraft proved a tough opponent, and versions existed which could carry two 2,205-lb (1000-kg) bombs internally, or were armed with a single 50-mm gun or combinations of 30-mm, 20-mm and 15-mm guns. Me 410s were particularly active in raids over the UK during 1943-44, proving capable of being caught only by Mosquito night-fighters.

Increased pressure

The inexorable turn of fortune for the German forces in the East, following the debacle at Stalingrad, was accompanied by greatly increased pressure on the Luftwaffe. By the spring of 1943 the fruits of Russian industrial expansion for war purposes were evidenced with huge deliveries of such aircraft as the Ilyushin Il-2 *Shturmovik* ground-support machine but, more significantly, by the appearance of the Lacochkin La-5, an excellent radial-engine fighter of similar appearance and performance to the Fw 190. Henceforth Soviet forces would exercise an initiative to select their own battlegrounds and apply sufficient strength to overwhelm the local German forces.

Displaying one of many ad hoc winter camouflage schemes applied 'in the field' on the Russian Front, this Gustav (a Bf 109G-6) flew with IV. Gruppe, Jagdgeschwader 5, at Petsamo during the winter of 1943-44.

A short-finned Bf 109G-14 of IV./JG 53. The unit was commanded by Major Günther von Maltzahn and was heavily engaged in operations in the Mediterranean during 1943-44. Ultimately components were withdrawn for the defence of Germany.

German Warplanes of World War II

Junkers Ju 88

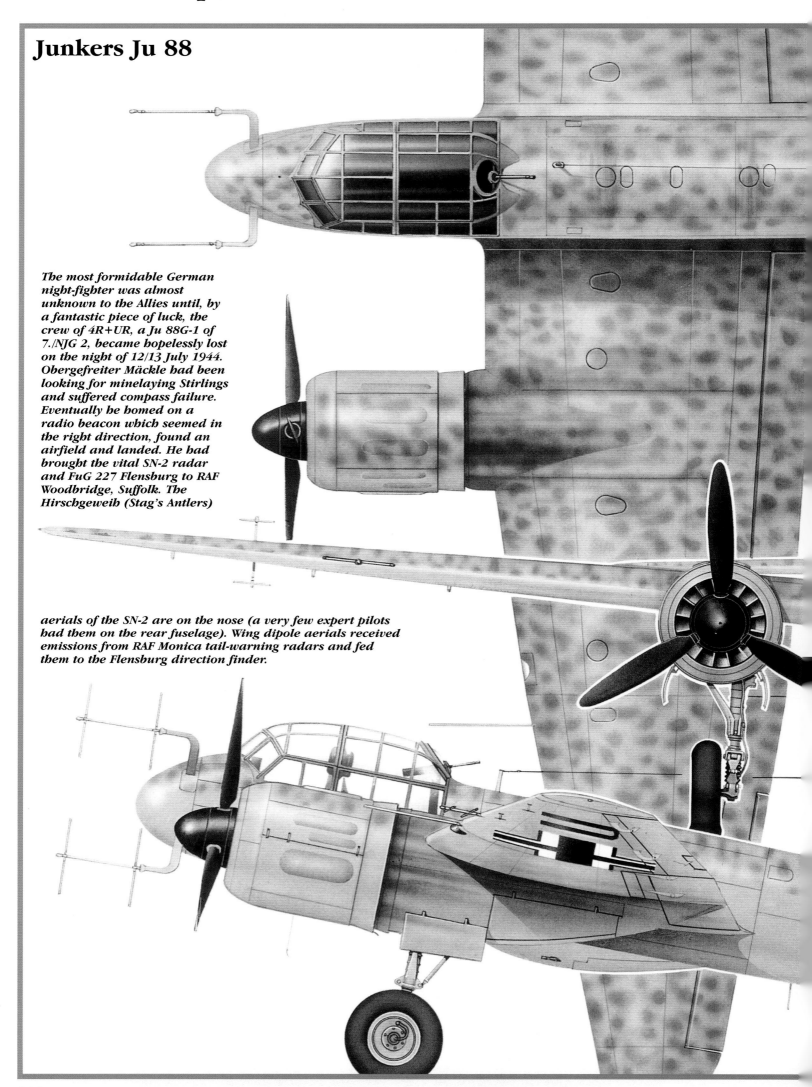

The most formidable German night-fighter was almost unknown to the Allies until, by a fantastic piece of luck, the crew of 4R+UR, a Ju 88G-1 of 7./NJG 2, became hopelessly lost on the night of 12/13 July 1944. Obergefreiter Mäckle had been looking for minelaying Stirlings and suffered compass failure. Eventually he homed on a radio beacon which seemed in the right direction, found an airfield and landed. He had brought the vital SN-2 radar and FuG 227 Flensburg to RAF Woodbridge, Suffolk. The Hirschgeweih (Stag's Antlers)

aerials of the SN-2 are on the nose (a very few expert pilots had them on the rear fuselage). Wing dipole aerials received emissions from RAF Monica tail-warning radars and fed them to the Flensburg direction finder.

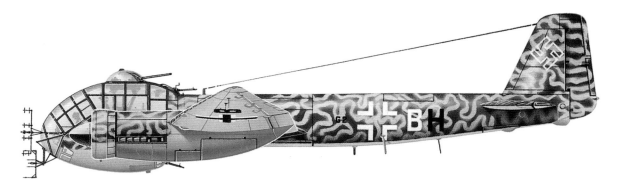

A Junkers Ju 188D-2 photo reconnaissance aircraft of 1.(F)/124, equipped with FuG 200 search radar and based at Kirkenes in northern Norway during 1944. This unit provided intelligence about Allied North Cape convoys for torpedo operations by KG 26.

Junkers Ju 88G-1
Type: three-seat night-fighter
Powerplant: two 1,700-hp (1268-kW) BMW 801D-2 14-cylinder radial piston engines
Performance: maximum speed 356 mph (573 km/h) with SN-2 array but no upward-firing guns; maximum endurance on internal fuel 4 hours; service ceiling 29,000 ft (8840 m)
Weights: empty (typical) 20,020 lb (9081 kg); normal loaded 28,870 lb (13095 kg); overload 32,385 lb (14690 kg)
Dimensions: wing span 65 ft 7 in (20.00 m); length (excluding radar) 47 ft 8 in (14.54 m), (including SN-2 aerials) 54 ft 1 in (16.50 m); height 15 ft 11 in (4.85 m); wing area 586.63 sq ft (54.50 m²)
Armament: (typically) four 20-mm MG 151 cannon in ventral compartment each with 200 rounds

Junkers Ju 88G-1

1   Starboard navigation light
2   Wingtip profile
3   FuG 227 Flensburg radar receiver antenna
4   Starboard aileron
5   Aileron control runs
6   Starboard flaps
7   Flap-fairing strip
8   Wing ribs
9   Starboard outer fuel tank (91-Imp gal/ 415-litre capacity)
10 Fuel filler cap
11 Leading-edge structure
12 Annular exhaust slot
13 Cylinder head fairings
14 Adjustable nacelle nose ring
15 Twelve-bladed cooling fan
16 Propeller boss
17 Variable-pitch VS 111 wooden propeller
18 Leading-edge radar array
19 FuG 220 Lichtenstein SN-2 intercept radar array
20 Nose cone

21 Forward armoured bulkhead
22 Gyro compass
23 Instrument panel
24 Armoured glass windscreen
25 Folding seat
26 Control column
27 Rudder pedal/brake cylinder
28 Control runs
29 Pilot's armoured seat
30 Sliding window section
31 Headrest
32 Jettisonable canopy roof section
33 Gun restraint
34 Wireless-operator/ gunner's seat
35 Rheinmetall Borsig MG 131 machine-gun (0.51-in/13-mm calibre)
36 Radio equipment (FuG 10P HF, FuG 16ZY VHF, FuG 25 IFF)
37 Ammunition box (500 rounds of 0.51-in/ 13-mm)
38 FuG 220 Lichtenstein SN-2 indicator box
39 FuG 227 Flensburg indicator box

40 Control linkage
41 Bulkhead
42 Armoured gunmount
43 Aerial post traverse check
44 Fuel filler cap
45 Whip aerial
46 Forward fuselage fuel tank (105-Imp gal/ 480-litre capacity)
47 Fuselage horizontal construction joint
48 Bulkhead
49 Fuel filler cap
50 Aft fuselage fuel tank (230-Imp gal/1045-litre capacity)
51 Access hatch
52 Bulkhead
53 Control linkage access plate
54 Fuselage stringers
55 Upper longeron
56 Maintenance walkway

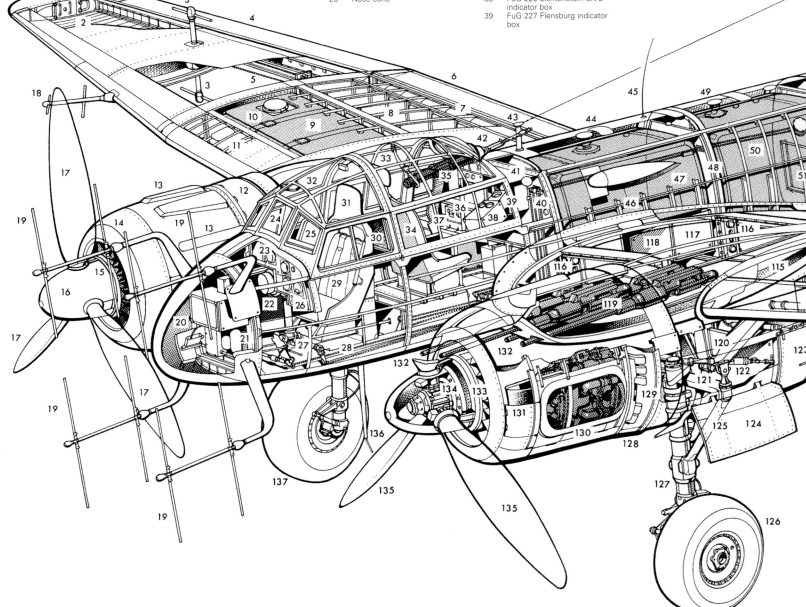

The Ju 88 really came into its own as a night-fighter when equipped with the schräge Musik (Jazz Music) armament of upward-firing cannon. This Ju 88G-6b (9W+CL) belonged to I./NGJ 10 and was based at Ingolstadt in December 1944.

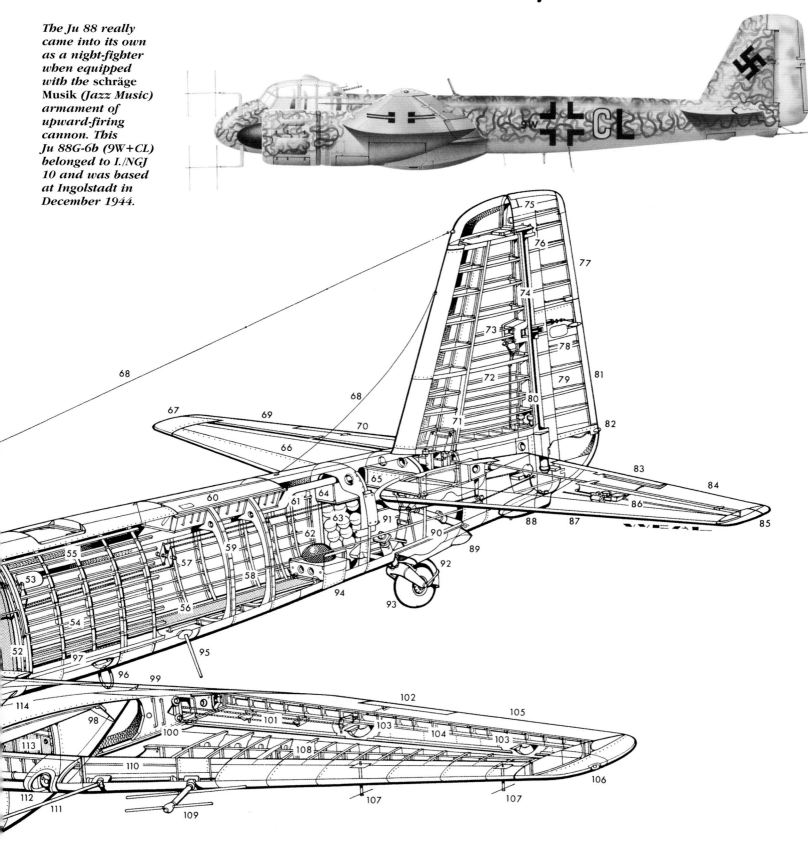

57	Control linkage	75	Rudder mass balance	92	Mudguard
58	Horizontal construction joint	76	Rudder upper hinge	93	Tailwheel
59	Z-section fuselage frames	77	Rudder tab (upper section)	94	Access hatch
60	Dinghy stowage	78	Inspection/ maintenance	95	Fixed antenna

57	Control linkage
58	Horizontal construction joint
59	Z-section fuselage frames
60	Dinghy stowage
61	Fuel vent pipe
62	Master compass
63	Spherical oxygen bottles
64	Accumulator
65	Tailplane centre section carry-through
66	Starboard tailplane
67	Elevator balance
68	Aerial
69	Starboard elevator
70	Elevator tab
71	Tailfin forward spar/ fuselage attachment
72	Tailfin structure
73	Rudder actuator
74	Rudder post
75	Rudder mass balance
76	Rudder upper hinge
77	Rudder tab (upper section)
78	Inspection/ maintenance handhold
79	Rudder structure
80	Tailfin aft spar/ fuselage attachment
81	Rudder tab (lower section)
82	Rear navigation light
83	Elevator tab
84	Port elevator
85	Elevator balance
86	Elevator tab actuator
87	Heated leading edge
88	Tail bumper/fuel vent outlet
89	Tailwheel doors
90	Tailwheel retraction mechanism
91	Shock absorber leg
92	Mudguard
93	Tailwheel
94	Access hatch
95	Fixed antenna
96	D/F loop
97	Lower longeron
98	Nacelle/flap fairing
99	Port flap
100	Wing centre/outer section attachment point
101	Aileron controls
102	Aileron tab (port only)
103	Aileron hinges
104	Rear spar
105	Port aileron
106	Port navigation light
107	FuG 101a radio altimeter antenna
108	Wing structure
109	Leading-edge radar array
110	Forward spar
111	Pitot head
112	Landing lamp
113	Mainwheel well rear bulkhead
114	Port outer fuel tank location (91-Imp gal/ 415-litre capacity)
115	Ventral gunpack (offset to port)
116	Ball-and-socket fuselage/wing attachment points
117	Port inner fuel tank location (934-Imp gal/ 425-litre capacity)
118	Ammunition boxes for MG 151 cannon (200 rpg)
119	Mauser MG 151/20 cannon (four) of 20-mm calibre
120	Mainwheel leg retraction yoke
121	Leg pivot member
122	Mainwheel door actuating jack
123	Mainwheel door (rear section)
124	Mainwheel door (forward section)
125	Leg support strut
126	Port mainwheel
127	Mainwheel leg
128	Annular exhaust slot
129	Exhaust stubs (internal)
130	BMW 801D air-cooled radial engine (partly omitted for clarity)
131	Annular oil tank
132	Cannon muzzles (depressed 5°)
133	Twelve-bladed cooling fan
134	Propeller mechanism
135	Variable-pitch wooden VS 111 propeller
136	FuG 167 antenna
137	Starboard mainwheel

Based at Werneuchen during the summer of 1944, this Fw 190A-6/R11 of 1.NGJ 10was flown by Knight's Cross holder Oberleutnant Hans Krause. The Wilde Sau (Wild Boar) insignia incorporates the pilot's nickname 'Illo'. Note the Neptun radar aerials. Krause scored 28 night victories.

Fw 190A-5 of II./JG 54 'Grünherz', based at Petseri, Estonia, during the spring of 1944. In this instance the yellow fuselage band was a 'theatre marking' denoting the Eastern Front.

Bearing a diminutive form of the wasp insignia, this Me 410B-2/U2/R4 was assigned to Zerstörergeschwader 1. The R4 conversion pack increased the forward armament of this version to no less than eight 20-mm cannon. The 'U' suffix in a designation referred to the application of an Umrüst-Bausätze (factory conversion kit) to the basic airframe, while 'R' related to Rüstsätzen (field conversion sets). These typically added revised equipment or weapons to an aircraft, the Rüstsätzen being added in the field, by regular groundcrew at operational bases, the Umrüst-Bausätze at the factory.

A Gotha Go 244B-1 powered glider. Aircraft of this type were used by KGrzbV 104 in Greece and KGrzbV 106 in Crete during 1942, but when flown in North Africa were very vulnerable to anti-aircraft fire and were quickly withdrawn.

These tactics imposed considerable strain upon the Luftwaffe's air supply units, and all manner of improvisation was taken to bolster the overworked *Transportgruppen*. The Heinkel He 111, by now recognised as being slow and vulnerable as a bomber, was pressed into service as a transport. It was first used as such during the Stalingrad operations, ancient He 111D and He 111F versions being joined by the He 111P and He 111H. Nevertheless, in the face of Soviet local air superiority, casualties were very heavy, no fewer than 165 He 111s being lost in a single month.

New transport types

Among other aircraft pressed into service as transports to join the Ju 52/3m, Me 323 and Ju 90 were the Arado Ar 232, Focke-Wulf Fw 200, Gotha Go 244 (a powered version of the Go 242 glider), Junkers Ju 252, Ju 290 and Ju 352, and Messerschmitt Me 264; most of these aircraft existed only in prototype or pre-production form.

In the great armoured Battle of Kursk of July 1943 the pattern of future ground-support operations was set. The advent of the excellent Russian T-34 tank in huge numbers brought about the creation of *Schlachtfliegergeschwader*

equipped primarily with the Fw 190, and other ad hoc units, such as armoured-fighter *Staffeln* within fighter groups (for example PzjAg/JG 51 'Mölders'). An offshoot of this new tactical concept was the development of the Night Assault Groups (*Nachtschlachtgeschwader*) whose task was to range over and behind the Soviet lines dropping light bombs and causing widespread disorganisation.

Night assault types

In due course about 15 such *Geschwader* were formed, not all on the Eastern Front, and flew an extraordinary variety of aircraft including the Arado Ar 66, Caproni Ca 314, Dornier Do 17, Fiat CR.42, Focke-Wulf Fw 158, Fokker C-V, Gotha Go 145, Henschel Hs 126, Heinkel He 46 and 50, Polikarpov Po-2 and Siebel Si 204.

By early 1944, as an Allied landing in western Europe obviously appeared imminent, as the Allies fought their way northwards in Italy and as Russia gradually beat back the German armies in the East, the Western air forces were piling on the agony from the air over the homeland. The perimeter of the Third Reich was now beginning to shrink, and the spectre of assault from enemies on all sides was now a reality.

The ugly Arado Ar 232B-0 was a four-engine development of the twin-engine Ar 232A of which only prototypes were produced. Nicknamed Tausendfüssler (millipede), a small number of aircraft served on special duties on the Eastern Front in 1944; the aircraft shown was flown by Transport-Staffel 5.

A Gotha Go 244B wearing the markings of 4./KGrzbV 106 early in 1943; by this time however the unit had almost entirely re-equipped with the Junkers Ju 52/3m.

Defence of the Reich

With British, American and Russian armies closing in on the frontiers of the German homeland, the Luftwaffe was forced to concentrate on desperate measures to combat the great bombing armadas that threatened to pulverise city after city into smoking ruin.

While the realists among Germany's air defence planners pressed for single-minded concentration upon the best Luftwaffe fighters, the Nazi leaders still pinned their faith on miraculous terror and retaliation weapons. At the beginning of 1944 development still continued of a huge six-engine bomber, the Junkers Ju 390 (which during trials reached to within 12 miles/20 km of New York before returning safely to its base in France); but even this was abandoned in favour of weapons to strike at targets nearer at hand.

When the Allies eventually launched their great invasion in Normandy in June 1944, there were inadequate Luftwaffe forces on the spot to dispute air superiority, most of the bombers in France being deployed for maritime operations over the Atlantic. Rapid redeployment brought together about 16 *Gruppen* of Fw 190As, including some of the new armoured-assault Focke-Wulf Fw 190A-8/R7s of IV. (Stürm)/JG 3, and several of Messerschmitt Bf 109Gs. Reconnaissance over the invasion area was undertaken by Bf 109G-8s of 3./NAGr 12. In due course German bombers

began attempts to attack the swiftly expanding beachhead, Hs 293-armed Dornier Do 217s attacking a number of key bridges, but British and American air attacks had already destroyed most of the Junkers Ju 88s and Junkers Ju 188s on their French bases.

Flying bomb attacks

Meanwhile a new form or air warfare was being introduced with the launching of the Fieseler Fi 103 (or V1) flying-bombs against southern England (and later Paris and Brussels). Development of these unmanned, pulse jet-powered missiles had gone ahead for almost two years in the face of Allied air attacks on their experimental establishments in Germany. The first weapons were launched against London from sites in northern France shortly after the Allies landed in Normandy, and launches continued for several months until these sites were overrun or flattened by the heavy air attacks mounted against them.

There followed another phase at the end of 1944 in which the bombs were launched from the air by Heinkel

Left: Despite its heavy armament and greatly superior speed, the Messerschmitt Me 262 jet fighter was on several occasions engaged and shot down by Allied fighters (such as the P-51 Mustang and Hawker Tempest); this is a gun-camera frame from a USAAF P-51.

Below: The Focke-Wulf Ta 152 was potentially the best German piston-engined fighter ever built but only appeared in small numbers in the very last weeks of the war; illustrated here is the Ta 152C V7 which was flown in March 1945. Its top speed was in the region of 435 mph (700 km/h).

German Warplanes of World War II

The big Junkers Ju 390 was designed as an ultra-long range heavy bomber. The first prototype made its maiden flight in August 1943; the second prototype, carrying search radar and heavy gun armament, flew with Fernaufklärungsgruppe 5 from Mont de Marsan to within 12 miles (20 km) of New York.

During the final days of the Third Reich Heinkel He 111s were employed to drop supplies to isolated German forces. This He 111H-20 (5J+GH) belonged to I./KG-4 'General Wever' based at Dresden-Klotzsche in April 1945.

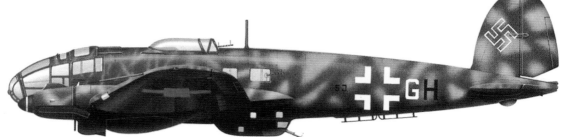

He 111s of KG 3 'Blitz' and KG 53 'Legion Condor' (although one such raid had been carried out against Southampton as early as 7 July). With one of these unwieldy weapons carried under its wing root, the He 111 proved to be exceedingly vulnerable and these flying-bomb carriers suffered heavy casualties from the guns of de Havilland Mosquito night-fighters. By the end of the war some 30,000 flying-bombs had been produced, of which 2,400 hit London and a similar number fell on Antwerp; around 5,000 others struck areas in England, France, Belgium and the Netherlands.

As the flying-bomb offensive reached its climax in September 1944, examples of Hitler's second terror

weapon, the A4 (or V2) rocket, were beginning to fall in southern England. These weapons, the first in the era of ballistic missiles, were launched from sites in the Netherlands and, carrying a warhead of some 2,149 lb (975 kg), fell to earth some 200 miles (320 km) distant.

Around 6,000 V2s were produced, of which 1,054 fell in the UK and 1,675 on the Continent. Although they, and the flying-bombs, were unpleasant but forlorn attempts to dis-

As the Allies overran the V1 launching sites the Luftwaffe resorted to carrying the weapon beneath Heinkel He 111s. An He 111H-22 of I./KG 53, with a flying bomb under its starboard wing, is seen here being inspected by German officials in October 1944.

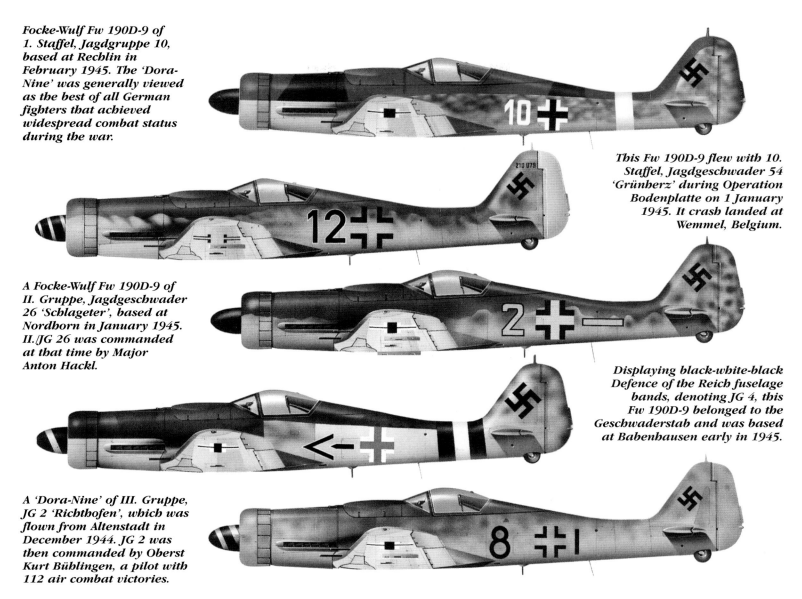

Focke-Wulf Fw 190D-9 of 1. Staffel, Jagdgruppe 10, based at Rechlin in February 1945. The 'Dora-Nine' was generally viewed as the best of all German fighters that achieved widespread combat status during the war.

This Fw 190D-9 flew with 10. Staffel, Jagdgeschwader 54 'Grünherz' during Operation Bodenplatte on 1 January 1945. It crash landed at Wemmel, Belgium.

A Focke-Wulf Fw 190D-9 of II. Gruppe, Jagdgeschwader 26 'Schlageter', based at Nordhorn in January 1945. II./JG 26 was commanded at that time by Major Anton Hackl.

Displaying black-white-black Defence of the Reich fuselage bands, denoting JG 4, this Fw 190D-9 belonged to the Geschwaderstab and was based at Babenhausen early in 1945.

A 'Dora-Nine' of III. Gruppe, JG 2 'Richthofen', which was flown from Altenstadt in December 1944. JG 2 was then commanded by Oberst Kurt Bühlingen, a pilot with 112 air combat victories.

courage the Allies in their war aims, they nevertheless represented only the spearhead of other substantial research work that was being undertaken on other devastating weapons. These would almost certainly have been used had the Allied invasion of Europe been delayed beyond mid-1944.

As it was, the Allied air attacks on the V1 and V2 (*Vergeltungswaffe* 1 and 2, or Retaliation Weapons 1 and 2) launch sites proved only a short respite from the devastating raids on German cities, and it was to counter these that greatest effort was now made by the Luftwaffe, a phase generally referred to as the Defence of the Reich. But for the intervention by Hitler himself, the most effective

Powered by a DB 603G driving a huge four-bladed propeller, the high altitude Fw 190 V18 was intended as a prototype for the proposed Fw 190 C-series. Equipped with turbo-supercharger and cabin pressurisation, this aircraft reportedly had a top speed in excess of 480 mph (772 km/h).

German Warplanes of World War II

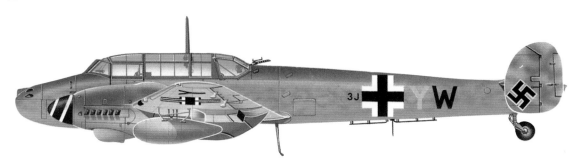

A Bf 110G-2 (3J+YW) of 12./NGJ 3, based at Stavanager, Norway in April 1945. The diminutive Geschwader codes were adopted by most night fighter units during the last 18 months of the war.

fighter that could have significantly blunted the Allied air attacks on Germany (particularly by day) was the Messerschmitt Me 262 jet-propelled fighter and also, given time, the Messerschmitt Me 163 rocket interceptor.

The first combat jets

Germany had been hard at work since before the war to develop a turbojet engine, and had indeed flown a research jet aircraft, the Heinkel He 178, on 27 August 1939. Various jet prototypes had flown since, including the He 280 fighter, but it was the Me 262 which was destined to become the world's first combat jet fighter. Powered by two 1,862-1b (8.28-kN) thrust Junkers 109-004A turbojets, this aircraft had first flown on 18 July 1942 and before long Hitler was insisting that it should be developed as a bomber. By mid-1944 about 25 prototypes and development aircraft had been completed before Hitler reluctantly sanctioned the development of fighter versions.

By the end of the year the first operational units had been formed, including JG 7 'Nowotny' (with fighters) and IV./KG 51 'Edelweiss' (with bombers). Casualties were at first high, a consequence of hurried development and training, but gradually the Me 262 was recognised by the Allies as being a dangerous new opponent with its speed of 536 mph (868 km/h) and armament of four 30-mm cannon.

Me 262 operations

During the last four months of the war a new unit, Jagdverband 44 (staffed by some of the best fighter pilots of the Luftwaffe and led by General Adolf Galland), was equipped with Me 262s and in the space of a month, during which seldom more than six aircraft were available, destroyed at least 45 Allied aircraft. Me 262s were also delivered to a number of bomber units whose personnel received hurried training as fighter pilots, including KG(J)/6, KG(J)/27 and I.KG(J)/54. Other Me 262s (the

Left: The Heinkel He 178 was the world's first aircraft to fly purely on turbojet power; its first true flight took place at Marienebe on 27 August 1939 with Flugkapitän Erich Warsitz at the controls.

Below: The first flight of a jet-powered aircraft designed from the outset as a fighter was made by the Heinkel He 280 V1, seen here during that flight on 2 April 1941 with Fritz Schäfer at the controls; the He 280 did not however reach production.

Defence of the Reich

Displaying the red 'Defence of the Reich' fuselage band, this Fw 190A-8 served with I. Gruppe, Jagdgeschwader 1, at Twenthe, Holland, in December 1944. The muted fuselage markings were commonplace among Luftwaffe aircraft at this late stage of the war.

This Fw 190F-8 of Schlachtgeschwader 4 was among the many aircraft assembled for Operation Bodenplatte on 1 January 1945. It flew from Köln-Wahn and Köln-Ostheim.

An Arado Ar 234B-2 of 9./KG 76, commanded by Major Hans-Georg Bätcher and based at Rheine and Achmer. II./KG 76 became fully operational in February 1945, losing its first aircraft in action on the 24th to P-47s near Segelsdorf.

Right: An Arado Ar 234B Blitz twin-jet bomber. A photo recce served with I./Versuchsverband Oberbefehlshaber der Luftwaffe in 1944. The type proved flew numerous high altitude sorties over Britain and was wholly immune from interception by Allied fighters.

Below: A Messerschmitt Me 262B-1a/U1 two-seat jet night fighter with Lichenstein SN-2 radar; aircraft of this type were flown by Kommando Welter in defence of Berlin during March 1945. The This example was captured by the Allies and shipped to the USA.

The prototype for the Focke-Wulf Fw 190 'Dora' series was the Fw 190 V53, powered by a Jumo 213A inline engine in annular cowling. Armament comprised four 20-mm wing cannon and two 13-mm (0.51-in) guns in the nose.

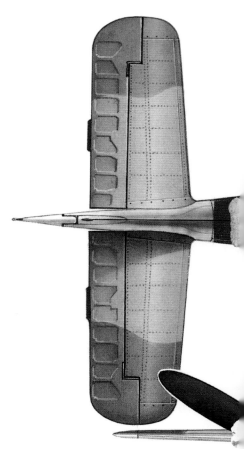

Focke-Wulf Fw 190

The Fw190A-8 'Panzerbock' was one of the major production versions of the Focke-Wulf Fw 190. This example is shown in its basic configuration and carrying a 300-litre (66-Imp gal) drop tank. The tank obscures the fact that the ETC 501 centre-line store rack was moved forward 20 cm (7.9 in). Armament comprised four long-barrelled 20-mm MG 151/20 cannon in the wings and two MG 17 machine-guns in the nose. 'Red 19' was flown by Unteroffizier Ernst Schroder of 5. Staffel/Jagdgeschwader 300, in Defence of the Reich operations during October and November 1944. II (Sturm) Gruppe of JG 300 had been formed with Fw 190A-8s in July 1944 under Major Kurd Peters (awarded the Knight's Cross in October that year), and was one of the fighter units opposing the Western Allies during the invasion of Europe, adopting Wilde Sau night-fighting tactics during the autumn. Staffelkapitän of 5. Staffel was Oberleutnant Klaus Bretschneider, also a Knight's Cross holder, of whose 31 combat victories 14 were gained during Wilde Sau sorties, and who was shot down and killed in combat with P-51s on 24 December 1944.

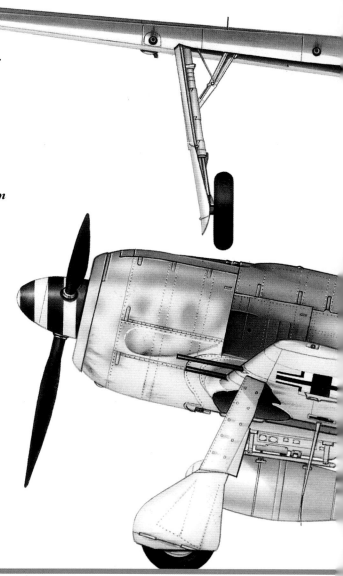

Focke-Wulf Fw 190A-8
Type: single-seat fighter and fighter-bomber
Powerplant: one 2100-hp (1567-kW) BMW 801D-2 14-cylinder radial piston engine
Performance: maximum speed (clean) 408 mph (654 km/h); initial climb rate 2,363 ft (720 m) per minute; normal range 500 miles (805 km); service ceiling 37,400 ft (11400 m)
Weights: empty 7,000 lb (3170 kg); maximum loaded 10,800 lb (4900 kg)
Dimensions: wing span 34 ft 5½ in (10.50 m); length 29 ft 0 in (8.84 m); height 13 ft 0 in (3.96 m); wing area 196.98 sq ft (18.3 m²)
Armament: (A-8/R2) two 7.9-mm (0.31-in) MG 17 machine-guns, four 20-mm MG 151/20 cannon, one SC 500 (500-kg/1,102-lb) and two SC 250 (250-kg/551-lb) bombs, or one 300-litre (66-lmp gal) drop tank

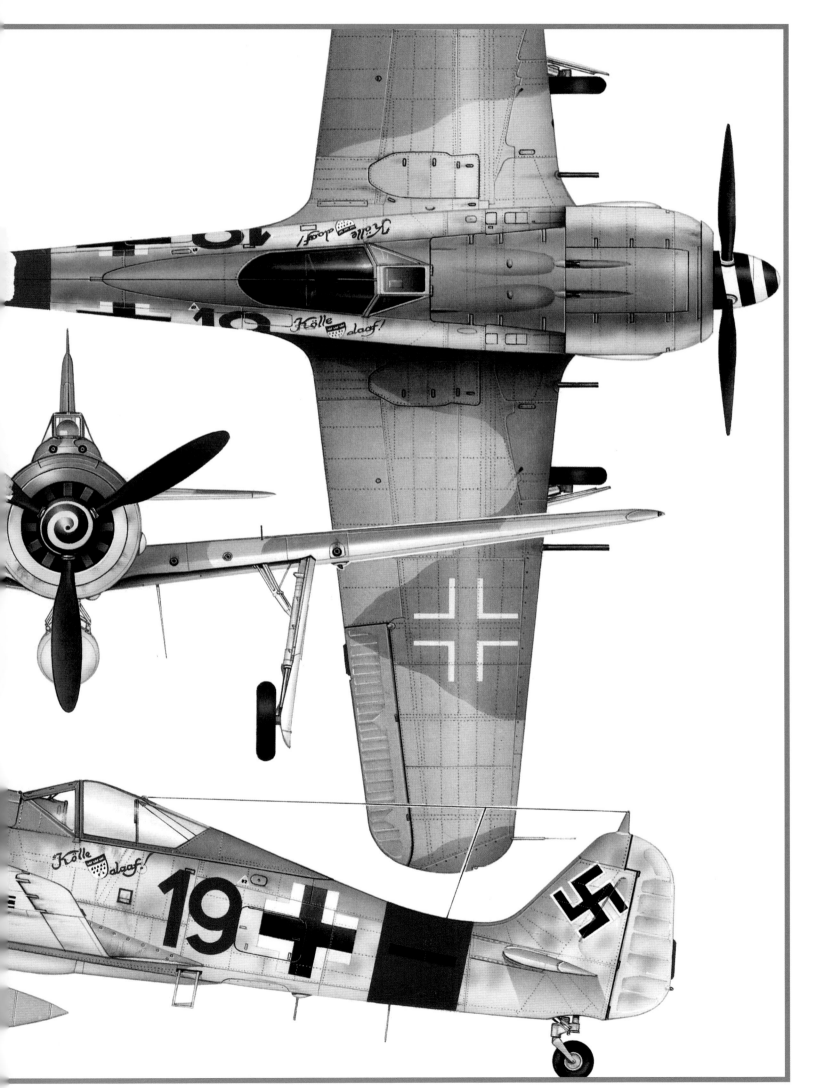

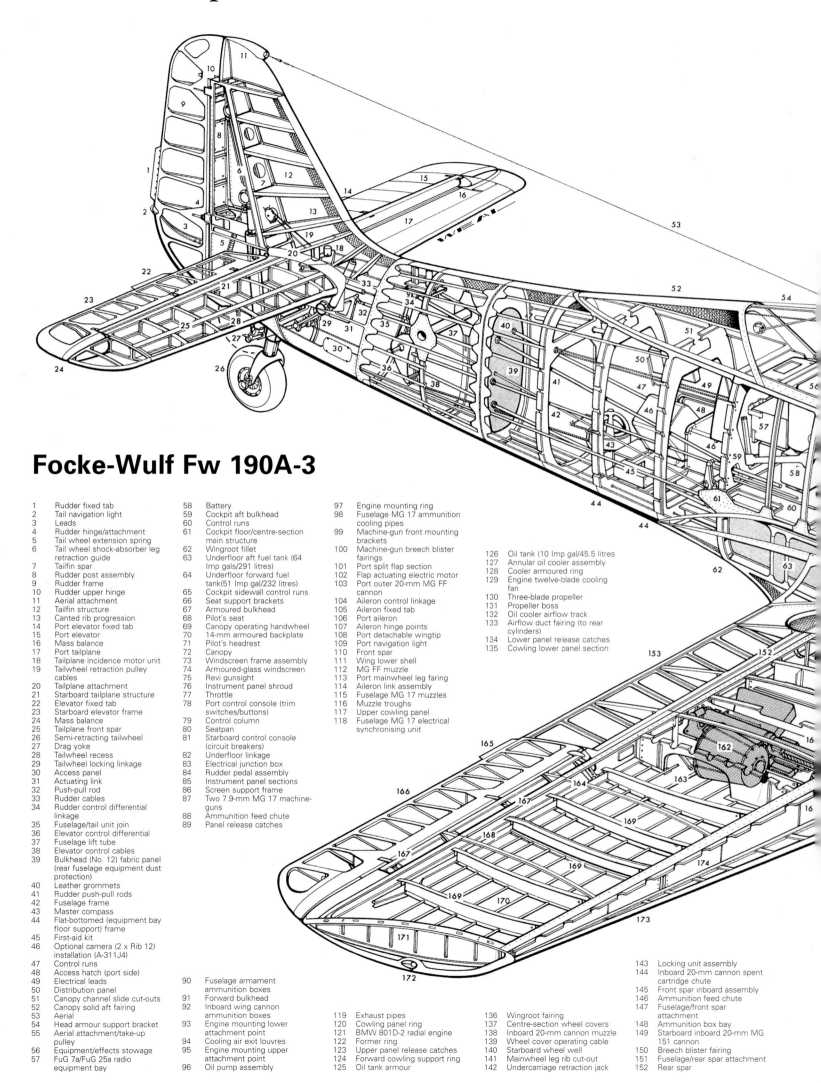

Focke-Wulf Fw 190A-3

1 Rudder fixed tab
2 Tail navigation light
3 Leads
4 Rudder hinge/attachment
5 Tail wheel extension spring
6 Tail wheel shock-absorber leg retraction guide
7 Tailfin spar
8 Rudder post assembly
9 Rudder frame
10 Rudder upper hinge
11 Aerial attachment
12 Tailfin structure
13 Canted rib progression
14 Port elevator fixed tab
15 Port elevator
16 Mass balance
17 Port tailplane
18 Tailplane incidence motor unit
19 Tailwheel retraction pulley cables
20 Tailplane attachment
21 Starboard tailplane structure
22 Elevator fixed tab
23 Starboard elevator frame
24 Mass balance
25 Tailplane front spar
26 Semi-retracting tailwheel
27 Drag yoke
28 Tailwheel recess
29 Tailwheel locking linkage
30 Access panel
31 Actuating link
32 Push-pull rod
33 Rudder cables
34 Rudder control differential linkage
35 Fuselage/tail unit join
36 Elevator control differential
37 Fuselage lift tube
38 Elevator control cables
39 Bulkhead (No. 12) fabric panel (rear fuselage equipment dust protection)
40 Leather grommets
41 Rudder push-pull rods
42 Fuselage frame
43 Master compass
44 Flat-bottomed (equipment bay floor support) frame
45 First-aid kit
46 Optional camera (2 x Rib 12) installation (A-311J4)
47 Control runs
48 Access hatch (port side)
49 Electrical leads
50 Distribution leads
51 Canopy channel slide cut-outs
52 Canopy solid aft fairing
53 Aerial
54 Head armour support bracket
55 Aerial attachment/take-up pulley
56 Equipment/effects stowage
57 FuG 7a/FuG 25a radio equipment bay

58 Battery
59 Cockpit aft bulkhead
60 Control runs
61 Cockpit floor/centre-section main structure
62 Wingroot fillet
63 Underfloor aft fuel tank (64 Imp gals/291 litres)
64 Underfloor forward fuel tank(51 Imp gal/232 litres)
65 Cockpit sidewall control runs
66 Seat support brackets
67 Armoured bulkhead
68 Pilot's seat
69 Canopy operating handwheel
70 14-mm armoured backplate
71 Pilot's headrest
72 Canopy
73 Windscreen frame assembly
74 Armoured-glass windscreen
75 Revi gunsight
76 Instrument panel shroud
77 Throttle
78 Port control console (trim switches/buttons)
79 Control column
80 Seatpan
81 Starboard control console (circuit breakers)
82 Underfloor linkage
83 Electrical junction box
84 Rudder pedal assembly
85 Instrument panel sections
86 Screen support frame
87 Two 7.9-mm MG 17 machine-guns
88 Ammunition feed chute
89 Panel release catches

90 Fuselage armament ammunition boxes
91 Forward bulkhead
92 Inboard wing cannon ammunition boxes
93 Engine mounting lower attachment point
94 Cooling air exit louvres
95 Engine mounting upper attachment point
96 Oil pump assembly

97 Engine mounting ring
98 Fuselage MG 17 ammunition cooling pipes
99 Machine-gun front mounting brackets
100 Machine-gun breech blister fairings
101 Port split flap section
102 Flap actuating electric motor
103 Port outer 20-mm MG FF cannon
104 Aileron control linkage
105 Aileron fixed tab
106 Port aileron
107 Aileron hinge points
108 Port detachable wingtip
109 Port navigation light
110 Front spar
111 Wing lower shell
112 MG FF muzzle
113 Port mainwheel leg faring
114 Aileron link assembly
115 Fuselage MG 17 muzzles
116 Muzzle troughs
117 Upper cowling panel
118 Fuselage MG 17 electrical synchronising unit

119 Exhaust pipes
120 Cowling panel ring
121 BMW 801D-2 radial engine
122 Former ring
123 Upper panel release catches
124 Forward cowling support ring
125 Oil tank armour

126 Oil tank (10 Imp gal/45.5 litres
127 Annular oil cooler assembly
128 Cooler armoured ring
129 Engine twelve-blade cooling fan
130 Three-blade propeller
131 Propeller boss
132 Oil cooler airflow track
133 Airflow duct fairing (to rear cylinders)
134 Lower panel release catches
135 Cowling lower panel section

136 Wingroot fairing
137 Centre-section wheel covers
138 Inboard 20-mm cannon muzzle
139 Wheel cover operating cable
140 Starboard wheel well
141 Mainwheel leg rib cut-out
142 Undercarriage retraction jack

143 Locking unit assembly
144 Inboard 20-mm cannon spent cartridge chute
145 Front spar inboard assembly
146 Ammunition feed chute
147 Fuselage/front spar attachment
148 Ammunition box bay
149 Starboard inboard 20-mm MG 151 cannon
150 Breech blister fairing
151 Fuselage/rear spar attachment
152 Rear spar

This Fw 190A-3 had been relegated to fighter training by the last months of the war. It served with Erhanzungsgeschwader 1 (Replacement Fighter Wing, EJG 1) at Bad Eibling in May 1945.

153 Starboard flap assembly
154 Inboard solid ribs
155 Rotating drive undercarriage retraction unit
156 Radius rod hinge
157 Outboard 20-mm cannon muzzle
158 Mainwheel leg strut mounting assembly
159 Undercarriage actuation drive motor

160 Starboard outboard 20-mm MG FF cannon
161 Front spar assembly
162 Ammunition drum
163 Rib cut-out
164 Aileron control linkage
165 Aileron fixed tab
166 Starboard aileron frame
167 Aileron hinge points
168 Rear spar
169 Wing lower shell outer 'floating ribs'

1945

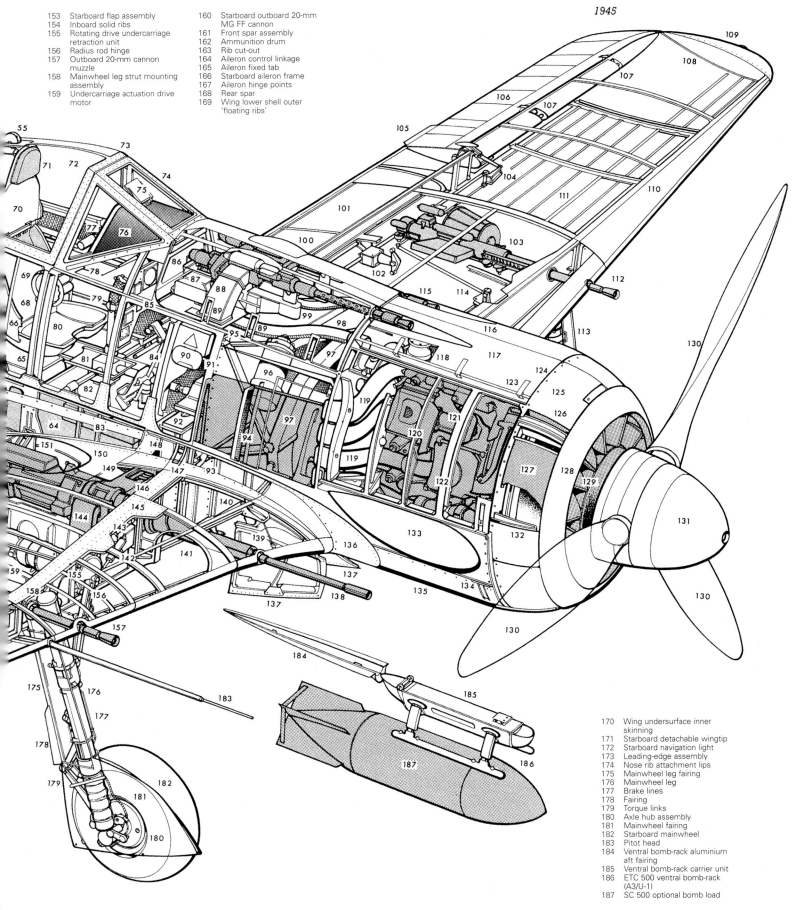

170 Wing undersurface inner skinning
171 Starboard detachable wingtip
172 Starboard navigation light
173 Leading-edge assembly
174 Nose rib attachment lips
175 Mainwheel leg fairing
176 Mainwheel leg
177 Brake lines
178 Fairing
179 Torque links
180 Axle hub assembly
181 Mainwheel fairing
182 Starboard mainwheel
183 Pitot head
184 Ventral bomb-rack aluminium aft fairing
185 Ventral bomb-rack carrier unit
186 ETC 500 ventral bomb-rack (A3/U-1)
187 SC 500 optional bomb load

227

This Me 163B-1 wears the Geschwaderzeichen of JG 400; the badge displays a rocket-powered flea and the words 'Wie ein Floh, aber Oho! (Only a flea, but Oh-Oh!). The prominent 'T' and 'C' stencils on the aircraft indicated refuelling points for its two liquid fuels, T-Stoff and C-Stoff respectively. Accidental contact between the two fuels resulted in catastrophic results.

Me 262B-la/U1) were developed and used operationally as two-seat radar-equipped night-fighters in the defence of the German capital, Berlin.

Another aircraft that entered service as a jet bomber was the twin-jet Arado Ar 234 Blitz (lightning) and this equipped KG 76 during the last three months of the war. Its top speed of 461 mph (742 km/h) rendered it almost immune from interception by Allied fighters and there were plans to introduce a four-jet version, the Ar 234C; a night-fighter version saw service before the end of the war.

An even more imaginative interceptor was the Messerschmitt Me 163 Komet rocket aircraft which started to equip a special fighter unit, JG 400, in mid-1944 near Leipzig. This extraordinary aircraft, with a top speed of 596 mph (960 km/h), an armament of two 30-mm cannon and an endurance of only 8 minutes under full power, was dogged by handling hazards with its extremely sensitive rocket fuels, and many pilots lost their lives in shattering explosions on the ground following fuel leakage. However, although some 300 Komets were produced, they destroyed fewer than a dozen enemy aircraft. Certainly no Allied fighter could match them in air combat.

One other expedient in air defence is worth mentioning here, the small single-jet Heinkel He 162 Volksjäger (or people's fighter), or Salamander as it was often termed. With an armament of two 30-mm cannon, it was a single-

Messerschmitt Me 163

Messerschmitt Me 163B Komet
Type: rocket-powered target-defence interceptor
Powerplant: one Walter HWK 509A-1 or A-2 rocket motor pump-fed with hyperbolic (spontaneously reacting) T-stoff and C-stoff, with high-altitude thrust of 3,748 lb st (16.67 kN)
Performance: maximum speed about 510-520 mph (830 km/h) at low levels, rising to 597 mph (960 km/h) above 9,845 ft (3000 m); initial climb 16,080 ft (4900 m) per minute; service ceiling 39,370 ft (12000 m); maximum rocket endurance (allowing for periods at reduced thrust) 7 minutes 30 seconds; practical range about 80 miles (130 km) not allowing for combat
Weights: empty 4,190 lb (1900 kg); maximum take-off 9,502 lb (4310 kg)
Dimensions: wing span 30 ft 7 in (9.40 m); length 19 ft 2 in (5.85 m); height (on take-off dolly) 9 ft 0 in (2.76 m); wing area 199.1 sq ft (18.50 m²)
Armament: two 30-mm Rheinmetall MK 108 cannon each with 60 rounds

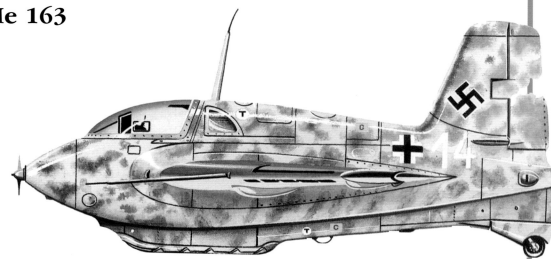

The Messerschmitt Me 163B-1 Komet rocket interceptor suffered all the problems of radical design in conditions of overwhelming chaos and privation in late-war Germany.

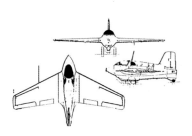

Messerschmitt Me 163B

Right: Operational Me 163B-1 Komets of Jagdgeschwader 400, the only combat unit to fly the extraordinary little fighter.

Defence of the Reich

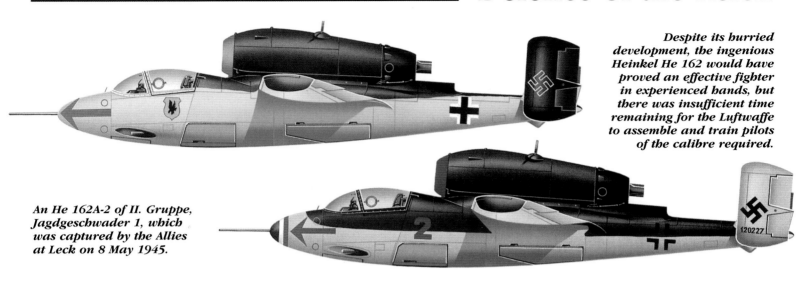

Despite its hurried development, the ingenious Heinkel He 162 would have proved an effective fighter in experienced hands, but there was insufficient time remaining for the Luftwaffe to assemble and train pilots of the calibre required.

An He 162A-2 of II. Gruppe, Jagdgeschwader 1, which was captured by the Allies at Leck on 8 May 1945.

Displaying a green 'Defence of the Reich' fuselage band, this Messerschmitt Bf 109K-4 served with I. Gruppe, Jagdgeschwader 27 at Rheine in December 1944. The application of the 'Afrika' badge, reminiscent of happier hunting by JG 27 in 1941, is somewhat ironic.

seat aircraft built largely of wood for ease and speed of production; the BMW 109-003 engine was mounted on top of the fuselage behind the cockpit. He 162s were issued to Einsatzkommando Bär (commanded by Oberst Heinz Bär, a pilot who gained 220 air victories during the war) and later to JG 1. By the end of the war about 275 aircraft had been flown and a further 800 were nearing completion.

While these advanced aircraft were evidence of Germany's enormous technological potential, the chaotic conditions brought about by shortage of materials and destruction of her research and manufacturing facilities ensured greater dependence upon established aircraft, albeit aircraft with considerable improvement.

Piston-engine developments

The splendid Messerschmitt Bf 109G had been joined in service by the Bf 109K with boosted DB 605D engine, the Bf 109K-4 having a top speed of 452 mph (728 km/h) and the Bf 109K-6 an armament of three 30-mm cannon and two 13-mm (0.51 -in) machine-guns. As a macabre postscript to this superb fighter, the final operation which it

fought during the war was by Rammkommando Elbe on 7 April 1945, when 120 Bf 109s took off to ram American bombers in an approaching raid; only 15 returned.

Enter the 'Dora-Nine'

The Focke-Wulf Fw 190 appeared in much developed form during the autumn of 1944 with a boosted Jumo 213A inline engine in a lengthened radial-type cowling. This version, the 'long-nose' Fw 190D (of which the Fw 190D-9, or 'Dora-Nine', was the most widely used) had a top speed of 426 mph (685 km/h) and was certainly a match for any Allied fighter. Large numbers of Fw 190D-9s were completed but, like so many other operations, dire shortages of fuel kept most of them grounded during the final desperate weeks of the Defence of the Reich. The 'Dora-Nine' was generally regarded as the best of all Germany's piston-engined fighters of the war and became the foundation for Kurt Tank's Ta 152. This was a excellent high-altitude fighter with a top speed of 472 mph (760 km/h) at over 41,010 ft (12500 m), which was just reaching fighter units at the end of the war.

The Focke-Wulf Ta 152 was potentially one of the best German fighters of the war but only appeared in numbers during the very last weeks of the war Illustrated here is the Ta 152C V7. Intended primarily as a Zerstörer, the Ta 152C series featured short-span wings and the Daimler-Benz DB 603 engine, a big improvement in terms of power over the Jumo 213. The V7 prototype, otherwise known as the Ta 152C-0/R11, featured Rüstsätz bad-weather equipment and an MW 50-boosted DB 603EM engine.

Messerschmitt Me 262

This Messerschmitt Me 262A-1a wears the markings of 9.Staffel of Jagdgeschwader 7, based at Parchim in March 1945 under 1.Jagddivision of I Jagdkorps operating in the defence of the Reich. After capture at the end of the war, this particular aircraft, Nr 500491, was given the code FE-111 by the technical branch of the USAAF for evaluation. In the course of 1979 the aircraft was stripped down, refurbished and rebuilt in over 6,000 hours of work, and placed on display at the National Air and Space Museum, Washington, DC, where it remains to this day. The illustration beautifully portrays the Me 262's sleek lines. The airframe alone, and in particular the wing design, was considered by the Allies to be far ahead of their own attainments in the field of high-speed flight.

Messerschmitt Me 262A-1a
Type: single-seat air-superiority fighter
Powerplant: two Junkers Jumo 004B-1, -2 or -3 axial-flow turbojets each rated at 1,984 lb (8.83 kN) static thrust
Performance: maximum speed 514 mph (827 km/h) at sea level, 532 mph (856 km/h) at 26,245 ft (8000 m); initial climb rate 3,937 ft (1200 m) per minute; service ceiling above 40,000 ft (12190 m); range 652 miles (1050 km) at 29,530 ft (9000 m)
Weights: empty 8,378 lb (3795 kg); empty equipped 9,742 lb (4413 kg); maximum take-off 14,080 lb (6387 kg)
Dimensions: wing span 40 ft 11 in (12.50 m); length 34 ft 9 in (10.58 m); height 12 ft 7 in (3.83 m); wing area 234 sq ft (21.73 m²)
Armament: four 30-mm Rheinmetall-Borsig MK 108A-3 cannon with 100 rounds per gun for the upper pair and 80 rounds per gun for the lower pair, plus provision for 12 R4M air-to-air rockets on racks under each wing

Messerschmitt Me 262-1a

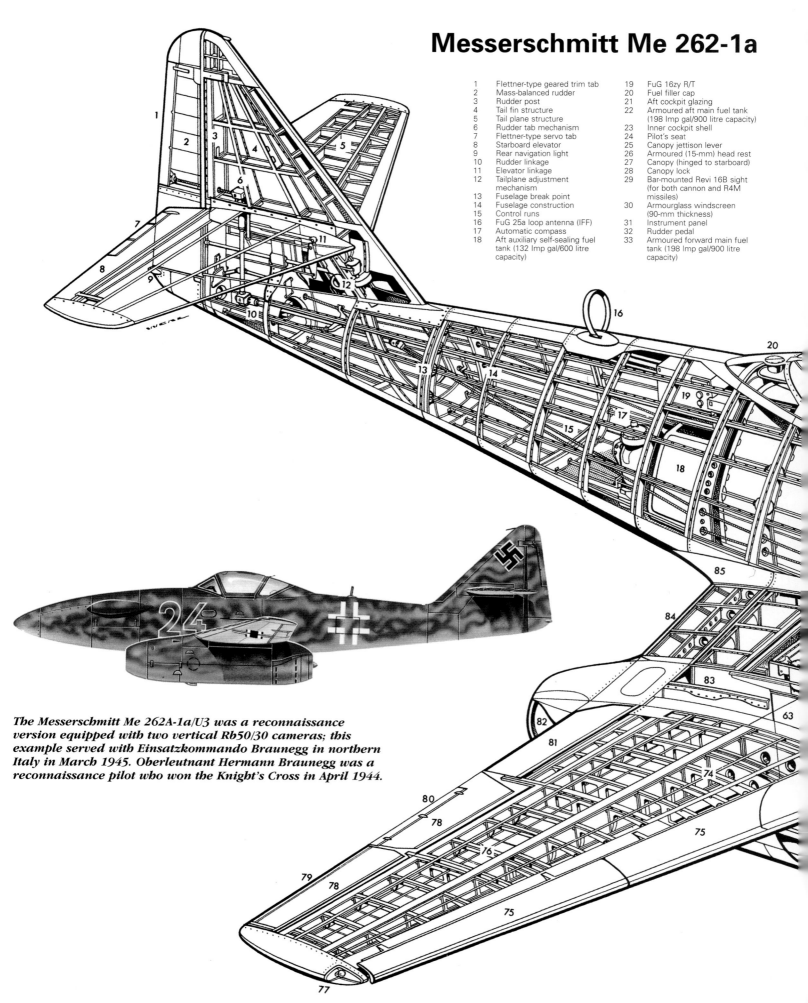

1	Flettner-type geared trim tab	19	FuG 16zy R/T
2	Mass-balanced rudder	20	Fuel filler cap
3	Rudder post	21	Aft cockpit glazing
4	Tail fin structure	22	Armoured aft main fuel tank (198 Imp gal/900 litre capacity)
5	Tail plane structure		
6	Rudder tab mechanism	23	Inner cockpit shell
7	Flettner-type servo tab	24	Pilot's seat
8	Starboard elevator	25	Canopy jettison lever
9	Rear navigation light	26	Armoured (15-mm) head rest
10	Rudder linkage	27	Canopy (hinged to starboard)
11	Elevator linkage	28	Canopy lock
12	Tailplane adjustment mechanism	29	Bar-mounted Revi 16B sight (for both cannon and R4M missiles)
13	Fuselage break point		
14	Fuselage construction	30	Armourglass windscreen (90-mm thickness)
15	Control runs		
16	FuG 25a loop antenna (IFF)	31	Instrument panel
17	Automatic compass	32	Rudder pedal
18	Aft auxiliary self-sealing fuel tank (132 Imp gal/600 litre capacity)	33	Armoured forward main fuel tank (198 Imp gal/900 litre capacity)

The Messerschmitt Me 262A-1a/U3 was a reconnaissance version equipped with two vertical Rb50/30 cameras; this example served with Einsatzkommando Braunegg in northern Italy in March 1945. Oberleutnant Hermann Braunegg was a reconnaissance pilot who won the Knight's Cross in April 1944.

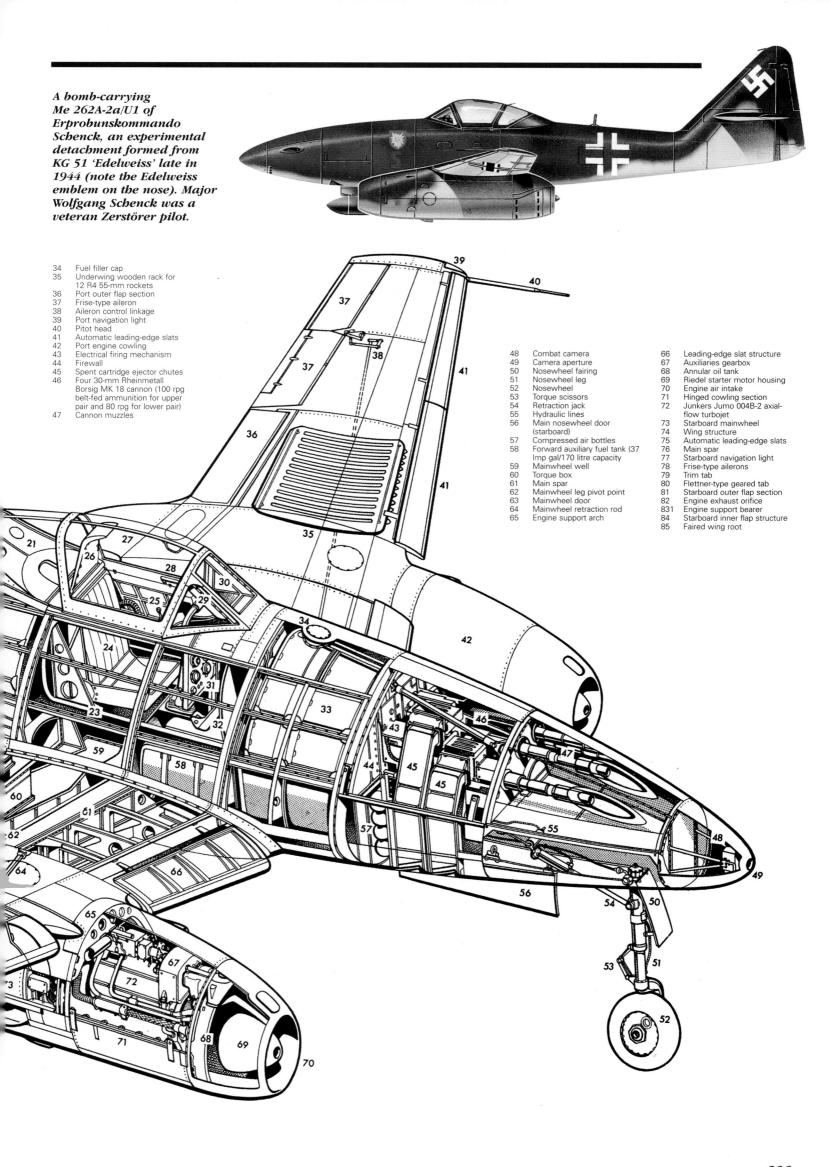

A bomb-carrying Me 262A-2a/U1 of Erprobunskommando Schenck, an experimental detachment formed from KG 51 'Edelweiss' late in 1944 (note the Edelweiss emblem on the nose). Major Wolfgang Schenck was a veteran Zerstörer pilot.

34 Fuel filler cap
35 Underwing wooden rack for 12 R4 55-mm rockets
36 Port outer flap section
37 Frise-type aileron
38 Aileron control linkage
39 Port navigation light
40 Pitot head
41 Automatic leading-edge slats
42 Port engine cowling
43 Electrical firing mechanism
44 Firewall
45 Spent cartridge ejector chutes
46 Four 30-mm Rheinmetall Borsig MK 18 cannon (100 rpg belt-fed ammunition for upper pair and 80 rpg for lower pair)
47 Cannon muzzles

48 Combat camera
49 Camera aperture
50 Nosewheel fairing
51 Nosewheel leg
52 Nosewheel
53 Torque scissors
54 Retraction jack
55 Hydraulic lines
56 Main nosewheel door (starboard)
57 Compressed air bottles
58 Forward auxiliary fuel tank (37 Imp gal/170 litre capacity
59 Mainwheel well
60 Torque box
61 Main spar
62 Mainwheel leg pivot point
63 Mainwheel door
64 Mainwheel retraction rod
65 Engine support arch

66 Leading-edge slat structure
67 Auxiliaries gearbox
68 Annular oil tank
69 Riedel starter motor housing
70 Engine air intake
71 Hinged cowling section
72 Junkers Jumo 004B-2 axial-flow turbojet
73 Starboard mainwheel
74 Wing structure
75 Automatic leading-edge slats
76 Main spar
77 Starboard navigation light
78 Frise-type ailerons
79 Trim tab
80 Flettner-type geared tab
81 Starboard outer flap section
82 Engine exhaust orifice
831 Engine support bearer
84 Starboard inner flap structure
85 Faired wing root

Above: The Mistel 1 pair comprised a Messerschmitt Bf 109F-1 atop a Junkers Ju 88A-4. 109 and Ju 88. This weapon probably belonged to 5.(Beleuchter) Staffel, Kampfgeschwader 200, in December 1944.

Left. Over 180 attacks were made using the Mistel weapon during the last 10 months of the war. An attack against the British fleet at Scapa Flow was also planned.

The appaling losses suffered by the Luftwaffe's *Kampfgeschwader* in 1943-44, their redeployment in other roles and the priority eventually bestowed on fighter production all contributed to the demise of the German bomber force towards the end of the war, and the last quasi-strategic operations by Germany's true heavy bomber (the Heinkel He 177) were those by KG 1 on the Russian front in June and July 1944, but it was the general shortage of fuel as much as Soviet fighter opposition that finally brought an end to these operations.

Instead the Luftwaffe undertook the use of yet another extraordinary weapon, the *Mistel* (mistletoe) composite weapon, involving the mounting of a manned single-seat fighter (usually a Bf 109 or Fw 190) on the top of an explosive-packed Junkers Ju 88. The composite weapon was flown to the target area where the Ju 88 was released and

This front view of a Heinkel He 162 emphasises the radical concept of this small fighter, in particular the location of the turbojet, the narrow-track undercarriage and the sharply angled-down wing tips – the latter found necessary to improve stability in high-g turns. Despite its hurried development, the ingenious Heinkel He 162 would have proved an effective fighter in experienced hands, but there was insufficient time remaining for the Luftwaffe to assemble and train pilots of the calibre required.

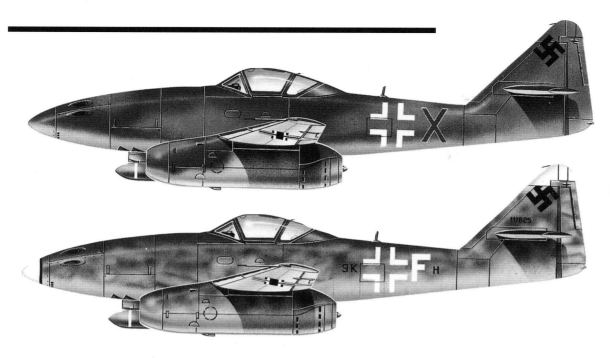

The Me 262 was developed as a bomber at Hitler's personal insistence. This Me 262A-2a carries a pair of SC 500 bombs and was assigned to I./KG 51 'Edelweiss' in March 1945.

Shown here bearing the full codes, 9K+FH, this Me 262A-2a of I./KG 51 'Edelweiss' was based at Achmer in the last weeks of the war. Shortage of fuel eventually grounded this unit and its surviving aircraft were captured intact by the advancing Allies.

Above: The Dornier Do 335 twin tandem engine fighter was beginning to appear at the end of the war. Potentially the fastest piston-engine aircraft ever built, early versions had a top speed of 474 mph (763 km/h). The type just failed to reach operational status.

radio-controlled by the fighter pilot to strike its objective. During the final months of the war numerous *Mistel* attacks were launched (but one against the Scapa Flow naval base was not) with considerable success, particularly against targets behind the swiftly advancing Russian forces.

When the curtain finally fell on Germany in May 1945 the once-vaunted Luftwaffe was a spent force. Its best pilots were dead and had been replaced by inadequate tyros, its bases in ruins, the aircraft factories destroyed or captured and its aircraft grounded by lack of fuel. Yet in six years of war its aircrew and aircraft had matched anything the Allies had thrown against them. No sensible Allied air commander was ever so foolish as to underestimate the professionalism of the German airman or the ingenuity of German industry and dedication.

Below: With the war in Europe over, the Allies set about disposing of German war materiel. In some cases aircraft were removed for testing, in others they were simply scrapped. Here He 111s, Ju 52/3ms, Ju 88s, Ju 188s, Me 110s, Me 262s and other types are ready for scrapping.

Picture acknowledgments

11: Grumman Aircraft Corporation. **12:** US Air Force. **20:** US Navy. **30:** US Air Force. **36:** US Air Force. **37:** US Air Force. **44:** US Navy. **45:** US Navy. **46:** US Navy (two). **48:** Vought Corporation (two). **49:** Vought Corporation, US Navy. **54:** US Navy (three). **55:** US Navy (two). **56:** US Navy (two). **55:** US Navy. **62:** US Navy. **63:** US Navy (two). **64:** Harold G. Martin. **65:** US Air Force. **68:** US Air Force. **77:** US Air Force. **78:** US Air Force, North American. **79:** US Navy (two). **81:** US Navy. **85:** RAF Museum. **88:** RAF Museum (two). **89:** Imperial War Museum. **92:** Imperial War Museum. **94:** RAF Museum, Imperial War Museum. **96:** Imperial War Museum (three). **97:** RAF Museum. **99:** Fox Photos. **100:** Imperial War Museum, RAF Museum, Charles E. Brown. **101:** Imperial War Museum. **103:** Imperial War Museum. **104:** Imperial War Museum (two). **110:** RAF Museum, Imperial War Museum. **113:** Imperial War Museum. **114:** Imperial War Museum. **115:** Charles E. Brown. **120:** Imperial War Museum, Charles E. Brown. **121:** John Rawlings. **122:** Imperial War Museum, Charles E. Brown/RAF Museum. **123:** Charles E. Brown. **125:** Charles E. Brown. **126:** Imperial War Museum. **127:** Imperial War Museum (two). **132:** RAF Museum. **133:** Charles E. Brown. **135:** Charles E. Brown. **136:** Imperial War Museum (two). **137:** Imperial War Museum. **138:** Imperial War Museum, Charles E. Brown/RAF Museum, Fox Photos. **139:** Charles E. Brown/RAF Museum, RAF Museum. **140:** Charles E. Brown/RAF Museum, RAF Museum. **143:** Imperial War Museum. **144:** Charles E. Brown. **145:** Imperial War Museum (two). **146:** Imperial War Museum (two). **147:** RAF Museum, Imperial War Museum. **150:** Imperial War Museum. **152:** Charles E. Brown. **153:** Imperial War Museum. **155:** Matthew Nathan. **156:** RAF Museum (two). **157:** Charles E. Brown (three). **158:** RAF Museum, Charles E. Brown. **159:** Charles E. Brown. **163:** Charles E. Brown. **172:** Imperial War Museum (two). **173:** Imperial War Museum. **183:** Bundesarchiv. **190:** Bundesarchiv. **192:** Bundesarchiv. **195:** Bundesarchiv. **199:** Bundesarchiv. **205:** US Air Force. **206:** Imperial War Museum. **210:** Imperial War Museum. **218:** US Air Force. **223:** US Air Force.